SCOTTISH DEERHOUNDS
KW-217

Photography: *Isabelle Francais, Ron Moat, Robert Pearcy, Vince Serbin, and Sally Anne Thompson.*

Drawings: Scott Boldt, Richard Crammer, Richard Davis, Andrew Prendimano, John Quinn, and Alexandra Suchenka.

Title page: Stunning Scottish Deerhound owned by Ellen Bonacarti and Jean Gentner.

The text of this book is the result of the joint efforts of the author and the staff of T.F.H. Publications, Inc., which is the originator of all sections of this book except the chapters entitled "Introducing the Scottish Deerhound" and "Grooming the Deerhound." Additionally, the portrayal of canine pet products in this book is for general instructive value only. The appearance of such products does not necessarily constitute an endorsement by the author, the publisher, or the owners of the dogs portrayed in this book.

636·753

19. OCT 1993

COVENTRY CITY LIBRARIES

t.f.h.

Distributed in the UNITED STATES to the Pet Trade by T.F.H. Publications, Inc., One T.F.H. Plaza, Neptune City, NJ 07753; distributed in the UNITED STATES to the Bookstore and Library Trade by National Book Network, Inc. 4720 Boston Way, Lanham MD 20706; in CANADA to the Pet Trade by H & L Pet Supplies Inc., 27 Kingston Crescent, Kitchener, Ontario N2B 2T6; Rolf C. Hagen Ltd., 3225 Sartelon Street, Montreal 382 Quebec; in CANADA to the Book Trade by Macmillan of Canada (A Division of Canada Publishing Corporation), 164 Commander Boulevard, Agincourt, Ontario M1S 3C7; in ENGLAND by T.F.H. Publications, PO Box 15, Waterlooville PO7 6BQ; in AUSTRALIA AND THE SOUTH PACIFIC by T.F.H. (Australia), Pty. Ltd., Box 149, Brookvale 2100 N.S.W., Australia; in NEW ZEALAND by Brooklands Aquarium Ltd., 5 McGiven Drive, New Plymouth, RD1 New Zealand; in the PHILIPPINES by Bio-Research, 5 Lippay Street, San Lorenzo Village, Makati, Rizal; in SOUTH AFRICA by Multipet Pty. Ltd., P.O. Box 35347, Northway, 4065, South Africa. Published by T.F.H. Publications, Inc. Manufactured in the United States of America by T.F.H. Publications, Inc.

SCOTTISH DEERHOUNDS

AUDREY M. BENBOW

The typical Scottish Deerhound expression is one of dignity and nobility. Owner, Gayle Bontecov.

Contents

Introducing the Scottish Deerhound

The statement that "a Deerhound should resemble a roughcoated Greyhound of larger size and bone" does nothing to convey the rugged beauty, grace, and dignity of the ancient Scottish hounds, which Sir Walter Scott described as "the most perfect creatures of Heaven." As the tapestries bedecking great ancient halls indicate that the Deerhound has inspired both painters and sculptors, the breed's beauty in modern times has also impressed screen writers and directors. The film *Out of Africa* portrayed Danish aristocrat Karen Blixen, played by American film star Meryl Streep, with her handsome Deerhounds, enchanting viewers who had never before seen these Scottish beauties.

The Deerhound is a large dog of rugged, graceful appearance, standing 28 to 32 inches at the shoulder and weighing 75 to 110 pounds. As a companion the Deerhound has many advantages. His gray coat does not show dirt; his legs and feet are relatively free of long hair, so they do not collect mud; the wiry textured coat does not mat and does not shed to any extent—even burrs come out easily.

Years of close companionship with man at work and leisure may account for the Deerhound's air of gentle dignity. He is aware of his size when playing with children and smaller animals and has infinite patience. Although bred and raised to hunt, the Deerhound does not wander but stays close to his home, his master, and family.

Deerhounds are quiet and obedient—my "Kestrel" was four years old before I ever heard her bark. As guard dogs they are alert but not aggressive—their size alone is usually sufficient to deter prowlers.

It is never necessary to use physical punishment on a Deerhound. A cross word or a note of displeasure in your voice is sufficient to make him lie down and cover his face with his paws—a typical Deerhound gesture.

HISTORY OF THE SCOTTISH DEERHOUND

The exact origin of the Scottish Deerhound is shrouded in the mists of antiquity, but it is evident that even prior to 1526 there was a long-established thriving race of large dogs in Scotland that was used to hunt deer. Confusion arises from the fact that these hounds were referred to by various names—Rough Greyhounds, Irish Greyhounds, Scottish Staghounds, Scotch Greyhounds, and Highland Greyhounds. These hounds must have possessed great speed, power, and courage since the

Although many people think of or describe the Scottish Deerhound as a larger, more rough-coated Greyhound, anyone who has seen a member of this breed is aware that mere words cannot describe it. Owner, James Gill Phinizy.

full-grown stag stands around four feet at the withers, weighs in the neighborhood of 300 pounds, and is well armed with a fine set of antlers.

The Highland chieftains prized and preserved their dogs with great zeal. *The Buik of Chronicles* recounts how the Picts' theft of King Crathlint's favorite hound precipitated a battle in which 100 Picts and 60 Scots perished. Further evidence

of the high value placed on these dogs appears in the *Accounts of the Lord High Treasurer*. "In the time of James VI these dogs were held in such high esteem that, in August 1594, the monarch sent ten of their breed in a present to the King of Denmark and in June 1599, nine others."

At the end of the 18th century and the early part of the 19th century, the breed was at a very

Although this adorable youngster appears small now, keep in mind that he will grow to be at least 30 inches tall and weigh close to 100 pounds, if not more.

low ebb. Several factors contributed—the collapse of the clan system in Scotland and the improvement of the sporting rifle. In 1815, at the end of the Napoleonic Wars, the sport of deerstalking came into vogue and the great forests were divided for purposes of letting. For stalking and shooting, the Deerhound was not only superfluous but an embarrassment, as he might well pursue his quarry into an adjacent forest. With the spread of cultivated lands and sheep farms, the Scottish Highlands, the last place where the stag remained numerous in the wild state, became the last stronghold of the Scottish Deerhound.

A great wave of renewed interest dates from around 1831, and the preservation of the breed can be credited to a few enthusiasts who spared no expense, bred extensively, and kept only the best. Among these people were Lord Colonsay, his brother Mr. Archibald McNeil, Cameron of Lochiel, and the Menzies of Chesthill.

The advent of organized dog shows in England in 1859 was probably a great boon to the Deerhound breed, as circumstances were against deer stalking on a wide scale. The first Deerhounds were shown in England in 1860, and most of the winners at the early shows were descended from the working strains. Today the Deerhound appears at most shows in Britain and in fair numbers but, as in the

The Scottish Deerhound is a sighthound through and through; some experts believe that, well over 1000 years ago, an African greyhound was crossed with shaggy European breeds to help create a dog that could withstand colder temperatures.

early days, credit must be given to a few dedicated individuals who carefully continued to preserve and promote this ancient breed of sighthound. In this respect, the kennel names of Ardlinglas, Enterkine, O'The Pentlands, Ross, and Rotherwood must be mentioned. The Deerhound Club was formed in 1886 and continues to be the voice of the breed in the United Kingdom.

THE SCOTTISH DEERHOUND IN THE U.S.

It is not clear when Scottish Deerhounds were first brought to North America, but mention is made of their hunting skill in several early letters. General Custer, on his campaigns in the

The Scottish Deerhound is a creature of the great outdoors; he has amazing speed and the incredible eyesight of a sighthound.

No, this is not Superdog, just a Deerhound (as he is known in Great Britain) taking a well-deserved rest.

West, owned and hunted three Deerhounds. Not until 1886 was the first Deerhound registered with the American Kennel Club—this was Bonnie Robin, owned by G.S. Paige of Stanley, New Jersey.

No history of the Deerhound would be complete without a suitable tribute to Mrs. A.H. Huntingdon, the renowned sculptress, who contributed more than anyone else to the past and future of the breed in America. To her Stanerigg kennels came some of the finest hounds from abroad, including the great English and American Champion Prophetic of Ross. The list of Deerhound champions bearing the Stanerigg prefix grew steadily until Mrs. Huntingdon retired from showing, but their names still appear in the pedigrees of some of the finest Deerhounds today.

Registrations indicate that interest in the breed is relatively constant. The Deerhound still ranks as a "rare breed," which in

itself creates a great pride of possession. In the hands of a few, the breed has survived and retained its purity for centuries.

Above: *And they're off! Scottish Deerhounds are usually coursed two at a time.* **Right:** *Rogue o' the Greenwood takes his mark and gets ready to go.* **Below:** *The Scottish Deerhound displays remarkable bursts of speed, especially when on the course.*

COURSING

Scottish Deerhounds today have little opportunity to hunt antlered game; in fact, in the United States and Canada it is illegal to run deer with dogs.

The object of coursing is not to kill but to see the hounds work and run—a thrilling sight indeed. Competitive coursing is run on the "knock-out" principle, with the winners of the first round going on to the second, and so on. When the hare is sighted it is given a fair amount of "law" (head start), and the hounds are slipped in pairs, each wearing a knitted collar of a different color. Points are scored on the work done, and the judge signals his decision by waving a red or white handkerchief.

The most important thing in a coursing hound is fitness—he

Above and left: *The Scottish Deerhound's tail is dropped or carried low when the dog is relaxing, but when he's in motion it is curved slightly upward but never out of line with the back.* **Below:** *Turning around and heading for home.*

cannot do his best if he is not in top condition. Steady roadwork to build up muscle is essential, combined with some galloping over rough ground. Greyhound people set great store by massage, which is also excellent for Deerhounds but takes a great deal of time.

Coursing is without doubt the greatest development in breed activities in recent years. It gives the hounds great pleasure, even if they do not chase their

traditional quarry. It provides an interest and an opportunity for owners and friends to get together at a time when there is more opportunity to talk than at most conformation shows, which are usually so rushed.

Deerhound after the course. Coursing is becoming more and more popular each year as more owners and canines become aware of its benefits.

Standard for the Breed

The Scottish Deerhound, like all other purebred dogs, is measured against a breed standard of perfection, a written description of what the ideal specimen should look like. Each dog-registering organization has its own set of standards, one for each breed of dog it recognizes; however, these standards vary, in the way they are worded, from registry to registry and from country to country. The Scottish Deerhound is accepted in both Great Britain and the United States; both the standard of the American Kennel Club (AKC) and the Kennel Club of Great Britain (KCGB) are presented here for your information. In Great Britain, the breed is known simply as Deerhound.

AKC STANDARD FOR THE SCOTTISH DEERHOUND

Head: Should be broadest at the ears, narrowing slightly to the eyes, with the muzzle tapering more decidedly to the nose. The muzzle should be pointed, but the teeth and lips level. The head should be long, the skull flat rather than round with a very slight rise over the eyes but nothing approaching a stop. The hair on the skull should

A trio of sighthound relations: an Irish Wolfhound (center), a Scottish Deerhound (right), and an Afghan Hound (left).

Standard for the Breed

Artist's rendering of a Scottish Deerhound. Deerhound ears are folded back when in repose yet raised above the head when excited.

be moderately long and softer than the rest of the coat. The nose should be black (in some blue fawns—blue) and slightly aquiline. In lighter colored dogs, the black muzzle is preferable. There should be a good mustache of rather silky hair and a fair beard.

Ears: Should be set on high; in repose, folded back like a Greyhound's, though raised above the head in excitement without losing the fold, and even in some cases semi-erect. A prick ear is bad. Big thick ears hanging flat to the head or heavily coated with long hair is a bad fault. The ears should be soft, glossy, like a mouse's coat to the touch and the smaller the better. There should be no long coat or long fringe, but there is sometimes a silky, silvery coat on the body of the ear and the tip. On all Deerhounds, irrespective of color of coat, the ears should be black or dark colored.

Neck and Shoulders: The neck should be long—of a length befitting the Greyhound character of the dog. Extreme length is neither necessary nor desirable. Deerhounds do not stoop to their work like the Greyhounds. The mane, which every good specimen should have, sometimes detracts from the apparent length of the neck. The neck, however, must be strong as is necessary to hold a stag. The nape of the neck should be very prominent where the head is set on, and the throat clean cut at the angle and prominent. Shoulders should be well sloped; blades well back and not too much width between them. Loaded and straight shoulders are very bad faults.

Tail: Should be tolerably long, tapering and reaching to within 1½ inches of the ground and about 1½ inches below the hocks. Dropped perfectly down or curved when the Deerhound is still, when in motion or excited,

Altair Alyssum of Vale Vue, owned by Mary Rose and Rosemary Page, standing in the show ring.

curved, but in no instance lifted out of the line of the back. It should be well covered with hair, on the inside, thick and wiry, underside longer and towards the end a slight fringe is not objectionable. A curl or ring tail is undesirable.

Eyes: Should be dark—generally dark brown, brown or hazel. A very light eye is not liked. The eye should be moderately full, with a soft look in repose, but a keen, far-away look when the Deerhound is roused. Rims of eyelids should be black.

Body: General conformation is that of a Greyhound of larger size and bone. Chest deep rather than broad but not too narrow or slab-sided. Good girth of chest is indicative of great lung power. The loin well arched and drooping to the tail. A straight back is not desirable, this

Mrs. Barb Davis evaluating the head of Altair Alyssum of Vale Vue.

Highstone's Tableau (left) *and Haystack of Vale Vue* (right) *in the ring. Note the proper harsh, wiry coat on both dogs.*

formation being unsuited for uphill work, and very unsightly.

Legs and Feet: Legs should be broad and flat, and good broad forearms and elbows are desirable. Forelegs must, of course, be as straight as possible. Feet close and compact, with well-arranged toes. The hindquarters drooping, and as broad and powerful as possible, the hips being set wide apart. A narrow rear denotes lack of power. The stifles should be well bent, with great length from hip to hock, which should be broad and flat. Cowhocks, weak pasterns, straight stifles and splay feet are very bad faults.

Coat: The hair on the body, neck and quarters should be harsh and wiry, about three or four inches long; that on the head, breast and belly much softer. There should be a slight fringe on the inside of the forelegs and hindlegs but nothing approaching the "feather" of a Collie. A woolly

Joie, owned by Gayle Bontecov, being gaited in the ring. The gait of the Scottish Deerhound should be easy, active and true.

coat is bad. Some good strains have a mixture of silky coat with the hard which is preferable to a woolly coat. The climate of the United States tends to produce the mixed coat. The ideal coat is a thick, close-lying ragged coat, harsh or crisp to the touch.

Color: is a matter of fancy, but the dark blue-gray is most preferred. Next come the darker and lighter grays or brindles, the darkest being generally preferred. Yellow and sandy red or red fawn, especially with black ears and muzzles, are in equally high estimation. This was the color of the oldest known strains—the McNeil and Chesthill Menzies. White is condemned by all authorities, but a white chest and white toes, occurring as they do in many of the darkest colored dogs, are not objected to, although the less the better, for the Deerhound is a self-colored dog. A white blaze on the head, or a white collar, should entirely disqualify. The less white the better but a slight white tip to the stern occurs in some of the best strains.

Height: *Height of Dogs—* From 30 to 32 inches, or even more if there be symmetry without coarseness, which is rare. *Height of Bitches—* From 28 inches upwards. There is no objection to a bitch being large, unless too coarse, as even at her greatest height she does not approach that of the dog, and therefore could not be too big for work as overbig dogs are.

Weight: From 85 to 110 pounds in dogs, and from 75 to 95 pounds in bitches.

Points of the Deerhound Arranged in Order of Importance

1. *Typical*—The Deerhound should resemble a rough-coated Greyhound of larger size and bone.

2. *Movements*—Easy, active and true.

3. As tall as possible consistent with quality.

4. *Head*—Long, level, well balanced, carried high.

5. *Body*—Long, very deep in brisket, well-sprung ribs and great breadth across hips.

More important than the exact height measurement of the Scottish Deerhound is the overall balance of the dog or bitch.

6. *Forelegs*—Strong and quite straight, with elbows neither in nor out.

7. *Thighs*—Long and muscular, second thighs well muscled, stifles well bent.

8. *Loins*—Well arched, and belly well drawn up.

9. *Coat*—Rough and hard, with softer beard and brows.

10. *Feet*—Close, compact, with well-knuckled toes.

11. *Ears*—Small (dark) with Greyhoundlike carriage.

12. *Eyes*—Dark, moderately full.

13. *Neck*—Long, well arched, very strong with prominent nape.

14. *Shoulders*—Clean, set sloping.

15. *Chest*—Very deep but not too narrow.

16. *Tail*—Long and curved slightly, carried low.

17. *Teeth*—Strong and level.

18. *Nails*—Strong and curved.

Disqualification: *White blaze on the head, or a white collar.*

KCGB STANDARD FOR THE DEERHOUND
General Appearance: Resembles a rough-coated Greyhound of larger size and bone.

Juniper of Vale Vue, owned by Norma Sellers, being checked for soundness of front.

The build of the Scottish Deerhound suggests speed, power and endurance—enough to pull down a stag or run along the shore.

Characteristics: The build suggests the unique combination of speed, power and endurance necessary to pull down a stag, but general bearing is one of gentle dignity.

Temperament: Gentle and friendly. Obedient and easy to train because eager to please. Docile and good tempered, never suspicious, aggressive or nervous. Carries himself with dignity.

Head and Skull: Broadest at ears, tapering slightly to eyes, muzzle tapering more decidedly to nose, lips level. Head long, skull flat rather than round, with very slight rise over eyes, with no stop. Skull coated with moderately long hair, softer than rest of coat. Nose slightly aquiline and black. In lighter coloured dogs, black muzzle preferred. Good moustache of rather silky hair and some beard.

Eyes: Dark. Generally dark brown or hazel. Light eyes undesirable. Moderately full with a soft look in repose, but keen, far-away look when dog is roused.

Standard for the Breed

Ears: Set on high and in repose folded back. In excitement raised above head without losing the fold and in some cases semi-erect. A big thick ear hanging flat to the head or a prick ear most undesirable. Ear soft, glossy and like a mouse's coat to the touch; the smaller the better, no long coat or fringe. Ears black or dark coloured.

Mouth: Jaws strong, with a perfect, regular and complete scissors bite, i.e., the upper teeth closely overlapping the lower teeth and set square to the jaws.

The jaws of the Scottish Deerhound are strong and powerful. The muzzle should be pointed but the lips level.

The Scottish Deerhound neck is very strong and is often longer than it appears, as the mane sometimes disguises its reach. However, there should never be any sign of throatiness.

Neck: Very strong, with good reach sometimes disguised by mane. Nape of neck very prominent where head is set on, no throatiness.

Forequarters: Shoulders well laid, not too far apart. Loaded and straight shoulders undesirable. Forelegs straight, broad and flat, a good broad forearm and elbow being desirable.

Body: Body and general conformation that of a Greyhound of larger size and bone. Chest deep rather than broad, not too narrow and flat-sided. Loin well arched and drooping to tail. Flat topline undesirable.

Hindquarters: Drooping, broad and powerful, hips set wide apart. Hindlegs well bent at stifle with great length from hip

Standard for the Breed

to hock. Bone broad and flat.

Feet: Compact and well knuckled. Nails strong.

Tail: Long, thick at root, tapering and reaching almost to ground. When standing dropped perfectly straight down or curved. Curved when moving, never lifted above line of back. Well covered with hair; on upper side, thick and wiry; on under side, longer; and towards end, a slight fringe is not objectionable. A curl or ring tail is undesirable.

Gait/Movement: Easy, active and true, with a long stride.

Coat: Shaggy, but not overcoated. Woolly coat unacceptable. The correct coat is thick, close-lying, ragged; harsh or crisp to the touch. Hair on body, neck and quarters harsh and wiry, about 7 cm (3 inches) to 10 cm (4 inches) long; that on head, breast and belly much softer. A slight hairy fringe on inside of fore and hindlegs.

Colour: Dark blue-grey, darker and lighter greys or brindles and yellows, sandy-red or red fawns with black points. A white chest, white toes and a slight white tip to stern are permissible but the less white the better, since it is a self-coloured dog. A white blaze on head or white collar unacceptable.

Weight and Size: *Dogs—* Minimum desirable height at withers 76 cm (30 inches). Weight about 45.5 kg (100 pounds). *Bitches—*Minimum

desirable height at withers 71 cm (28 inches). Weight about 36.5 kg (80 pounds).

Faults: *Any departure from the foregoing points should be considered a fault and the seriousness with which the fault should be regarded should be in exact proportion to its degree.*

Note: *Male animals should have two apparently normal testicles fully descended into the scrotum.*

Facing page: *Sonnet being stacked just prior to being judged. Stacking involves positioning the dog to show off its best features—in other words presenting a proper picture of breed conformation to the judge. Stacking helps create a good first impression, and it may help catch the judge's eye.*

Grooming the Deerhound

In general, Scottish Deerhounds are remarkably free of doggy odor and should be bathed as seldom as possible. However, you should begin accustoming your pet to regular combing and brushing sessions from the time he is a puppy.

GROOMING PROCEDURE

The following is a grooming procedure used by professionals. You may find it helpful to visit a salon and watch the process before attempting it yourself. Before you begin grooming, assemble the following items, which are available at your local pet shop:

- sisal (natural bristle) brush
- fine metal comb
- toenail clipper
- medicated ear powder
- eye drops (eye stain remover)

The Scottish Deerhound, unlike the Miniature Poodle he is pictured with here, does not require a lot of grooming time.

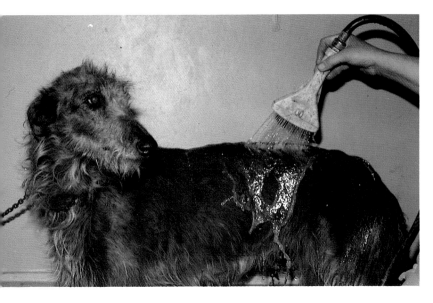

Always keep in mind that you should bathe your Scottish Deerhound as little as possible, since bathing tends to dry out the coat by removing essential oils. **Above:** The first step is, of course, wetting the coat. A spray hose attachment is very useful for this task. **Right:** Always use a high-quality canine shampoo—human shampoos will dry out the coat. Dog shampoos are available at your local pet shop.

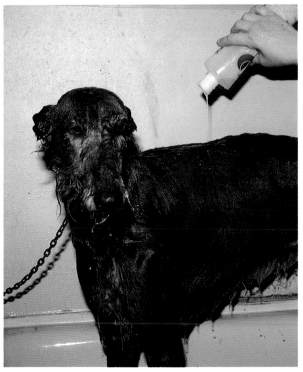

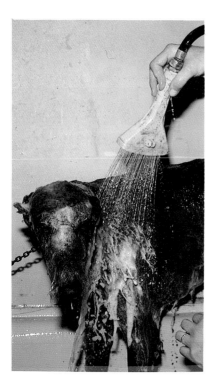

Left: *Always be sure to rinse out every last trace of shampoo from the coat, as leftover traces of soap will irritate your dog's skin.*
Below: *Dry your Deerhound thoroughly with a towel or a hair dryer, if he will allow it.*

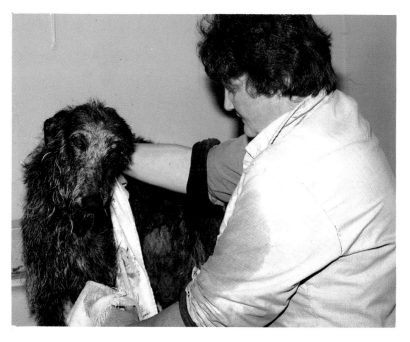

- stripping knife
- scissors
- thinning shears
- cotton balls

1. Brush through the coat.

2. Clean inside the ears.

3. Clean the eyes by wiping with cotton that has been moistened with eye drops.

4. Cut the nails with a toenail clipper, being careful not to cut the quick.

5. Put a cotton ball in each ear to prevent water from entering the ear canals. After you have done this, bathe the dog and cage dry him.

6. Lightly brush through the coat with the sisal brush.

7. With the thinning shears or stripping knife, trim any straggly hair from the top of the head and ears.

8. With the thinning shears, trim any straggly hair from the sides of the face, the neck, and the chest.

9. Lightly scissor around the whiskers and the beard, making this hair square and full.

10. With the scissors, snip hair from between the pads and toes

If the temperature is very warm and there are no cold breezes, you may wish to let your pet dry off in the sun.

of the feet and around the edges. This gives a neat appearance to the feet.

11. Trim the front leg fringes to make them even.

12. With scissors or thinning shears, trim any straggly hair from the hocks down to the feet on the hindlegs.

13. Holding the tail out, comb the hair down and trim the lower edge, making it wide at the base and tapering toward the tip.

14. Brush through the entire coat with the sisal brush.

Regular combing and brushing will help keep your pet's coat clean and healthy. It will also help your dog feel better about himself.

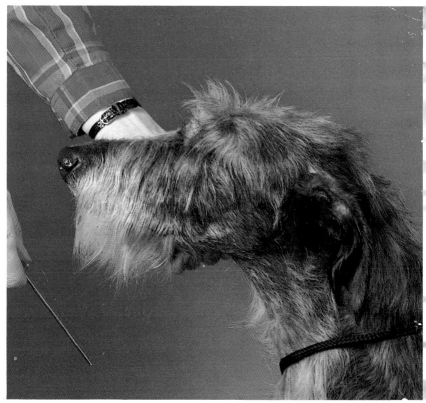

Selecting Your Dog

Now that you have decided which dog breed suits your needs, your lifestyle, and your own temperament, there will be much to consider before you make your final purchase. Buying a puppy on impulse may only cause heartbreak later on; it makes better sense to put some real thought into your canine investment, especially since it is likely that he will share many happy years with you. Which individual will you choose as your adoring companion? Ask yourself some questions as you analyze your needs and preferences for a dog, read all that you can about your particular breed, and visit as many dog shows as possible. At the shows you will be surrounded by people who can give you all the details about the breed that you are interested in buying. Decide if you want a household pet, a dog for breeding, or a show dog. Would you prefer a male or female? Puppy or adult?

Ask the seller to help you with your decision. When you have settled on the dog you want, discuss with the seller the dog's temperament, the animal's positive and negative aspects, any health problems it might have, its feeding and grooming requirements, and whether the dog has been immunized. Reputable sellers will be willing to answer any questions you

might have that pertain to the dog you have selected, and often they will make themselves available if you call for advice or if you encounter problems after you've made your purchase.

A pair of Scottish Deerhound puppies and a friend. Choosing a particular puppy may be the hardest part of acquiring your new pet.

A bit too big?
A little **too** small.
Too fuzzy for me!
Too fat to crawl.

Before you wrap it tight
And crate it home,
Behold its appetite
And room to roam.

A sloppy yap, a barking slur,
Puppy eyes to be let free,
A him? a her? an unmarked cur,
Let's pout to see its pedigree.

The perfect pet quest:
Which pup for me is best?

ANDREW DE PRISCO

Most breeders and sellers want to see their dogs placed in loving, responsible homes; they are careful about who buys their animals. So as the dog's new owner, prepare yourself for some interrogation from the from the person who sells you your pet.

WHERE TO BUY

You can choose among several places to buy your dog. Many people think of their local pet shop as the first source for buying a puppy, and very often they're right; you should

Best-of-breed Scottish Deerhound proudly wearing his ribbon. Before purchasing your dog, decide whether you want a pet- or show-quality specimen.

remember, however, that a pet shop cannot possibly stock all breeds of dog. If your pet shop does not carry the type of dog you desire, there are other places to look. One is a kennel whose business is breeding show-quality dogs; such kennels may have extra pups for sale. Another source is the one-dog owner who wants to sell the puppies from an occasional litter to pay the expenses of his small-scale breeding operation. To find such kennels and part-time breeders and hobbyists, check the classified section of your local newspaper or look in your telephone directory.

Whichever source you choose, you can usually tell in a very short time whether the puppies will make healthy and happy pets. If they are clean, plump, and lively, they are probably in good health. Sometimes you will have the advantage of seeing the puppies' dam and perhaps their sire and other relatives. Remember that the mother, having just raised a demanding family, may not be looking her best; but if she is sturdy, friendly, and well-mannered, her puppies should be too. If you feel that something is lacking in the care or condition of the dogs, it is better to look elsewhere than to buy hastily and regret it afterward. Buy a healthy dog with a good disposition, one that has been properly socialized and

Never leave your dog in a closed car—if you do you may be signing his death warrant. If you must leave your dog unattended for a short while, roll down the windows or tether your dog outside of the car.

likes being around people.

If you cannot find the dog you want locally, write to the secretary of the national breed club or kennel club and ask for names of breeders near you or to whom you can write for information. Puppies are sometimes shipped, sight unseen, from reputable breeders. In these instances, pictures and pedigree information are usually sent beforehand to help you decide.

Breeders can supply you with further details and helpful guidance, if you require it. Many breed clubs provide a puppy referral service, so you may want to look into this before making your final decision.

PET OR SHOW DOG

Conscientious breeders strive to maintain desirable qualities in their breed. At the same time, they are always working to improve on what they have already achieved, and they do this by referring to the breed standard of perfection. The standard describes the ideal dog, and those animals that come close to the ideal are generally selected as show

Owners of purebred dogs too often forget that all breeds of dog are interrelated. The ancient canine that is the believed ancestor of all dogs is known as Tomarctus. As packs traveled and inhabited various lands, types evolved through the process of adaptation. Later, as dogs and man joined forces, type became further diversified. This chart sketches one commonly accepted theory of the domesticated dog's development. Where does your dog fit in? With a few exceptions, dogs evolve or change as a result of a specific functional need.

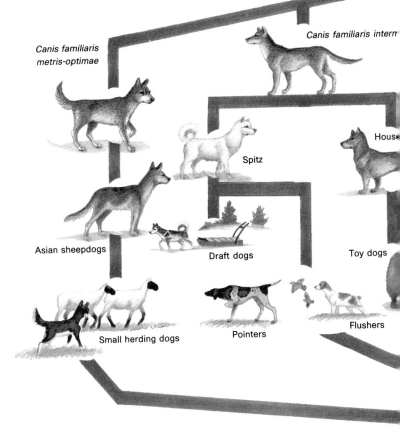

Canis familiaris intern

Canis familiaris
metris-optimae

Hous

Spitz

Asian sheepdogs

Draft dogs

Toy dogs

Small herding dogs

Pointers

Flushers

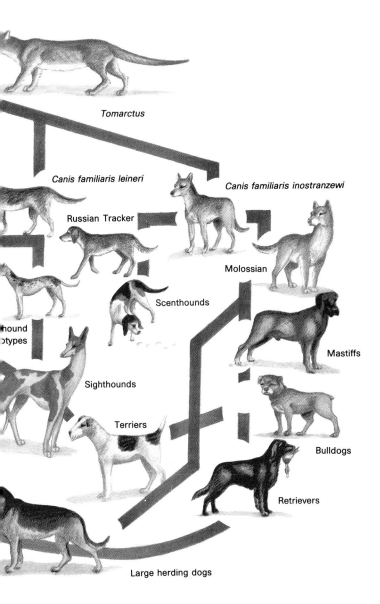

Tomarctus

Canis familiaris leineri

Canis familiaris inostranzewi

Russian Tracker

Molossian

Scenthounds

hound
otypes

Mastiffs

Sighthounds

Terriers

Bulldogs

Retrievers

Large herding dogs

stock; those that do not are culled and sold as pets. Keep in mind that pet-quality purebred dogs are in no way less healthy or attractive than show-quality specimens. Sometimes these dogs even prove more hardy. It's just that the pet may have undesirable features (such as

Paisley Piper of Vale Vue, owned by Judy Olsen and Norma Sellers, at a show. If you do wish to get involved in showing, it is a good idea to buy an older dog rather than a young puppy whose looks might change.

ears that are too large or eyes that are the wrong color for the breed) which would be faults in the show ring. Often these so-called "flaws" are detectable only by experienced breeders or show judges. Naturally the more perfect animal, in terms of its breed standard, will cost more—even though he seems almost identical to his pet-quality littermate.

If you think you may eventually want to show your dog or raise a litter of puppies, by all means buy the best you can afford. You will save expense and disappointment later on. However, if the puppy is strictly to be a pet for the children, or a companion for you, you can afford to look for a bargain. The pup that is not show material, or the older pup for which there is often less demand, or the grown dog that is not being used for breeding is occasionally available and offers opportunities to save money. Remember that your initial investment may be a bargain, but it takes good food and care—and plenty of both—to raise a healthy, vigorous puppy through to adulthood.

Facing page: *Note the calm, even expression displayed by this Deerhound.*

The price you pay for your dog is little compared to the love and devotion he will return over the many years he'll be with you. With proper care and affection, your pup should live to a ripe old age; thanks to modern veterinary science and improvements in canine nutrition, dogs today are better maintained and live longer. It is not uncommon to see dogs living well into their teens.

Generally speaking, small dogs live longer than big ones. With love and the proper care any dog will live to its optimum age. Many persons, however, opt for a particular breed because of its proven longevity. This, of course, is purely a personal decision.

MALE OR FEMALE

Let us first disregard the usual generalizations and misconceptions applied to male vs. female dogs and consider the practical concerns. If you intend to show your new dog, a male will likely closer adhere to the

Size variation in the dog family is extreme. The consideration of size must be a high priority when choosing a breed. The amount of housing, exercise, and food required, as well as the animal's lifespan are just some of the factors involved.

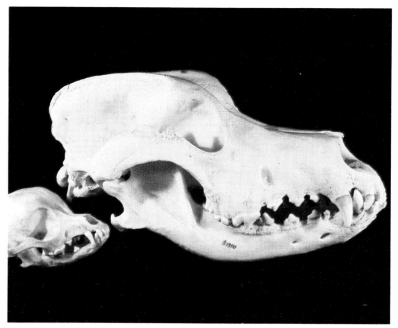

breed standard, though ring competition for males is stiffer. A female chosen to show cannot be spayed and the owner must contend with the bitch's heat period. If it is solely a pet—and pet animals should *not* be bred—castration or spaying is necessary. Neutered pets have longer lifespans and have a decreased risk of cancer. Males are more economical to neuter than are females. You might also consider that females are generally smaller than males, easier to housetrain, may be more family-oriented and protective of home and property. Any dog will roam—male or female—castration will not affect roaming in most cases. Males are larger and stronger, proving better guard-dog candidates. Of course, a dog of either sex, if properly trained, can make a charming, reliable, and loving pet. Male vs. female is chiefly a matter of personal preference—go with your first instinct.

ADULT OR PUP

Whether to buy a grown dog or a young puppy is another question. It is surely an undeniable pleasure to watch your dog grow from a lively pup to a mature, dignified dog. If you don't have the time to spend on the more frequent meals, housebreaking, and other training a puppy needs in order to become a dog you can be

Life Expectancy	
Dog's Age in Years	Comparative Human Age in Years
1	15
2	24
3	28
4	32
5	36
6	40
7	44
8	48
9	52
10	56
11	60
12	64
13	68
14	72
15	76
16	80
17	84
18	88
19	92
20	96
21	100

This chart is designed to provide a comparative view of ages between a dog and its human counterpart. Necessarily it is an oversimplification since larger breeds often have shorter lifespans than do average or medium-sized dogs; likewise working dogs may tend to live shorter lives than the easygoing pet dog. These factors, and many others, must be taken into account when considering this chart.

proud of, then choose an older, partly trained adolescent or a grown dog. If you want a show dog, remember that no one, not even an expert, can predict with one hundred percent accuracy what a puppy will be like when he grows up. The dog may seem to exhibit show potential *most* of the time, but six months is the earliest age for the would-be exhibitor to select a prospect and know that its future is in the show ring.

If you have a small child, it is best to get a puppy big enough to defend itself, one not less than four or five months old.

Older children will enjoy playing with and helping to take care of a baby pup; but at less than four months, a puppy wants to do little else but eat and sleep, and he must be protected from teasing and overtiring. You cannot expect a very young child to understand that a puppy is a fragile living being; to the youngster he is a toy like his

A pair of puppies from the Birchwood Kennels resting after a hard day of play.

If you have young children, it may be a good idea to get an older dog, one who can safely handle a little rough-housing.

stuffed dog. Children, therefore, must learn how to handle and care for their young pets.

We recommend that you start with a puppy so you can raise and train it according to the rules you have established in your own home. While a dog is young, its behavior can be more easily shaped by the owner, whereas an older dog, although trainable, may be a bit set in his ways.

WHAT TO LOOK FOR IN A PUPPY

In choosing a puppy, assuming that it comes from healthy, well-bred parents, look for one that is friendly and outgoing. The biggest pup in the litter is apt to be somewhat coarse as a grown dog, while the appealing "runt of the litter" may turn out to be a timid shadow—or have a Napoleonic complex! If you want a show dog and have no experience in choosing a prospect, study the breed standard and listen carefully to the breeder on the finer points of show conformation. A breeder's prices will be in accord with his puppies' expected worth, and he will be honest with you about each pup's potential because it is to his own advantage. He wants his top-quality show puppies placed in the public eye to reflect glory on him—and to attract future buyers. Why should he sell a potential show champion to someone who just wants a pet?

Now that you have paid your money and made your choice, you are ready to depart with puppy, papers, and instructions. Make sure that you know the youngster's feeding routine, and take along some of his food. For the trip home, place him in a comfortable, sturdy carrier. Do not drive home with a puppy on your lap! If you'll be travelling for a few hours, at the very least bring along a bottle of water from the breeder and a small water dish.

PEDIGREE AND REGISTRATION

Owners of puppies are often misled by sellers with such ruses as leading the owner to believe his dog is something special. The term *pedigree papers* is quite different from the term *registration papers.* A pedigree is nothing more than a statement made by the breeder of the dog;

If you have never been to a dog show, whether you're interested in show dogs or not, by all means—Go! An all-breed dog show will give you hands-on experience with different breeds of dog, the chance to meet their owners and breeders, and the answers to many of your questions.

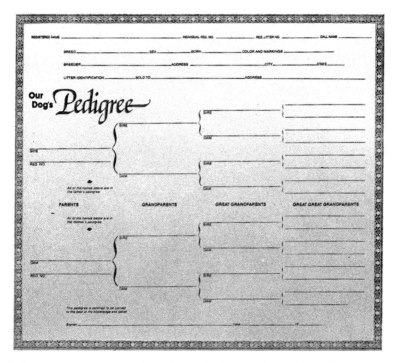

The pedigree form contains the following labels:

REGISTERED NAME ___ INDIVIDUAL REG. NO. ___ REG LITTER NO. ___ CALL NAME ___

BREED ___ SEX ___ BORN ___ COLOR AND MARKINGS ___

BREEDER ___ ADDRESS ___ CITY ___ STATE ___

LITTER IDENTIFICATION ___ SOLD TO ___ ADDRESS ___

Our Dog's *Pedigree*

SIRE

REG NO.

All of the names above are in the father's pedigree

PARENTS GRANDPARENTS GREAT GRANDPARENTS GREAT GREAT GRANDPARENTS

All of the names below are in the mother's pedigree

DAM

REG NO.

This pedigree is correct to be correct to the best of my knowledge and belief.

Signed: ___ City ___ 19 ___

Pedigree papers can trace a dog's lineage back several generations. They do not, however, guarantee that a puppy is purebred, healthy or sound.

and it is written on special pedigree blanks, which are readily available from any pet shop or breed club, with the names of several generations from which the new puppy comes. It records your puppy's ancestry and other important data, such as the pup's date of birth, its breed, its sex, its sire and dam, its breeder's name and address, and so on. If your dog has had purebred champions in his background, then the pedigree papers are valuable as evidence of the good breeding behind your dog; but if the names on the pedigree paper are meaningless, then so is the paper itself. Just because a dog has a pedigree doesn't necessarily mean he is registered with a kennel club.

Registration papers from the American Kennel Club or the United Kennel Club in the United States or The Kennel Club of Great Britain attest to the fact that the mother and father of your puppy were purebred dogs of the breed represented by your puppy and that they were registered with a particular club. Normally every registered dog also has a complete pedigree available. Registration papers, which you receive when you buy a puppy, merely enable you to register your puppy. Usually the breeder has registered only the litter, so it is the new owner's responsibility to register and name an individual pup. The papers should be filled out and sent to the appropriate address printed on the application, along with the fee required for the registration. A certificate of registration will then be sent to you.

Pedigree and registration, by the way, have nothing to do with licensing, which is a local regulation applying to purebred and mongrel alike. Find out what the local ordinance is in your town or city and how it applies to your dog; then buy a license and keep it on your dog's collar for identification.

Prancing Scottish Deerhound owned by Shawnine Hogan.

The New Family Member

It is a good idea to have all of your new pet's necessities—such as food, dishes, and a crate or doggy bed—in place before you bring him home.

At long last, the day you have all been waiting for, your new puppy will make its grand entrance into your home. Before you bring your companion to his new residence, however, you must plan carefully for his arrival. Keep in mind that the puppy will need

The New Family Member

time to adjust to life with a different owner. He may seem a bit apprehensive about the strange surroundings in which he finds himself, having spent the first few weeks of life with his dam and littermates, but in a couple of days, with love and patience on your part, the transition will be complete.

First impressions are important, especially from the puppy's point of view, and these may very well set the pattern of his future relationship with you. You must be consistent in the

The puppy's bed will provide a place of refuge and privacy. Make sure that the puppy's toilet needs have been met before sending him to bed for the night.

way you handle your pet so that he learns what is expected of him. He must come to trust and respect you as his keeper and master. Provide him with proper care and attention, and you will be rewarded with a loyal companion for many years. Considering the needs of your puppy and planning ahead will surely make the change from his former home to his new one easier.

ADVANCE PREPARATION

In preparing for your puppy's arrival, perhaps more important than anything else is to find out from the seller how the pup was maintained. What brand of food was offered and when and how often was the puppy fed? Has

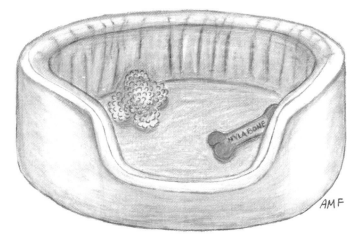

BASIC PUPPY NEEDS

- Canned and dry food/diet schedule
- Feeding and water bowls
- Carrying/sleeping crate
- Bed
- Collar and leash
- Grooming supplies (brushes, shampoo, etc.)
- Outdoor lead and/or pen
- Muzzle/first-aid kit
- Flea collar and preparations
- Safe chew products (Nylabone®, Gumabone®)
- Edible chew products (treats/rewards)

the pup been housebroken; if so, what method was employed? Attempt to continue whatever routine was started by the person from whom you bought your puppy; then, gradually, you can make those changes that suit you and your lifestyle. If, for example, the puppy has been paper trained, plan to stock up on newspaper. Place this newspaper toilet facility in a selected spot so that your puppy learns to use the designated area as his "bathroom." And keep on hand a supply of the dog food to which he is accustomed, as a sudden switch to new food could cause digestive upsets.

Another consideration is sleeping and resting quarters. Be sure to supply a dog bed for your pup, and introduce him to his special cozy corner so that he

This chart lists some of the many items that the dog owner should have on hand before he brings home his new charge.

knows where to retire when he feels like taking a snooze. You'll need to buy a collar (or harness) and leash, a safe chew item (such as Nylabone® or Gumabone®), and a few grooming tools as well. A couple of sturdy feeding dishes, one for food and one for water, will be needed; and it will be necessary, beforehand, to set up a feeding station.

FINDING A VETERINARIAN

An important part of your preparations should include finding a local veterinarian who can provide quality health care in the form of routine check-ups, inoculations, and prompt medical attention in case of illness or emergency. Find out if the animal you have selected has been vaccinated against canine diseases, and make certain you secure all health certificates at the time of purchase. This information will be valuable to your veterinarian, who will want to know the puppy's complete medical history. Incidentally, don't wait until your puppy becomes sick before you seek the services of a vet; make an appointment for your pup before or soon after he takes up residence with you so that he starts out with a clean bill of health in his new home.

CHILDREN AND PUPPIES

Instruct the young members of the household on pet care. Children should learn not only to love their charges but to respect them and treat them with the consideration that one would give all living things. It must be emphasized to youngsters that the puppy has certain needs, just as humans have, and all family members must take an active role in ensuring that these needs are met. Someone must feed the puppy. Someone must walk him a couple of times a day or clean up after him if he is trained to relieve himself on newspaper. Someone must groom his coat, clean his ears, and clip his nails from time to time. Someone

must see to it that the puppy gets sufficient exercise and attention each day.

A child who has a pet to care for learns responsibility; nonetheless, parental guidance is an essential part of this learning experience. Many a child has been known to "love a pet to death," squeezing and hugging the animal in ways which are irritating or even painful. Others have been found guilty of teasing, perhaps unintentionally, and disturbing their pet while the animal is eating or resting. One must teach a child, therefore, when and how to stroke and fondle a puppy gently. In time, the child can learn how to pick up and handle the pup with care. A dog should always be supported with both hands, *not* lifted by the scruff of the neck. One hand placed under the chest, between the front legs, and the other hand supporting the dog's rear end will be comfortable and will restrain the animal as you hold and carry it. Always demonstrate to children the proper way to lift a dog.

BE A GOOD NEIGHBOR

For the sake of your dog's safety and well being, don't allow him to wander onto the property of others. Keep him confined at all times to your own yard or indoors where he won't become a nuisance. Consider what

The regality of the Scottish Deer-hound is explicit in the demeanor of this dog owned by Ellen Bonacarti.

Clockwise from upper right: *pokeweed, jimson weed, foxglove,* and *yew*. If ingested, any toxic plant can be dangerous to your dog.

ROVER WILL NOT BE HARMED IF YOU FOLLOW MY INSTRUCTIONS

AMF

Dog theft is not an uncommon event. Dognappers will steal either a purebred or mongrel puppy so all owners must always be wary.

dangers lie ahead for an unleashed dog that has total freedom of the great outdoors, particularly when he is unsupervised by his master. There are cars and trucks to dodge on the streets and highways. There are stray animals with which to wrangle. There are poisons all around, such as car antifreeze in driveways or toxic plants and shrubs, which, if swallowed, could prove fatal. There are dognappers and sadistic people who may steal or bring harm to your beloved pet. In short, there are all sorts of nasty things waiting to hurt him. Did you know that if your dog consumes rotting garbage, there is the possibility he could go into shock or even die? And are you aware that a dog left to roam in a wooded area or field could become infected with any number of parasites if he plays with or ingests some small prey, such as a rabbit, that might be carrying these parasitic organisms? A thorn from a rosebush imbedded in the dog's foot pad, tar from a newly paved road stuck to his coat, and a wound inflicted by a wild animal all can be avoided if you take the precaution of keeping your dog in a safe enclosure where he will be protected from such dangers. Don't let your dog run loose; he is likely to stray from home and get into all sorts of trouble.

The New Family Member

GETTING ACQUAINTED

Plan to bring your new pet home in the morning so that by nightfall he will have had some time to become acquainted with you and his new environment. Avoid introducing the pup to the family around holiday time, since the extra excitement will only add to the confusion and frighten him. Let the puppy enter your home on a day when the routine is normal. For those people who work during the week, a Saturday morning is an ideal time to bring the puppy to his new home. Let the puppy explore, under your watchful eye, of course, and let him come to know his new home without stress and fear.

Resist the temptation to handle him too much during these first few days. And, if there are other dogs or animals around the house, make certain that all are properly introduced. If you observe fighting among the animals, or some other problem, you may have to separate all parties until they learn to accept one another. Remember that neglecting your other pets while

Scottish Deerhound on a blustery day. Owner, S.J. de Haan.

Facing page: *A lovely pair of Deerhounds owned by Ellen Bonacarti and Jean Gentner.*

showering the new puppy with extra attention will only cause animosity and jealousy. Make an effort to pay special attention to the other animals as well.

On that eventful first night, try not to give in and let the puppy sleep with you; otherwise, this could become a difficult habit to break. Let him cry and whimper, even if it means a night of restlessness for the entire family. Some people have had success with putting a doll or a hot water bottle wrapped in a towel in the puppy's bed as a surrogate mother, while others have placed a ticking alarm clock in the bed to simulate the heartbeat of the pup's dam and littermates. Remember that this furry little fellow is used to the warmth and security of his mother and siblings, so the adjustment to sleeping alone will take time. Select a location away from drafts and away from the feeding station for placement of his dog bed. Keep in mind, also, that the bed should be roomy enough for him to stretch out in; as he grows older, you may need to supply a larger one.

Prior to the pup's arrival, set up his room and partition it the way you would to keep an infant out of a particular area. You may want to keep his bed, his feeding station, and his toilet area all in the same room—in separate locations—or you may want to set the feeding station up in your kitchen, where meals for all family members are served. Whatever you decide, do it ahead of time so you will have that much less to worry about when your puppy finally moves in with you.

Above all else, be patient with your puppy as he adjusts to life in his new home. If you purchase a pup that is not housebroken, you will have to spend time with the dog—just as you would with a small child—until he develops proper toilet habits. Even a housebroken puppy may feel nervous in strange new surroundings and have an occasional accident. Praise and encouragement will elicit far better results than punishment or scolding. Remember that your puppy wants nothing more than to please you, thus he is anxious to learn the behavior that is required of him.

Feeding Requirements

Perhaps more than any other single aspect of your dog's development, proper feeding requires an educated and responsible dog owner. The importance of nutrition on your dog's bone and muscle growth cannot be overemphasized. Soon after your puppy comes to live with you, he will need to be fed. Remember to ask the seller what foods were given to the youngster and stay with that diet for a while. It is important for the puppy to keep eating and to avoid skipping a meal, so entice him with the food to which he is accustomed. If you prefer to switch to some other brand of dog food, each day begin to add small quantities of the new brand to the usual food offering. Make the portions of the new food progressively larger until the pup is weaned from his former diet.

What should you feed the puppy and how often? His diet is really quite simple and relatively inexpensive to prepare. Puppies need to be fed small portions at frequent intervals, since they are growing and their activity level is high. You must ensure that your pup gains weight steadily; with an adult dog, however, growth slows down and weight must be regulated to prevent obesity and a host of other problems. At one time, it was thought that home-cooked meals were the answer, with daily rations of meat,

Choosing a quality dog food from your pet shop is easy—deciding how much to feed may not be as straightforward. Feedings must always be carefully monitored.

vegetables, egg yolk, cereal, cheese, brewer's yeast, and vitamin supplements. With all of the nutritionally complete commercial dog food products readily available, these time-consuming preparations really are unnecessary now. A great deal of money and research has resulted in foods that we can serve our dogs with confidence and pride; and most of these commercial foods have been developed along strict guidelines according to the size, weight, and age of your dog. These products are reasonably priced,

Scottish Deerhound puppy posing with his Nylabone®. Nylabones®, available at pet shops, are the premier canine tension relievers—no one wants their pet to get stressed out!

easy to find, and convenient to store.

THE PUPPY'S MEALS

After a puppy has been fully weaned from its mother until approximately three months of age, it needs to be fed four times a day. In the morning and evening, offer kibble (dog meal) soaked in hot water or broth, to which you have added some canned meat-based food or fresh raw meat cut into small chunks. At noon and bedtime feed him a bit of kibble or whole-grain cereal moistened with milk (moistening, by the way, makes the food easier to digest, since dogs don't typically chew their food). From three to six months, increase the portion size and offer just three meals—one milk

A pair of Scottish Deerhounds at a show. If you think you might be interested in showing someday, buy the best possible dog you can afford.

and two meat. At six months, two meals are sufficient; at one year, a single meal can be given, supplemented with a few dry biscuits in the morning and evening. During the colder months, especially if your dog is active, you might want to mix in some wheat germ oil or corn oil or meat drippings with the meal to add extra calories. Remember to keep a bowl of cool, fresh water always on hand to help your dog regulate his body temperature and to aid in digestion.

From one year on, you may continue feeding the mature dog a single meal (in the evening, perhaps, when you have your supper), or you may prefer to divide this meal in two, offering half in the morning and the other half at night. Keep in mind that while puppies require foods in small chunks or nuggets, older dogs can handle larger pieces of food at mealtime. Discuss your dog's feeding schedule with your veterinarian; he can make suggestions about the right diet for your particular canine friend.

COMPARISON SHOPPING
With so many fine dog-food products on the market today, there is something for

everyone's pet. You may want to serve dry food "as is" or mix it with warm water or broth. Perhaps you'll choose to combine dry food with fresh or canned preparations. Some canned foods contain all meat, but they are not complete; others are mixtures of meat and grains, which have been fortified with additional nutrients to make them more complete and balanced. There are also various packaged foods that can be served alone or as supplements and that can be left out for a few hours without spoiling. This self-feeding method, which works well for dogs that are not prone to weight problems, allows the animal to serve himself whenever he feels hungry. Many people who work during the day find these dry or semi-moist rations convenient to use, and these foods are great to bring along if you travel with your dog.

Be sure to read the labels carefully before you make your dog-food purchases. Most

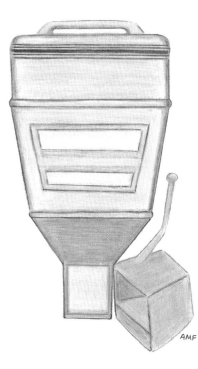

Feeder bins are used by many kennel owners as well as pet owners. These devices help to conveniently store and distribute dry foods in a sanitary, efficient way.

Pet shops offer a variety of dry kibbles. Though the nutritional values of these foods are essentially equivalent, compare the manufacturer's labels.

reputable pet-food manufacturers list the ingredients and the nutritional content right on the can or package. Instructions are usually included so that you will know how much to feed your dog to keep him thriving and in top condition. A varied, well-balanced diet that supplies the proper amounts of protein, carbohydrate, fat, vitamins, minerals, and water is important to keep your puppy healthy and to guarantee his normal development. Adjustments to the diet can be made, under your veterinarian's supervision, according to the individual puppy, his rate of growth, his activity level, and so on. Liquid or powder vitamin and mineral supplements, or those in tablet form, are available and can be given if you need to feel certain that the diet is balanced.

Proper nutrition, plenty of fresh clean water, and ample fresh air and exercise will keep your Deerhound healthy and happy throughout his life.

THE WORLD'S LARGEST SELECTION OF PET AND ANIMAL BOOKS

.F.H. Publications publishes more than 900 books covering many hobby aspects (dogs,

. . . BIRDS . .

. . CATS . . .

. . . ANIMALS . . .

. . . DOGS . .

. . FISH . . .

cats, birds, fish, small animals, etc.), plus books dealing with more purely scientific aspects of the animal world (such as books about fossils, corals, sea shells, whales and octopuses). Whether you are a beginner or an advanced hobbyist you will find exactly what you're looking for among our complete listing of books. For a free catalog fill out the form on the other side of this page and mail it today. All T.F.H. books are recyclable.

Since 1952, *Tropical Fish Hobbyist* has been the source of accurate, up-to-the-minute, and fascinating information on every facet of the aquarium hobby. Join the more than 50,000 devoted readers world-wide who wouldn't miss a single issue.

DEVELOPING GOOD EATING HABITS

Try to serve your puppy his meals at the same time each day and in the same location so that he will get used to his daily routine and develop good eating habits. A bit of raw egg, cottage cheese, or table scraps (leftover food from your own meals) can

Feeding your dog is made easy by the use of sturdy non-tip, easy-clean bowls. Pet shops offer the best selection of colors, styles and sizes.

be offered from time to time; but never accustom your dog to eating human "junk food." Cake, candy, chocolate, soda, and other snack foods are for people, not dogs. Besides, these foods provide only "empty" calories that your pet doesn't need if he is to stay healthy. Avoid offering spicy, fried, fatty, or starchy foods; rather, offer leftover meats, vegetables, and gravies. Get in the habit of feeding your puppy or your grown dog his *own* daily meals of dog food. If ever you are in doubt about what foods and how much to serve, consult your veterinarian.

Feeding Requirements

FEEDING GUIDELINES

Some things to bear in mind with regard to your dog's feeding regimen follow.

● Nutritional balance, provided by many commercial dog foods, is vital; avoid feeding a one-sided all-meat diet. Variety in the kinds of meat (beef, lamb, chicken, liver) or cereal grains (wheat, oats, corn) that

Automatic feeders are handy modern devices, available from most good pet shops. Overfeeding can be a drawback of this method of feeding.

you offer your dog is of secondary importance compared to the balance or "completeness" of dietary components.

● Always refrigerate opened canned food so that it doesn't spoil. Remember to remove all uneaten portions of canned or moistened food from the feeding dish as soon as the pup has finished his meal. Discard the leftover food immediately and thoroughly wash and dry the feeding dish, as a dirty dish is a breeding ground for harmful germs.

● When offering dry foods, always keep a supply of water on hand for your dog. Water should be made available at all times, even if dry foods are not left out for self-feeding. Each day the water dish should be washed with soap and hot water, rinsed well, and dried; a refill of clean, fresh water should be provided daily.

● Food and water should be served at room temperature, neither too hot nor too cold, so that it is more palatable for your puppy.

● Serve your pup's meals in sturdy hard-plastic, stainless steel, or earthenware containers, ones that won't tip over as the dog gulps his food down. Some bowls and dishes are weighted to prevent spillage, while others fit neatly into holders which offer support. Feeding dishes should be large enough to hold each meal.

- Whenever the nutritional needs of your dog change—that is to say, when it grows older or if it becomes ill, obese, or pregnant; or if it starts to nurse its young—special diets are in order. Always contact your vet for advice on these special dietary requirements.

- Hard foods, such as biscuits and dog meal, should be offered regularly. Chewing on these hard, dry morsels helps the dog keep its teeth clean and its gums conditioned.

- Never overfeed your dog. If given the chance, he will accept and relish every in-between-meal tidbit you offer him. This pampering will only put extra weight on your pet and cause him to be unhealthy.

New treats on the block by Chooz®. These crunchy dog bones are delectable and affordable.

- Feed your puppy at the same regular intervals each day; reserve treats for special occasions or, perhaps, to reward good behavior.

- Do not encourage your dog to beg for food from the table while you are eating your meals.

- Food can be effectively used by the owner to train the dog. Doggie treats are practical and often nutritional—choose your chew treats choosily.

FEEDING CHART

Age and No. of Feedings Per Day	Weight in Lbs.	Weight in Kg.	Caloric Requirement kcal M.E./Day
Puppies—Weaning to 3 months Four per day	1–3 3–6 6–12 12–20 15–30	.5–1.4 1.4–2.7 2.7–5.4 5.4–9.1 6.8–13.6	124–334 334–574 574–943 943–1384 1113–1872
Puppies—3 to 6 months Three per day	3–10 5–15 12–25 20–40 30–70	1.4–4.5 2.3–6.8 5.4–11.3 9.1–18.2 13.6–31.8	334–816 494–1113 943–1645 1384–2352 1872–3542
Puppies—6 to 12 months Two per day	6–12 12–25 20–50 40–70 70–100	2.7–5.4 5.4–11.3 9.1–22.7 18.2–31.8 31.8–45.4	574–943 943–1645 1384–2750 2352–3542 3542–4640
Normally Active Adults One or two per day	6–12 12–25 25–50 50–90 90–175	2.7–5.4 5.4–11.3 11.3–22.7 22.7–40.8 40.8–79.4	286–472 472–823 823–1375 1375–2151 2151–3675

This chart presents general parameters of the dog's caloric requirements, based on weight. The total caloric intake comes from a complete, balanced diet of quality foods. To assist owners, dog food companies generally provide the nutritional information to their product right on the label.

Accommodations

Puppies newly weaned from their mother and siblings should be kept warm at all times. As they get older, they can be acclimated gradually to cooler temperatures. When you purchase your dog, find out from the seller whether he is hardy and can withstand the rigors of outdoor living. Many breeds have been known to adapt well to a surprising number of environments, so long as they are given time to adjust. If your pup is to be an indoor

for your pooch; or you may find that a heated garage or finished basement works well as your dog's living quarters. If your breed can tolerate living outside, you may want to buy or build him his own dog house with an attached run. It might be feasible to place his house in your fenced-in backyard. The breed that can live outdoors fares well when given access to some sort of warm, dry shelter during periods of inclement weather. As you begin thinking about where

companion, perhaps a dog bed in the corner of the family room will suffice; or you may want to invest in a crate for him to call his "home" whenever he needs to be confined for short intervals. You might plan to partition off a special room, or part of a room,

A bed for your dog gives him a place to call his own. His bed should be placed in a warm, dry, draft-free area.

69

your canine friend will spend most of his time, you'll want to consider his breed, his age, his temperament, his need for exercise, and the money, space, and resources you have available to house him.

your puppy something with which to snuggle, such as a laundered towel or blanket or an article of old clothing. Some dogs have been known to chew apart their beds and bedding, but you can easily channel this

THE DOG BED

In preparing for your puppy's arrival, it is recommended that a dog bed be waiting for him so that he has a place to sleep and rest. If you have provided him with his own bed or basket, ensure that it is placed in a warm, dry, draft-free spot that is private but at the same time near the center of family activity. Refrain from placing his bed near the feed and water dishes or his toilet area. You may want to give

Beds can have personality. Pet shops offer many different bedding options to the owner willing to explore.

chewing energy into more constructive behavior simply by supplying him with some safe toys or a Nylabone® pacifier for gnawing. Pet shops stock dog beds, among other supplies that you might need for your pup. Select a bed that is roomy, comfortable, and easy to clean, keeping in mind that you may have to replace the smaller bed with a larger one as the puppy grows to adulthood. Remember to clean and disinfect the bed and sleeping area from time to time, as these can become parasitic playgrounds for fleas, lice, mites, and the like.

THE CRATE

Although many dog lovers may cringe at the mere mention of the word *crate,* thinking of it as a cage or a cruel means of confinement, this handy piece of equipment can be put to good use for puppies and grown dogs alike. Even though you may love your dog to an extraordinary degree, you may not want him to have free reign of the house, particularly when you are not home to supervise him. If used properly, a crate can restrict your dog when it is not convenient to have him underfoot, *i.e.,* when guests are visiting or during your mealtimes.

A surprising number of dog owners, who originally had negative feelings about crating their dogs, have had great success using crates. The crate itself serves as a bed, provided it is furnished with bedding material, or it can be used as an indoor dog house. Not all dogs

The wire crate is a most effective means to accelerate housebreaking and is the safest way to ensure that the puppy is safe when he cannot be supervised.

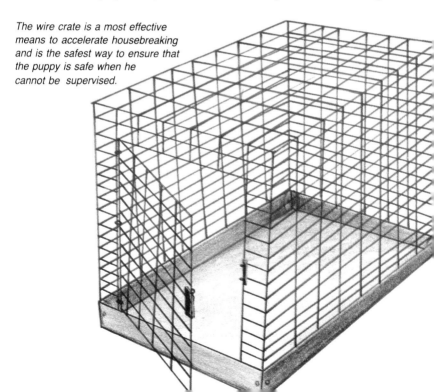

readily accept crates or being confined in them for short intervals, so for these dogs, another means of restriction must be found. But for those dogs that do adjust to spending time in these structures, the crate can be useful in many ways. The animal can be confined for a few hours while you are away from home or at work, or you can bring your

If your living arrangement allows, an outdoor run connected to the house by a swinging pet door can provide an ideal accommodation for your dog.

crated dog along with you in the car when you travel or go on vacation. Crates also prove handy as carriers whenever you have to transport a sick dog to the veterinarian.

Most crates are made of sturdy wire or plastic, and some of the collapsible models can be conveniently stored or folded so that they can be moved easily from room to room or from inside the house to the yard on a warm, sunny day. If you allow your puppy or grown dog to become acquainted with its crate by cleverly propping the door open and leaving some of his favorite toys inside, in no time he

will come to regard the crate as his own doggie haven. As with a dog bed, place the crate away from drafts in a dry, warm spot; refrain from placing food and water dishes in it, as these only crowd the space and offer opportunity for spillage.

If you need to confine your puppy so that he can't get into mischief while you're not home, remember to consider the animal's needs at all times. Select a large crate, one in which the dog can stand up and move around comfortably; in fact, bigger is better in this context. Never leave the animal confined for more than a few hours at a time without letting him out to exercise, play, and, if necessary, relieve himself. Never crate a dog for ten hours, for example, unless you keep the door to the crate open so that he can get out for food and water and to stretch a bit. If long intervals of confinement are necessary, consider placing the unlatched crate in a partitioned section of your house or apartment.

Crates have become the answer for many a dog owner faced with the dilemma of either getting rid of a destructive dog or living with him despite his bad habits. People who have neither the time nor the patience to train their dogs, or to modify undesirable behavior patterns, can at least restrain their pets during the times they can't be

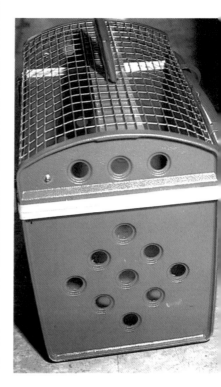

Traveling crates can provide safe and easy transport for your dog. Ventilation for travel is a most important consideration.

there to supervise. So long as the crate is used in a humane fashion, whereby a dog is confined for no more than a few hours at any one time, it can figure importantly in a dog owner's life. Show dogs,

The pet trade offers many commercially made dog houses and other outdoor living structures that make great temporary accommodations for your pet.

incidentally, learn at an early age that much time will be spent in and out of crates while they are on the show circuit. Many canine celebrities are kept in their crates until they are called to ringside, and they spend many hours crated to and from the shows.

THE DOG HOUSE

These structures, often made of wood, should be sturdy and offer enough room for your dog to stretch out in when it rests or sleeps. Dog houses that are elevated or situated on a platform protect the animal from cold and dampness that may seep through the ground. For the breeds that are temperature hardy and will live outdoors, a dog house is an excellent option for daytime occupancy. Owners who cannot provide indoor accommodations for their chosen dog should consider a smaller breed since no dog should lead an exclusively outdoor existence.

If you have no option but to accommodate your dog with only an outdoor house, it will be necessary to provide him with a more elaborate house, one that really protects him from the elements. Make sure the dog's house is constructed of waterproof materials. Furnish him with sufficient bedding to burrow into on a chilly night and provide extra insulation to keep out drafts and wet weather. Add a partition (a kind of room divider which separates the entry area from the main sleeping space) inside his house or attach a swinging door to the entrance to help keep him warm when he is inside his residence. The

Indoor-outdoor dog houses offer pest-free, sanitary conditions for your dog. These attractive living options can be acquired from pet shops, supply outlets or mail-order catalogues.

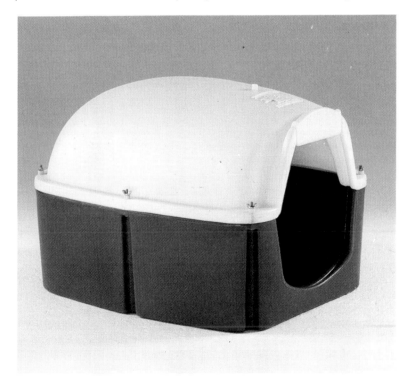

swinging door facilitates entry to and from the dog house, while at the same time it provides protection, particularly from wind and drafts.

Some fortunate owners whose yards are enclosed by high freedom is a dog kennel or run which attaches to or surrounds the dog's house. This restricts some forms of movement, such as running, perhaps, but it does provide ample room for walking, climbing, jumping, and

An anchored lead can provide efficient temporary restraint. This is not a viable substitute for a fenced-in yard and no dog should be left unsupervised on such a lead for any length of time.

fencing allow their dogs complete freedom within the boundaries of their property. In these situations, a dog can leave his dog house and get all the exercise he wants. Of course such a large space requires more effort to keep it clean. An alternative to complete backyard stretching. Another option is to fence off part of the yard and place the dog house in the enclosure. If you need to tether your dog to its house, make certain to use a fairly long lead so as not to hamper the animal's need to move and exercise his limbs.

CLEANLINESS

No matter where your dog lives, either in or out of your home, be sure to keep him in surroundings that are as clean and sanitary as possible. His excrement should be removed and disposed of every day without fail. No dog should be forced to lie in his own feces. If your dog lives in his own house, the floor should be swept occasionally and the bedding should be changed regularly if it becomes soiled. Food and water dishes need to be scrubbed with hot water and detergent and rinsed well to remove all traces of soap. The water dish should be refilled with a supply of fresh water. The dog and his environment must be kept free of parasites (especially fleas and mosquitoes, which can carry disease) with products designed to keep these pests under control. Dog crates need frequent scrubbing, too, as do the floors of kennels and runs. Your pet must be kept clean and comfortable at all times; if you exercise strict sanitary control, you will keep disease and parasite infestation to a minimum.

EXERCISE

A well-balanced diet and regular medical attention from a qualified veterinarian are essential in promoting good health for your dog, but so is

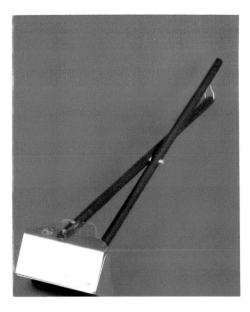

Most cities and towns require dog owners to clean up after their pets. Commercial pooper scoopers can make curbing your dog more convenient and sanitary.

daily exercise to keep him fit and mentally alert. Dogs that have been confined all day while their owners are at work or school need special attention. There should be some time set aside each day for play—a romp with a family member, perhaps. Not everyone is lucky enough to let his dog run through an open meadow or along a sandy beach, but even a ten-minute walk in the fresh air will do Dogs that are house-bound, particularly those that live in apartments, need to

Flying discs are popular with most dog owners, child and adult alike. Many dogs display a natural talent for Frisbee® games.

be walked out-of-doors after each meal so that they can relieve themselves. Owners can make this daily ritual more pleasant both for themselves

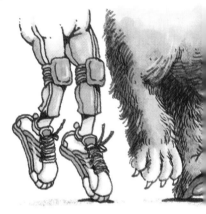

and their canine companions by combining the walk with a little "roughhousing," that is to say, a bit of fun and togetherness.

Whenever possible, take a stroll to an empty lot, a playground, or a nearby park. Attach a long lead to your dog's collar, and let him run and jump and tone his body through aerobic activity. This will help him burn calories and will keep him trim, and it will also help relieve tension and stress that may have had a chance to develop while you were away all day. For people who work Monday through Friday, weekend jaunts can be especially beneficial, since there will be more time to spend with your canine friend. You might want to engage him in a simple game of fetch with a stick or a rubber ball. Even such basic tricks as rolling over, standing on

by all means do it. Don't neglect your pet and leave him confined for long periods without attention from you or time for exercise.

the hindlegs, or jumping up (all of which can be done inside the home as well) can provide additional exercise. But if you plan to challenge your dog with a real workout to raise his heart rate, remember not to push him too hard without first warming up with a brisk walk. Don't forget to "cool him down" afterwards with a rhythmic trot until his heart rate returns to normal. Some dog owners jog with their dogs or take them along on bicycle excursions.

At the very least, however, play with your dog every day to keep him in good shape physically and mentally. If you can walk him outdoors, or better yet run with him in a more vigorous activity,

Fitness and exercise are on the move. Getting in on the trim-and-active side ain't just a doggie obsession—owners should sneak in too!

EXERCISING FOR YOU AND YOUR DOG

Dogs are like people. They come in three weights: overweight, underweight, and the correct weight. It is fair to say that most dogs are in better shape than most humans who own them. The reason for this is that most dogs accept exercise without objection—people do not! Follow your dog's lead towards exercise and the complete enjoyment of the outdoors—your dog is the ideal work-out partner. There are toys

at your local pet shop which are designed just for that purpose: to allow you to play and exercise with your dog. Here are a few recommended exercise toys for you and your dog.

Frisbee® Flying Discs Most dog owners capitalize on the dog's natural instinct to fetch or retrieve, and the Frisbee® flying disc is standard fare for play. The original Frisbee® is composed of polyethylene plastic, ideal for flying and great for games of catch between two humans. Since humans don't usually chew on their flying discs, there is no need for a "chew-worthy" construction material. Dogs, on the other

The most popular in flying discs designed especially for dogs is the Nylabone Frisbee®, a toy that outlasts plastic discs by ten times. The molded dog bone on the top makes for easy retrieves by your dog.

hand, do chew on their Frisbees® and therefore should not be allowed to play with a standard original Frisbee®. These discs will be destroyed quickly by the dog and the rigid plastic can cause intestinal complications.

Nylon Discs More suitable for playing with dogs are the Frisbee® discs that are constructed from nylon. These durable Frisbee® discs are designed especially for dogs and the nearly indestructible manufacturing makes them ideal for aggressive chewing dogs. For play with dogs, the nylon discs called Nylabone Frisbee® are guaranteed to last ten times as long as the regular plastic Frisbee®. Owners should carefully consider the size of the nylon Frisbee® they purchase. A rule of thumb is choose the largest disc that your dog can comfortably carry. Nylabone manufactures two sizes only— toy and large—so the choice should be apparent.

Polyurethane Flexible Floppy Flying Discs The greatest advance in flying discs came with the manufacture of these discs from polyurethane. The polyurethane is so soft that it doesn't hurt you, your dog, or the window it might strike accidentally. The polyurethane Gumadisc® is floppy and soft. It can be folded and fits into your pocket. It is also much tougher than cheap plastics, and most pet shops guarantee that it will last ten times longer than cheap plastic discs.

Making the polyurethane discs even more suited to dog play is the fact that many of the Gumabone® Frisbee® Flexible Fly Discs have the advantage of a dog bone molded on the top. Very often a Frisbee® without the bone molded on the top is difficult for a dog to pick up

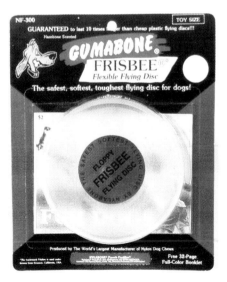

Made of durable and flexible polyurethane, the Gumabone Frisbees® prove chew-worthy and good-smelling to dogs. These and other Nylabone® discs are available in pet shops and other stores.

*Frisbee® is a trademark of the Kransco Company, California, and is used for their brand of flying disc.

when it lands on a flat surface. The molded ones enable the dog to grasp it with his mouth or turn it with his paw. Dogs love pawing at the bone and even chew on it occasionally.

This product has one further capacity—it doubles as a temporary drinking dish while out running, hiking and playing. The Gumabone Frisbee® flyers may also be flavored or scented, besides being annealed, so your dog can find it more easily if it should get lost in woods or tall grass.

with your canine friend. Basically, you play with the dog and the disc so the dog knows the disc belongs to him. Then you throw it continuously,

Toys made for doggie tug-of-wars are popular with lots of pet owners. These tug toys are durable and last a long time.

Flying discs manufactured by the Nylabone® Company may cost more than some of its imitators, but an owner can be assured that the product will last and not be quickly destroyed.

With most flying discs made for dogs comes an instruction booklet on how to use the disc

increasing the distance, so that the dog fetches it and brings it back to you.

The exercise for you comes in when your dog stops fetching it, or when you have a partner. The two of you play catch. You stand as far apart as available space allows—usually 30–35 m (100

Great for the athletic dog and less-active owner are commercially designed retractable leads which give the dog much freedom when exercising in an open field or cleared area.

feet) is more than enough room. You throw the disc to each other, arousing your dog's interest as he tries to catch it. When the disc is dropped or veers off, the dog grabs it and brings it back (hopefully). Obviously you will have to run to catch the disc before your dog does.

There are contests held all over the world where distance, height, and other characteristics are measured competitively. Ask your local pet shop to help you locate a Frisbee® Club near you.

Tug Toys A tug toy is a hard rubber, cheap plastic, or polyurethane toy which allows a

*Frisbee® is a trademark of the Kransco Company, California, and is used for their brand of flying disc.

The more consideration given to the canine's needs, the better the outdoor accommodations will be. Owners planning an outdoor kennel set-up must consider the elements (sun, rain, and wind) as well as sanitation and security.

dog and his owner to have a game of tug-o-war. The owner grips one end while the dog grips the other—then they pull. The polyurethane flexible tug toy is the best on the market at the present time. Your pet shop will have one to show you. The polyurethane toys are clear in color and stay soft forever. Cheap plastic tug toys are indisputably dangerous, and the hard-rubber tug toys get brittle too fast and are too stiff for most dogs; however, there *is* a difference in price—just ask the advice of any pet shop operator.

Balls Nobody has to tell you about playing ball with your dog. The reminder you may need is that you should not throw the ball where traffic might interfere with the dog's catching or fetching of it. The ball should not be cheap plastic (a dog's worst enemy as far as toys are concerned) but made of a substantial material. Balls made of nylon are practically indestructible, but they are very hard and must be rolled, never thrown. The same balls made of polyurethane are great—they bounce and are soft. The Nylaballs® and Gumaballs® are scented and flavored, and dogs can easily find them when lost.

Other manufacturers make balls of almost every substance, including plastic, cotton, and wood. Soft balls, baseballs, tennis balls, and so on, have all been used by dog owners who want their dogs to play with them in a game of catch. A strong caveat is that you use only those balls made especially for dogs.

It pays to invest in entertainment toys and exercise devices which are marketed particularly for dogs. These products outlast everyday play things and are much safer for your pet. The Gumaball® is a great example of a dog toy worth the price of admission.

Housebreaking is required training for all puppies and even some older dogs who come in to new homes. There are many experience-based rules for the housebreaking owner to follow, including the use of a restricted area and close supervision. If approached thoughtfully and intelligently, housebreaking should proceed smoothly to its completion.

Housebreaking and Training

The value of the news may be waning in recent years, but newspaper will always have a worthwhile purpose to the new dog owner.

HOUSEBREAKING

The new addition to your family may already have received some basic house training before his arrival in your home. If he has not, remember that a puppy will want to relieve himself about half a dozen times a day; it is up to you to specify where and when he should "do his business." Housebreaking is your first training concern and should begin the moment you bring the puppy home.

Ideally, puppies should be taken outdoors after meals, as a full stomach will exert pressure on the bladder and colon. What

goes into the dog must eventually come out; the period after his meal is the most natural and appropriate time. When he eliminates, he should be praised, for this will increase the likelihood of the same thing happening after every meal. He should also be encouraged to

that your pet will associate the act of elimination with a particular word of your choice rather than with a particular time or place which might not always be convenient or available. So whether you are visiting an unfamiliar place or don't want to go outside with your dog in sub-

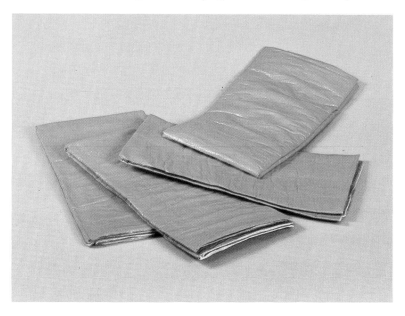

Housebreaking pads, used by many cautious owners instead of the ever trusty press, can be purchased in pet shops and pet supply outlets.

use the same area and will probably be attracted to it after frequent use.

Some veterinarians maintain that a puppy can learn to urinate and defecate on command, if properly trained. The advantage of this conditioning technique is

zero temperatures, he will still be able to relieve himself when he hears the specific command word. Elimination will occur after this "trigger" phrase or word sets up a conditioned reflex in the dog, who will eliminate anything contained in his bladder or bowel upon hearing it. The shorter the word, the more you can repeat it and imprint it on your dog's memory.

Your chosen command word should be given simultaneously with the sphincter opening events in order to achieve perfect and rapid conditioning. This is why it is important to familiarize yourself with the tell-tale signs preceding your puppy's elimination process. Then you will be prepared to say the word at the crucial moment. There is usually a sense of urgency on the dog's part; he

will soon learn to associate the act with the word. One word of advice, however, if you plan to try out this method: never use the puppy's name or any other word which he might frequently hear about the house—you can imagine the result!

Finally, remember that any training takes time. Such a conditioned response can be obtained with intensive practice with any normal, healthy dog over six weeks of age. Even Pavlov's salivating dogs required fifty repetitions before the desired response was achieved.

Crates assist in potty-training the puppy. The dog's natural instinct is never to soil his sleeping area.

may follow a sniffing and circling pattern which you will soon recognize. It is important to use the command in his usual area only when you know the puppy can eliminate, i.e., when his stomach or bladder is full. He

Patience and persistence will eventually produce results—do not lose heart!

Indoors, sheets of newspapers can be used to cover the specific area where your dog should relieve himself. These should be placed some distance away from his sleeping and feeding area, as a puppy will not urinate or defecate where he eats. When the newspapers are changed, the bottom papers should be placed on top of the new ones in order to reinforce the purpose of

the run of the house, the sheer size of the place will seem overwhelming and confusing and he might leave his "signature" on your furniture or clothes! There will be time later to familiarize him gradually with his new surroundings.

The choke collar and walking lead are commonly used in training.

the papers by scent as well as by sight. The puppy should be praised during or immediately after he has made use of this particular part of the room. Each positive reinforcement increases the possibility of his using that area again.

When he arrives, it is advisable to limit the puppy to one room, usually the kitchen, as it most likely has a linoleum or easily washable floor surface. Given

PATIENCE, PERSISTENCE, AND PRAISE

As with a human baby, you must be patient, tolerant, and understanding of your pet's mistakes, making him feel loved and wanted, not rejected and isolated. You wouldn't hit a baby for soiling his diapers, as you would realize that he was not yet able to control his bowel movements; be as compassionate with your canine infant. Never rub his nose in his excreta. Never indulge in the common practice of punishing him with a rolled-up newspaper. Never hit a puppy with your hand. He will only become "hand-shy" and learn to fear you. Usually the punishment is meted out sometime after the offense and loses its efficacy, as the bewildered dog cannot connect the two events. Moreover, by association, he will soon learn to be afraid of you and anything to do with newspapers—including, perhaps, that area where he is *supposed* to relieve himself!

A simple dog collar or leash can be deceiving. Never be afraid to ask your pet shop proprietor exactly how a particular device is intended to work.

Most puppies are eager to please. Praise, encouragement, and reward (particularly the food variety) will produce far better results than any scolding or physical punishment. Moreover, it is far better to dissuade your puppy from doing certain things, such as chewing on chair legs or other furniture, by making those objects particularly distasteful to him. Some pet shops stock bitter apple sprays or citronella compounds for application to furniture legs. These products are generally safer than old-fashioned home remedies. An owner may soon discover that application of these products may indeed make it seem as if the object itself was administering the punishment whenever he attempted to chew it. He probably wouldn't need a second reminder and your furniture will remain undamaged.

Remember that the reason a dog has housebreaking or behavior problems is because his owner has allowed them to develop. This is why you must begin as you intend to continue, letting your dog know what is acceptable and unacceptable behavior. It is also important that you be consistent in your

A choke collar can be an effective training tool when properly used.

demands; you cannot feed him from the dining room table one day and then punish him when he begs for food from your dinner guests.

TRAINING

You will want the newest member of your family to be welcomed by everyone; this will not happen if he urinates in every room of the house or barks all night! He needs training in the correct forms of behavior in this new human world. You cannot expect your puppy to become the perfect pet overnight. He needs your help in his socialization process. Training greatly facilitates and enhances the relationship of the dog to his owner and to the rest of society. A successfully trained dog can be taken anywhere and behave well with anyone. Indeed, it is that one crucial word—*training*—which can transform an aggressive animal into a peaceful, well-behaved pet. Now, how does this "transformation" take place?

WHEN AND HOW TO TRAIN

Like housebreaking, training should begin as soon as the puppy enters the house. The formal training sessions should be short but frequent, for example, ten to fifteen minute periods three times a day. These are much more effective than long, tiring sessions of half an hour which might soon become boring. You are building your relationship with your puppy during these times, so make them as enjoyable as possible. It is a good idea to have these sessions *before* the puppy's meal, not after it when he wouldn't feel like exerting himself; the dog will then

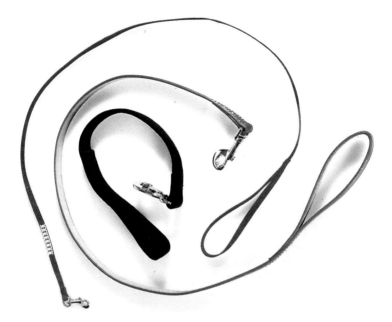

associate something pleasurable with his training sessions and look forward to them.

THE COLLAR AND LEASH

Your puppy should become used to a collar and leash as soon as possible. If he is very young, a thin, choke-chain collar can be used, but you will need a larger and heavier one for training when he is a little older. Remember to have his name and address on an identification tag attached to his collar, as you don't want to lose your pet if he should happen to leave your premises and explore the neighborhood!

Nylon and leather leads are the most popular with pet owners.

Let the puppy wear his collar until he is used to how it feels. After a short time he will soon become accustomed to it and you can attach the leash. He might resist your attempts to lead him or simply sit down and refuse to budge. Fight him for a few minutes, tugging on the leash if necessary, then let him relax for the day. He won't be trained until he learns that he must obey the pull under any circumstance, but this will take a few sessions. Remember that a dog's period of concentration is short, so LITTLE and OFTEN is the wisest course of action—and patience is the password to success.

For safety purposes, as well as the comfort of your pet, be sure to choose the right-sized collar and a sensible leash for your daily walks.

GIVING COMMANDS

When you begin giving your puppy simple commands, make them as short as possible and use the same word with the same meaning at all times, for example, "Heel," "Sit," and "Stay." You must be consistent; otherwise your puppy will become confused. The dog's name should prefix all commands to attract his attention. Do not become impatient with him however many times you have to repeat your command.

A good way to introduce the "Come" command is by calling the puppy when his meal is ready. Once this is learned, you can call your pet to you at will, always remembering to praise him for his prompt obedience. This "reward," or positive reinforcement, is such a crucial part of training that a Director of the New York Academy of Dog Training constructed his whole teaching program upon the methods of "Love, Praise, and Reward." Incidentally, if you use the command "Come," use it every time. Don't switch to "Come here" or "Come boy," as this will only confuse your dog.

It is worth underlining the fact that punishment is an ineffective teaching technique. We have already seen this in housebreaking. For example, if your pup should run away, it would be senseless to beat him when he eventually returns; he would only connect the punishment with his return, not with running away! In addition, it is unwise to call him to you to punish him, as he will soon learn not to respond when you call his name.

Harnesses can be used for daily walks, though some dogs do not find them comfortable. Heavily coated dogs especially may object, and the harness can eventually wear on the dog's coat.

Housebreaking and Training

SOME SPECIFIC COMMANDS

"Sit" This is one of the easiest and most useful commands for your dog to learn, so it is a good idea to begin with it. The only equipment required is a leash, a collar, and a few tasty tidbits. Take your dog out for some exercise before his meal. After about five minutes, call him to you, praise him when he arrives,

Praise must be given when the dog correctly assumes the sit position. If praise is given before sitting or after the dog makes motion to rise, the dog may become confused.

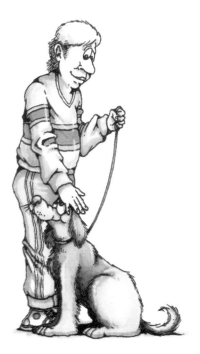

and slip his collar on him. Hold the leash tightly in your right hand; this should force the dog's head up and focus his attention on you. As you say "Sit" in a loud, clear voice, with your left hand press steadily on his rump until he is in a sitting position. As soon as he is in the correct position, praise him and give him the tidbit you have in your hand. Now wait a few minutes to let him rest and repeat the routine. Through repetition, the dog soon associates the word with the act. Never make the lesson too long. Eventually your praise will be reward enough for your puppy. Other methods to teach this command exist, but this one, executed with care and moderation, has proven the most effective.

"Sit-Stay/Stay" To teach your pet to remain in one place or "stay" on your command, first of all order him to the sitting position at your side. Lower your left hand with the flat of your palm in front of his nose and your fingers pointing downwards. Hold the leash high and taut behind his head so that he cannot move. Speak the command "Sit-stay" and, as you are giving it, step in front of him. Repeat the command and tighten the leash so the animal cannot follow you. Walk completely around him, repeating the command and keeping him motionless by holding the leash at arm's length above him to check his movement. When he remains in this position for about fifteen seconds, you can begin the second part of the training. You will have to exchange the leash for a nylon cord or rope about twenty to thirty feet long. Repeat the whole routine from the beginning and be ready to prevent any movement towards you with a sharp "Sit-stay." Move around him in ever-widening circles until you are about fifteen feet away from him. If he still remains seated, you can pat yourself on the back! One useful thing to remember is that the dog makes associations with what you say, how you say it, and what you do while you are saying it. Give this command in a firm, clear tone of voice, perhaps using an admonishing forefinger raised, warning the dog to "stay."

"Heel" When you walk your dog, you should hold the leash firmly in your right hand. The dog should walk on your left so you have the leash crossing your body. This enables you to have greater control over the dog.

Let your dog lead you for the first few moments so that he fully understands that freedom can be his if he goes about it properly. He already knows that when he wants to go outdoors the leash and collar are

Timing is all-important in sit training—be sure to say "sit" and press down on the dog's rump at the same time.

necessary, so he has respect for the leash. Now, if he starts to pull in one direction while walking, all you do is *stop walking.* He will walk a few steps and then find that he can't walk any further. He will then turn and look into your face. *This is the crucial point!* Just stand there for a moment and stare right back at him . . . now walk another ten feet and stop again. Again your dog will probably walk to the end of the leash, find he can't go any further, and turn around and look again. If he starts to pull and jerk, just stand there. After he quiets down, bend down and comfort him, as he may be frightened. Keep up this training until he learns not to outwalk you.

Once the puppy obeys the pull of the leash, half of your training is accomplished. "Heeling" is a necessity for a well-behaved dog, so teach him to walk beside you, head even with your knee. Nothing looks sadder than a big dog taking his helpless owner for a walk. It is annoying to passers-by and other dog owners to have a large dog, however friendly, bear down on them and entangle dogs, people, and packages.

To teach your dog, start off walking briskly, saying "Heel" in a firm voice. Pull back with a sharp jerk if he lunges ahead, and if he lags repeat the command and tug on the leash, not allowing him to drag behind. After the dog has learned to heel at various speeds on leash, you can remove it and practice heeling free, but have it ready to snap on again as soon as he wanders.

"Come" Your dog has already learned to come to you when you call his name. Why? Because you only call him when his food is ready or when you wish to play with him or praise him. Outdoors such a response is more difficult to achieve, if he is happily

When in the heel position, the dog should be at your left side. The lead should be held in your right hand, loosely except when checking him back to the desired position.

playing by himself or with other dogs, so he must be trained to come to you when he is called. To teach him to come, let him reach the end of a long lead, then give the command, gently pulling him towards you at the same time. As soon as he associates the word *come* with the action of moving towards you, pull only when he does not respond immediately. As he starts to come, move back to make him learn that he must come from a distance as well as when he is close to you. Soon you may be able to practice without a leash, but if he is slow to come or actively disobedient, go to him and pull him toward you, repeating the command. Always remember to reward his successful completion of a task.

"Down" Teaching the "down" command ideally begins while your dog is still a pup. During

Correct behavior deserves positive reinforcement. When your dog heels, let him know how pleased you are by giving a kind word or reward.

Be gentle and reassuring with your dog, especially during the early stages of the down training—he may not understand what you are doing and may even feel threatened.

puppyhood your dog frequently will lie down, as this position is one of the dog's most natural positions. Invest some time, and keep close watch over your pup. Each time he begins to lie, repeat in a low convincing tone the word "down." If for the first day of training, you concur a majority of the dog's sitting with your commands and continue with reinforcement and moderate praise your pup should conquer the "down" command in no time.

Teaching the "down" command to a mature dog likely will require more effort. Although the lying position is still natural to a dog, his being forced into it is not. Some dogs may react with

Once he is in the correct down position, lavish praise will tell him that he is doing well.

fear, anger, or confusion. Others may accept the process and prove quick learners. Have your dog sit and face you. If he is responsive and congenial, gently take his paws, and slowly pull them towards you; give the "down" command as he approaches the proper position. Repeat several times: moderate reinforcement of this procedure should prove successful.

For the dog that responds with anger or aggression, attach a lead (and a muzzle) and have the dog sit facing you at a close distance. There should be a J-loop formed by the lead. With moderate force, relative to the size and strength of your dog, step on the J-loop, forcing the dog down, while repeating the command "down" in a low forceful tone. When the dog is down, moderate praise should be given. If the dog proves responsive, you may attempt extending his legs to the "down" position—leaving the muzzle on, of course. Daily reinforcement of the training method will soon yield the desired results. The keys to remember are: patience, persistence, and praise.

Behavior Modification

"Problems with the Barking Dog" and "Aggressive Behavior and Dominance" are extracts from the veterinary monograph *Canine Behavior* (a compilation of columns from *Canine Practice,* a journal published by Veterinary Practice Publishing Company).

PROBLEMS WITH THE BARKING DOG

One of the most frequent complaints about canine behavior is barking. Aside from the biting dog, the barking dog is probably the pet peeve of many non-dog owners. I know of at least one city in which owners of dogs that bark excessively, and for which there are complaints on file, are required to take steps to eliminate the barking.

Canine practitioners are drawn into problems with barking when they are asked for their advice in helping an owner come up with a solution or, as a last resort, when they are requested to perform a debarking operation or even euthanasia. In this column I will deal with some of the factors that apparently cause dogs to bark and suggest some corrective approaches.

Barking is, of course, a natural response for many dogs. They have an inherited predisposition to bark as an alarm when other dogs or people approach their territory. Alarm barking makes

Only in the most extreme situations may trainers recommend electric-shock collars for correcting a dog's misbehavior.

many dogs valuable as household watchdogs and is not necessarily undesirable behavior. With a different vocal tone and pattern, dogs bark when they are playing with each other. On occasion dogs have a tendency to bark back at other dogs or join in with other barking dogs.

In addition to inherited barking tendencies, dogs can also learn to bark if the barking is followed, at least sometimes, by a reward. Thus dogs may bark when they wish to come in the house or to get out of a kennel. Some dogs are trained to bark upon hearing the command "speak" for a food reward.

One of the first approaches to take when discussing a barking problem is to determine if the behavior is a manifestation of a natural (inherited) tendency or is learned behavior which has been rewarded in the past.

praise again when it barks after being told to "speak," it will eventually stop this type of barking. This is the process of extinction and it implies that the behavior must be repeated but never again rewarded.

A more practical example of the possible use of extinction

Canine viciousness cannot be tolerated. Owners who train their dogs to be vicious are to blame for the strong anti-dog sentiment in our communities.

Can Barking Be Extinguished?

Extinction, as a way of eliminating a behavioral problem, may be considered when it is clear that the behavior has been learned and when one can identify the specific rewarding or reinforcing factors that maintain the behavior.

For example, the dog that barks upon hearing the command "speak" is periodically rewarded with food and praise. If a dog is never, ever given food or

would be in dealing with the dog that apparently barks because, at least occasionally, it is allowed in the house. By not allowing the dog in the house until the barking has become very frequent and loud, the owners may have shaped the barking behavior to that which is the most objectionable. If the dog is never allowed in the house again when barking, the barking should eventually be extinguished—at least theoretically.

How Should Punishment Be Used?

Sometimes it is not feasible to attempt to extinguish barking even if it seems to be the case that the behavior was learned. This brings up the advisability of punishment. Clients who seek advice in dealing with a barking problem may already have employed some type of punishment such as shouting at the dog or throwing something at it. That this type of punishment is ineffective is attested to by the fact that the client is seeking advice. By shouting at a dog or hitting, a person interferes with what effect the punishment may have on the behavior itself through the arousal of autonomic reactions and escape attempts or submissive responses by the dog.

The Water Bucket Approach

I am rather impressed by the ingenuity of some dog owners in

Sound-wave bark-control collars emit a noise that is inaudible to man but discomforting to the canine. These should not be used without professional supervision.

coming up with ways to punish a dog for barking without being directly involved in administering the punishment. One such harried dog owner I talked to, who was also a veterinarian, was plagued by his dog's barking in the kennel commencing at about 1:30 a.m. every night. A platform to hold a bucket of water was constructed over the area of the kennel in which the dog usually chose to bark. Through a system of hinges, ropes, and pulleys, a mechanism was devised so that the dog owner could pull a rope from his bedroom window, dumping a bucket of water on the dog when he started to bark. The bucket was suspended such that once it was dumped, it

Muzzles may prevent biting, but the root cause of biting must be extracted if the dog is to live as a trusted member of the human family.

uprighted itself and the owner could fill it again remotely by turning on a garden hose. After two appropriate dunkings, the dog's barking behavior was apparently eliminated.

In advising a client on the type of punishment discussed above, keep in mind one important consideration. From the time the owner is ready to administer punishment for barking, every attempt should be made to punish all undesirable barking from that point on and not to allow excessively long periods of barking to go unpunished. Thus it may be necessary to keep a dog indoors when away unless the dog will be punished for barking when the owner is gone.

Alternative Responses Barking dogs are, and probably always will be, one of the enduring problems of dog owners. Barking is relatively effortless, and it is such a natural response for many dogs that it is admittedly hard to eliminate with either punishment or a program of conditioning non-barking. In some instances it may be advisable to forget about eliminating barking and to suggest that the problem be dealt with by changing the circumstances which lead to barking. For example, a dog that

Pet gates are used to confine a dog to certain areas of the house. The dog must learn to accept any such restrictions and not attempt to overcome them.

barks continuously in the backyard while the owners are away may not bark if left in the house while they are gone. But the problem of keeping the dog in the house may be related to inadequate house training or the dog's shedding hair or climbing onto the furniture. It may be easier to correct these latter behavioral problems than it is to change the barking behavior.

AGGRESSIVE BEHAVIOR AND DOMINANCE

Aggressiveness can have many causes. Determining what kind of aggression an animal is manifesting is a prerequisite to successful treatment of the behavior. A frequent problem that is presented to the practitioner is one of aggression related to dominance.

Dogs, which are social animals, have a hierarchal system of dominance within their pack. This predisposition to take a dominant or submissive position relative to fellow canines also occurs in relationship to people. Only in unusual situations would a submissive dog threaten a dominant animal, and almost never would it physically assault its superior. The dominant dog, however, frequently threatens submissive individuals to maintain its position. In a household setting, a person may be the object of threats, and when the person backs off, the dog's position is reassured. The aggressive behavior is also reinforced, and when behavior is reinforced it is likely to recur.

Case History The following is a typical case history of a dog presented for aggression stemming from dominance.

Max was a two-year-old intact male Cocker Spaniel. He had been acquired by Mr. Smith, one year prior to his owner's marriage, as a puppy. He liked and was well liked by both Mr. and Mrs. Smith. He frequently solicited and received attention from both people. However, several times over the last few months, Max had snapped at Mrs. Smith and repeatedly growled at her. A detailed anamnesis revealed that such incidents usually occurred in situations where the dog wanted his own way or did not want to be bothered. He would growl if asked to move off a chair or if persistently commanded to do a specific task. He growled if Mrs. Smith came between him and a young female Cocker Spaniel acquired a year ago. He also refused to let Mrs. Smith take anything from his possession. Max never showed any of these aggressive behaviors toward Mr. Smith or strangers. Admittedly he did not have much opportunity to demonstrate such

behaviors toward strangers. A description of the dog's body and facial postures and circumstances under which the aggression occurred did not indicate that this was a case of fear-induced aggression, but rather one of assertion of dominance.

Mrs. Smith's reaction to the aggression was always to retreat, and, hence, the dog was rewarded for his assertiveness. She had never physically disciplined the dog and was afraid to do so. To encourage her to physically take control of the dog would likely have resulted in her being bitten. The dominance-submissive relationship had to be reversed in a more subtle manner.

Instructions to Client Mrs. Smith was instructed to avoid all situations which might evoke any aggressive signs from Max. This was to prevent any further reinforcement of his growling and threats.

Both she and her husband were not to indiscriminately pet or show affection towards the dog. For the time being, if Max solicited attention from Mr. Smith, he was to ignore the dog. Mrs. Smith was to take advantage of Max's desire for attention by giving him a command which he had to obey before she praised and petted him. She was also to take advantage of high motivation levels for other activities whenever such situations arose. Max had to obey a command before she gave him anything—before she petted him, before she let him out or in, etc.

Mrs. Smith also was to assume total care of the dog and coveted food rewards as well as praise. These were entirely fun and play sessions—but within a few days the dog had acquired the habit of quickly responding to commands. And this habit transferred over to the non-game situations.

There is a wide variety of collars and harnesses available to the dog owner. Talk with your pet shop proprietor to determine which one best satisfies your needs.

become "the source of all good things in life" for Max. She was to feed him, take him on walks, play with him, etc.

Mrs. Smith also spent 5–10 minutes a day teaching Max simple parlor tricks and obedience responses for

Results Within a few weeks, Max had ceased to growl and threaten Mrs. Smith in situations that he previously had. He would move out of her way or lie quietly when she would pass by him. She could order him off the furniture and handle the female

Cocker Spaniel without eliciting threats from Max.

Mrs. Smith still felt that she would not be able to take the objects from Max's possession. Additional instructions were given to her. She then began placing a series of objects at progressively closer distances to the dog while the dog was in a sit-stay position. After she placed the object on the floor for a short time, she would pick it up. If the dog was still in a sit-stay (which it always was), he received a reward of cheese and verbal praise. Eventually the objects were to be placed and removed from directly in front of the dog. At first she was to use objects that the dog did not care much about and then progressively use more coveted items. This was what she was

Treats can be effective in shaping behavior and establishing a rapport with your pet.

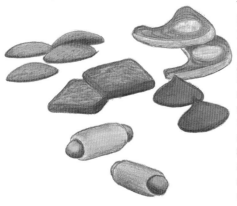

supposed to do, but before she actually had completed the program she called in excitedly to report that she had taken a piece of stolen food and a household ornament from Max's mouth. And he didn't even object! She said she had calmly told Max to sit. He did. He was so used to doing so, in the game and other situations, that the response was now automatic. She walked over, removed the item from his mouth, and praised him.

Mrs. Smith did resume the systematic presentation of objects and put the dog on an intermittent schedule of food and praise reinforcement during the practice sessions. Mr. Smith again began interacting with Max.

A progress check six months later indicated Max was still an obedient dog and had definitely assumed a submissive position relative to both of his owners. The dominance hierarchy between Max and Mrs. Smith had been reversed *without resorting to any physical punishment.* Mrs. Smith was instructed to reinforce her dominance position by frequently giving Max a command and reinforcing him for the appropriate response.

Summary The essential elements in treatment of such cases are as follows. First, of course, there must be a correct

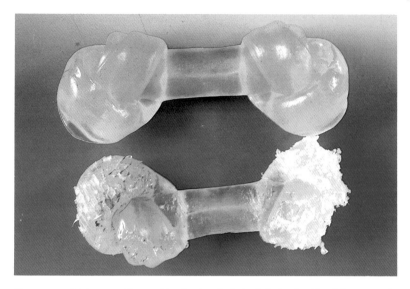

Owners must take an active part in shaping their dog's behavior. Providing a sensible chew device can help alleviate an animal's frustration and thereby eliminate some undesirable behavior.

diagnosis of what kind of aggressive behavior is occurring. During the course of treatment, the submissive person(s) should avoid all situations that might evoke an aggressive attitude by the dog. All other family members should totally ignore the dog during the treatment interim. The person most dominated by the dog should take over complete care of the dog in addition to spending 5–10 minutes a day teaching the dog tricks or simple obedience commands (sit-stay is a useful one to gain control of the dog in subsequent circumstances). These should be fun-and-games situations. Food rewards are highly recommended in addition to simple praise.

The person submissive to the dog should take the opportunity to give the dog a command, which must be obeyed, before doing anything pleasant for the dog.

It must be emphasized to the owner that no guarantee can be made that the dog will never threaten or be aggressive again. What is being done, as with all other aggression cases, is an attempt to reduce the likelihood, incidence, and intensity of occurrence of the aggressive behavior.

DESTRUCTIVE TENDENCIES

It is ironical but true that a dog's destructive behavior in the home may be proof of his love for his owner. He may be trying to get more attention from his owner or, in other cases, may be expressing his frustration at his owner's absence. An abundance of unused energy may also contribute to a dog's destructive behavior, and therefore the owner should ensure that his dog has, at least, twenty minutes of vigorous exercise a day.

As a dog's destructive tendencies may stem from his desire to get more attention from his owner, the latter should devote specific periods each day to his dog when he is actively interacting with him. Such a period should contain practice obedience techniques during which the owner can reward the dog with his favorite food as well as praise and affection.

Planned departure conditioning is one specific technique which has been used to solve the problem of destructive tendencies in a puppy. It eventually ensures the dog's good behavior during the owner's absence. A series of short departures, which are identical to real departures, should condition the dog to behave well in the owner's absence. How is this to be achieved? Initially, the departures are so short (2–5 minutes) that the dog has no opportunity to be destructive. The dog is always rewarded for having been good when the owner returns. Gradually the duration of the departures is increased. The departure time is also varied so that the dog does not know when the owner is going to return. Since a different kind of behavior is now expected, it is best if a new stimulus or "atmosphere" is introduced into the training sessions to permit the dog to distinguish these departures as different from previous departures when he was destructive.

This new stimulus could be the sound of the radio or television. The association which the dog will develop is that whenever the "signal" or "stimulus" is on, the owner will return in an unknown period of time and, if the dog has not been destructive, he will be rewarded. As with the daily owner-dog interaction, the food reward is especially useful.

If the dog misbehaves during his owner's absence, the owner should speak sternly to him and isolate him from social contact for at least thirty minutes. (Puppies hate to be ignored.) Then the owner should conduct another departure of a shorter time and generously reward good behavior when he returns. The owner should progress slowly enough in the program so that once the departure has been initiated, the dog is never given an opportunity to make a mistake.

If planned departures are working satisfactorily, the departure time may gradually be extended to several hours. To reduce the dog's anxiety when left alone, he should be given a "safety valve" such as the indestructible Nylabone® to play with and chew on.

While crates may be used principally for sleeping and traveling, some owners might opt to employ a crate for disciplining a dog, rather like sending a naughty child to his room.

Health Care

From the moment you purchase your puppy, the most important person in both your lives becomes your veterinarian. His

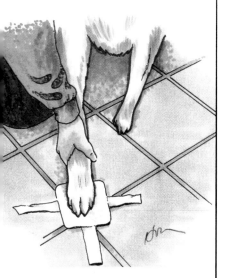

Bandaging a minor cut on the paw pad is one of many basic first-aid techniques that the dog owner should learn.

professional advice and treatment will ensure the good health of your pet. The vet is the first person to call when illness or accidents occur. Do *not* try to be your own veterinarian or apply human remedies to canine diseases. However, just as you would keep a first aid kit handy for minor injuries sustained by members of your family at home, so you should keep a similar kit prepared for your pet.

First aid for your dog would consist of stopping any bleeding, cleaning the wound, and preventing infection. Thus your kit might contain medicated powder, gauze bandages, and adhesive tape to be used in case of cuts. If the cut is deep and bleeding profusely, the bandage should be applied very tightly to help in the formation of a clot. A tight bandage should not be kept in place longer than necessary, so take your pet to the veterinarian immediately.

Walking or running on a cut pad prevents the cut from

Thoroughly clean the injury with peroxide and apply an antibiotic. Then place the injured pad in sterile gauze, secure with first-aid tape, and replace daily.

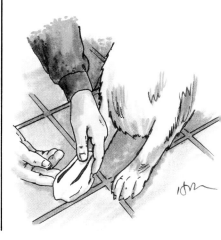

healing. Proper suturing of the cut and regular changing of the bandages should have your pet's wound healed in a week to ten days. A minor cut should be covered with a light bandage, for you want as much air as possible to reach the wound. Do not apply wads of cotton to a wound, as they will stick to the area and may cause contamination.

You should also keep some hydrogen peroxide available, as it is useful in cleaning wounds and is also one of the best and simplest emetics known. Cotton applicator swabs are useful for applying ointment or removing debris from the eyes. A pair of tweezers should also be kept handy for removing foreign bodies from the dog's neck, head or body.

Nearly everything a dog might contract in the way of sickness has basically the same set of symptoms: loss of appetite, diarrhea, dull eyes, dull coat, warm and/or runny nose, and a high temperature. Therefore, it is most important to take his temperature at the first sign of illness. To do this, you will need a rectal thermometer which should be lubricated with petroleum jelly. Carefully insert it into the rectum, holding it in place for at least two minutes. It must be held firmly; otherwise there is the danger of its being sucked up into the rectum or slipping out, thus giving an

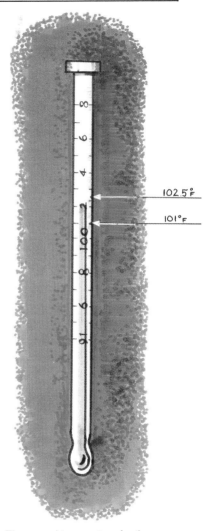

The normal temperature for the average dog ranges from 101°F to 102.5°F. This may vary during sleeping and exercise time.

inaccurate reading. The normal temperature for a dog is between 101° and 102.5°F. If your pet is seriously ill or injured in an accident, your veterinarian will advise you what to do before he arrives.

SWALLOWING FOREIGN OBJECTS

Most of us have had experience with a child swallowing a foreign object. Usually it is a small coin; occasionally it may be a fruit pit or something more dangerous. Dogs, *as a general rule,* will not swallow anything which isn't edible. There are, however, many dogs that swallow pebbles or small shiny objects such as pins, coins, and bits of cloth and plastic. This is especially true of dogs that are offered so-called "chew toys."

Chew toys are available in many sizes, shapes, colors and materials. Some even have whistles which sound when the dog's owner plays with it or when the dog chomps on it quickly. Most dogs attack the whistle first, doing everything possible to make it stop squeaking. Obviously, if the whistle is made of metal, a dog can injure its mouth, teeth, or tongue. Therefore, *never* buy a "squeak toy" made with a metal whistle.

Other chew toys are made of vinyl, a cheap plastic which is

soft to the touch and pliable. Most of the cute little toys that are figures of animals or people are made of this cheap plastic. They are sometimes hand-painted in countries where the cost of such labor is low. Not only is the paint used dangerous to dogs, because of the lead content, but the vinyl tears easily and is usually destroyed by the dog during the first hour. Small bits of vinyl may be ingested and cause blockage of the intestines. You are, therefore, reminded of these things before you buy anything vinyl for your dog!

Very inexpensive dog toys, usually found in supermarkets and other low-price venues, may

Natural chew bones can splinter and become lodged in a dog's throat. Nylon and polyurethane bones are safer for canine use.

Old discardable shoes should not be included in the dog's toy box. Such items are dangerous to a puppy or an adult dog.

be made of polyethylene. These are to be avoided completely, as this cheap plastic is, for some odd reason, attractive to dogs. Dogs destroy the toy in minutes and sometimes swallow the indigestible bits and pieces that come off. Most pet shops carry only safe toys.

WHAT TOYS ARE SAFE FOR DOGS?

Hard Rubber Toys made of hard rubber are usually safe for dogs, providing the toy is made of 100% hard rubber and not a compound of rubber and other materials. The rubber must be "virgin" and not re-ground from old tires, tubes, and other scrap rubber products. The main problem with rubber, even 100% virgin rubber, is that it oxidizes

quickly, especially when subjected to the ultraviolet rays of the sun and a dog's saliva. The rubber then tends to be brittle, to crack, to dust off, and to be extremely dangerous to dogs that like swallowing things.

Nylon Toys Toys made of nylon could well be the safest of all toys, *providing the nylon is annealed.* Nylon that is not annealed is very fragile, and if you smash it against a hard surface, it might shatter like glass. The same is true when the weather is cold and the nylon drops below freezing. Thus far there is only one line of dog toys that is made of annealed virgin nylon—Nylabone®. These toys not only are annealed but they are flavored and scented. The flavors and scents, such as hambone, are undetectable by humans, but dogs seem to find them attractive.

Some nylon bones have the flavor sprayed on them or molded into them. These cheaper bones are easy to detect—just smell them. If you

The Puppy Bone® by Nylabone® is multi-purpose, designed for teething, chew-pacification, teeth-cleaning and the elimination of behavioral problems before they become habitual.

discern an odor, you know they are poorly made. The main problem with the nylon toys that have an odor is that they are not annealed and they "smell up"

the house or car. The dog's saliva dilutes the odor of the bone, and when he drops it on your rug, this odor attaches itself to the rug and is quite difficult to remove.

Annealed nylon may be the best there is, but it is not 100% safe. The Nylabone® dog chews are really meant to be Pooch Pacifiers®. This trade name indicates the effect intended for the dog, which is to relieve the tension in your excited puppy or anxious adult dog. Instead of chewing up the furniture or some other object, he chews up his Nylabone® instead. Many dogs ignore the Nylabone® for weeks, suddenly attacking it when they have to relieve their doggie tensions.

The Nylabone® is designed for the most aggressive chewers. Even so, owners should be wary that some dogs may have jaws strong enough to chomp off a piece of Nylabone®, but this is extremely rare. *One word of caution:* the Nylabone® should be replaced when the dog has chewed down the knuckle. Most dogs slowly scrape off small slivers of nylon which pass harmlessly through their digestive tract. The resultant frizzled bone actually becomes a toothbrush.

One of the great characteristics of nylon bones is that they can be boiled and sterilized. If a dog loses interest in his Nylabone®, or it is too hard for him to chew due to his age and the condition of his teeth, you can cook it in some chicken or beef broth, allowing it to boil for 30 minutes. Let it cool down normally. It will then be perfectly sterile and re-flavored for the next dog. *Don't try this with plastic bones, as they will melt and ruin your pot.*

Polyurethane Toys Because polyurethane bones such as the Gumabone® are constructed of the strongest *flexible* materials known, some dogs (and their owners) actually prefer them to the traditional nylon bones. There are several brands on the market: ignore the ones which have scents that you can discern. Some of the scented polyurethane bones have an unbearable odor after the scent has rubbed off the bone and onto your rug or car seat. Again, look for the better-quality polyurethane toy. Gumabone® is a flexible material, the same as used for making artificial hearts and the bumpers on automobiles, thus it is strong and stable. It is not as strong as Nylabone®, but many dogs like it because it is soft.

If your dog is soft-mouthed and a less aggressive, more playful chewer, he will love the great taste and fun feel of the Gumabone® products.

The most popular of the

Gumabone® products made in polyurethane are the tug toys, knots, balls, and Frisbee® flying discs. These items are almost clear in color, have the decided advantage of lasting a long time, and are useful in providing exercise for both a dog and his master or mistress.

Gumabone® is available in different sizes and shapes. These are probably the most popular of all chew toys because dogs love them.

Gumabone® has also introduced new spiral-shaped dental devices under the name Plaque Attacker®. These unique products are fast becoming standards for all aggressive chewers. The Plaque Attacker Dental Device® comes in four fun sizes and each is designed to maximize gum and teeth

Attacker® products are patented and scented with hambone to make them even more enticing for the dog. Clinical findings support the assertion that a significant reduction in calculus accompanies use of the Gumbone® products.

Whatever dog toy you buy, be sure it is high quality. Pet shops

The Plaque Attacker® is a Dental Ball™, not just a plaything, designed to reduce plaque and tartar by use of its revolutionary "dental tips."

massage through its upraised "dental tips," which pimple the surface of the toy. Similarly, the Plaque Attacker Dental Ball® ensures a reduction in plaque and tartar. This one-of-a-kind product provides hours of fun for a dog. It bounces erratically and proves to be the most exciting of all polyurethane toys. All Plaque

and certain supermarkets, as a rule, always carry the better quality toys. Of course there may be exceptions, but you are best advised to ask your local pet shop operator—or even your veterinarian—what toys are suitable for *your* dog.

In conclusion, if your dog is a swallower of foreign objects,

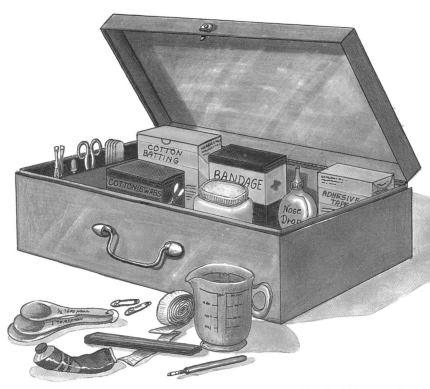

When emergencies occur, being prepared pays off. A first-aid kit should be accessible and always well stocked with medical accessories and supplies.

don't give him anything cheap to chew on. If he swallows a coin, you can hardly blame the Treasury! Unless your dog is carefully supervised, use only the largest size Nylabone® and Gumabone®, and replace them as soon as the dog chews down the knuckles. *Do not let the dog take the Nylabone® outdoors.* First of all he can hide and bury it, digging it up when his tensions rise. Then, too, all nylon becomes more brittle when it freezes, even Nylabone®.

IF YOUR PET SWALLOWS POISON

A poisoned dog must be treated instantly; any delay could cause his death. Different poisons act in different ways and require different treatments. If you know the dog has swallowed an acid, alkali, gasoline, or kerosene, do not induce vomiting. Give milk to dilute the poison and rush him to the vet. If you can find the bottle or container of poison, check the label to see if there is a recommended antidote. If not, try to induce vomiting by giving him a mixture of hydrogen peroxide and water. Mix the regular drugstore strength of hydrogen peroxide (3%) with an equal part of water, but do not attempt to pour it down your dog's throat, as that could cause inhalation pneumonia. Instead, simply pull the dog's lips away from the side of his mouth, making a pocket for depositing the liquid. Use at least a tablespoonful of the mixture for every ten pounds of your dog's

weight. He will vomit in about two minutes. When his stomach has settled, give him a teaspoonful of Epsom salts in a little water to empty the intestine quickly. The hydrogen peroxide, on ingestion, becomes oxygen and water and is harmless to your dog; it is the best antidote for phosphorus, which is often used in rat poisons. After you have administered this emergency treatment to your pet and his stomach and bowels have been emptied, rush him to your veterinarian for further care.

The contents of a full ashtray if consumed by the curious non-smoker dog may induce nicotine poisoning. Pet owners must dog-proof their home for the safety of their animals.

DANGER IN THE HOME

There are numerous household products that can prove fatal if ingested by your pet. These include rat poison, antifreeze, boric acid, hand soap, detergents, insecticides, mothballs, household cleansers, bleaches, de-icers, polishes and disinfectants, paint and varnish removers, acetone, turpentine, and even health and beauty aids

There is another danger lurking within the home among the household plants, which are almost all poisonous, even if swallowed in small quantities. There are hundreds of poisonous plants around us, among which are: ivy leaves, cyclamen, lily of the valley, rhododendrons, tulip bulbs, azalea, wisteria, poinsettia leaves, mistletoe, daffodils,

if ingested in large enough quantities. A word to the wise should be sufficient: what you would keep locked away from your two-year-old child should also be kept hidden from your pet.

Preparing for emergencies also requires that an owner understand such basic revival techniques as cardio-pulmonary resuscitation, chest compression, heart massage, heat stroke measures, and many others.

Checking for an animal's vital signs in the event of an emergency will help you to provide the veterinarian with the answers to his preliminary questions.

jimson weed—we cannot name them all. Rhubarb leaves, for example, either raw or cooked, can cause death or violent convulsions. Peach, elderberry, and cherry trees can cause cyanide poisoning if their bark is consumed.

There are also many insects that can be poisonous to dogs such as spiders, bees, wasps, and some flies. A few toads and frogs exude a fluid that can make a dog foam at the mouth—and even kill him—if he bites too hard!

There have been cases of dogs suffering nicotine poisoning by consuming the contents of full ashtrays which thoughtless smokers have left on the coffee table. Also, do not leave nails, staples, pins, or other sharp objects lying around. Likewise, don't let your puppy play with plastic bags which could suffocate him. Unplug, remove, or cover any electrical cords or wires near your dog. Chewing live wires could lead to severe mouth burns or death. Remember that an ounce of prevention is worth a pound of cure: keep all potentially dangerous objects out of your pet's reach.

VEHICLE TRAVEL SAFETY

A dog should never be left alone in a car. It takes only a few minutes for the heat to become unbearable in the summer, and to drop to freezing in the winter.

A dog traveling in a car or truck should be well behaved. An undisciplined dog can be deadly in a moving vehicle. The dog should be trained to lie on the back seat of the vehicle. Allowing your dog to stick its head out of the window is unwise. The dog may jump or it may get something in its eye. Some manufacturers sell seat belts and car seats designed for dogs.

Traveling with your dog in the back of your pick-up truck is an unacceptable notion and dangerous to all involved.

PROTECT YOURSELF FIRST

In almost all first aid situations, the dog is in pain. He may indeed be in shock and not appear to be suffering, until you move him. Then he may bite your hand or resist being helped at all. So if you want to help your dog, help yourself first by tying his mouth closed. To do this, use a piece of strong cloth four inches wide and three feet long, depending on the size of the dog.

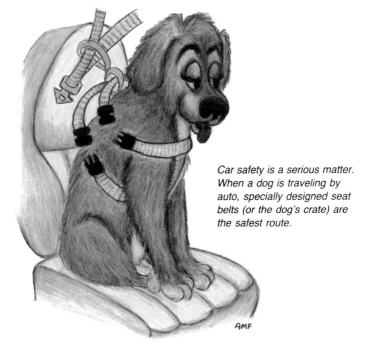

Car safety is a serious matter. When a dog is traveling by auto, specially designed seat belts (or the dog's crate) are the safest route.

AMF

Health Care

Make a loop in the middle of the strip and slip it over his nose with the knot under his chin and over the bony part of his nose. Pull it tight and bring the ends back around his head behind the ears and tie it tightly, ending with a bow knot for quick, easy release. Now you can handle the dog safely. As a dog perspires through his tongue, do not leave the "emergency muzzle" on any longer than necessary.

ADMINISTERING MEDICINE

When you are giving liquid medicine to your dog, it is a good idea to pull the lips away from the side of the mouth, form a lip pocket, and let the liquid trickle past the tongue. Remain at his side, never in front of the dog, as he may cough and spray you with the liquid. Moreover, you must never pour liquid medicine while the victim's tongue is drawn out, as

First aid, in the ideal sense, is the temporary care of an animal or person until professional help can be found. Recognizing the urgency in any given circumstance is the primary concern. Moving an injured animal with utmost care usually requires two persons and a clean blanket.

inhalation pneumonia could be the disastrous result.

Medicine in pill form is best administered by forcing the dog's mouth open, holding his forced to swallow the medicine. As the dog will not be feeling well, stroke his neck to comfort him and to help him swallow his medicine more easily. Do keep

Before attempting to transport an injured dog, be very careful to inspect for apparent wounds, burns or breaks while disturbing the animal as little as possible. Laying the dog in a flat position will make the carrying easier to manage.

head back, and placing the capsule as far back on his tongue as you can reach. To do this: put the palm of your hand over the dog's muzzle (his foreface) with your fingers on one side of his jaw, your thumb on the other. Press his lips hard against his teeth while using your other hand to pull down his lower jaw. With your two fingers, try to put the pill as far back on the dog's tongue as you can reach. Keep his mouth and nostrils closed and he should be an eye on him for a few moments afterward, however, to make certain that he does not spit it out.

IN CASE OF AN ACCIDENT

It is often difficult for you to assess the dog's injuries after a road accident. He may appear normal, but there might be internal hemorrhaging. A vital organ could be damaged or ribs broken. Keep the dog as quiet and warm as possible; cover him with blankets or your coat to let his own body heat build up. Signs of shock are a rapid and weak pulse, glassy-eyed appearance, subnormal temperature, and slow capillary refill time. To determine the last symptom, press firmly against the dog's gums until they turn white. Release and count the number of seconds until the gums return to their normal color. If it is more than 2–3 seconds, the dog may be going into shock. Failure to return to the reddish pink color indicates that the dog may be in serious trouble and needs immediate assistance.

If artificial respiration is required, first open the dog's mouth and check for obstructions; extend his tongue and examine the pharynx. Clear his mouth of mucus and blood and hold the mouth slightly open. Mouth-to-mouth resuscitation involves holding the dog's tongue to the bottom of his mouth with one hand and sealing his nostrils with the other while you blow into his mouth. Watch for his chest to rise with each inflation. Repeat every 5–6 seconds, the equivalent of 10–12 breaths a minute.

If the veterinarian cannot come to you, try to improvise a stretcher to take the dog to him. To carry a puppy, wrap him in a blanket that has been folded into several thicknesses. If he is in shock, it is better to pick him up by holding one hand under his chest, the other under the hindquarters. This will keep him stretched out.

It is always better to roll an injured dog than to try and lift him. If you find him lying beside the road after a car accident, apply a muzzle even if you have to use someone's necktie to make one. Send someone for a blanket and roll him gently onto it. Two people, one on each side, can make a stretcher out of the blanket and move the dog easily.

If no blanket is available and the injured dog must be moved, try to keep him as flat as possible. So many dogs' backs are broken in car accidents that one must first consider that possibility. However, if he can move his hind legs or tail, his spine is probably not broken. Get medical assistance for him immediately.

It should be mentioned that unfortunate car accidents, which can maim or kill your dog, can be avoided if he is confined at all times either indoors or, if out-of-doors, in a fenced-in yard or some other protective enclosure. *Never* allow your dog to roam free; even a well-trained dog may, for some unknown reason, dart into the street—and the result could be tragic.

If you need to walk your dog, leash him first so that he will be protected from moving vehicles.

It is the smooth, efficient execution of first-aid technique that saves lives. Costly mistakes happen when haste and frenzy take over. When moving an injured dog, keep calm and be focused on the situation at hand. Act swiftly and maintain control at all times.

PROTECTING YOUR PET

It is important to watch for any tell-tale signs of illness so that you can spare your pet any unnecessary suffering. Your dog's eyes, for example, should normally be bright and alert, so if the haw is bloodshot or partially covers the eye, it may be a sign of illness or irritation. If your dog has matter in the corners of his eyes, bathe them with a mild eye wash; obtain ointment or eye drops from your veterinarian to treat a chronic condition.

If your dog seems to have something wrong with his ears which causes him to scratch at them or shake his head, cautiously probe the ear with a cotton swab. An accumulation of wax will probably work itself out. Dirt or dried blood, however, is indicative of ear mites or infection and should be treated immediately. Sore ears in the summer, due to insect bites, should be washed with mild soap and water, then covered with a soothing ointment and wrapped in gauze if necessary. Keep your pet away from insects until his ears heal, even if this means confining him indoors.

VACCINATION SCHEDULE

Age	Vaccination
6-8 weeks	Initial canine distemper, canine hepatitis, tracheobronchitis, canine parvovirus, as well as initial leptospirosis vaccination.
10-12 weeks	Second vaccination for all given at 6-8 weeks. Initial rabies and initial Lyme disease to be given at this time.
14-16 weeks	Third vaccination for all given at 6-8 and 10-12 weeks.Re-vaccinate annually, hereafter. Second rabies and second Lyme disease to be given at this time, and then re-vaccinated annually.

INOCULATIONS

Periodic check-ups by your veterinarian throughout your puppy's life are good health insurance. The person from whom your puppy was purchased should tell you what inoculations your puppy has had and when the next visit to the vet is necessary. You must make certain that your puppy has been vaccinated against the following infectious canine diseases: distemper, canine hepatitis, leptospirosis, rabies, parvovirus, and parainfluenza. Annual "boosters" thereafter provide inexpensive protection for your dog against such serious diseases. Puppies should also be checked for worms at an early age.

Vaccination schedules should be confirmed with your vet.

DISTEMPER

Young dogs are most susceptible to distemper, although it may affect dogs of all ages. Some signs of the disease are loss of appetite, depression, chills, and fever, as well as a watery discharge from the eyes and nose. Unless treated promptly, the disease goes into advanced stages with infections of the lungs, intestines, and nervous system. Dogs that recover may be impaired with paralysis, convulsions, a twitch, or some other defect, usually spastic in nature. Early inoculations in puppyhood should be followed by an annual booster to help protect against this disease.

CANINE HEPATITIS

The signs of hepatitis are drowsiness, loss of appetite, high temperature, and great thirst. These signs may be accompanied by swellings of the head, neck, and abdomen. Vomiting may also occur. This disease strikes quickly, and death may occur in only a few hours. An annual booster shot is needed after the initial series of puppy shots.

LEPTOSPIROSIS

Infection caused by either of two serovars, *canicola* or *copehageni,* is usually begun by the dog's licking substances contaminated by the urine or feces of infected animals. Brown rats are the main carriers of *copehageni.* The signs are weakness, vomiting, and a yellowish discoloration of the jaws, teeth, and tongue, caused by an inflammation of the kidneys. A veterinarian can administer the bacterins to protect your dog from this disease. The frequency of the doses is determined by the risk factor involved.

RABIES

This disease of the dog's central nervous system spreads by infectious saliva, which is

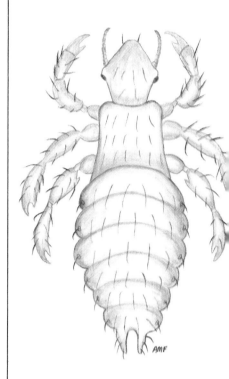

Lice are not a common problem in dogs and usually only infest dogs that are poorly cared for. Proper care of your dog will prevent lice infestation.

transmitted by the bite of an infected animal. Of the two main classes of signs, the first is "furious rabies," in which the dog shows a period of melancholy or depression, then irritation, and finally paralysis. The first period can be from a few hours to several days, and during this time the dog is cross

129

and will change his position often, lose his appetite, begin to lick, and bite or swallow foreign objects. During this phase the dog is spasmodically wild and has impulses to run away. The dog acts fearless and bites everything in sight. If he is caged or confined, he will fight at the bars and possibly break teeth or fracture his jaw. His bark

The deer fly has a wicked bite that can cause a welt; all flies can carry disease and germs.

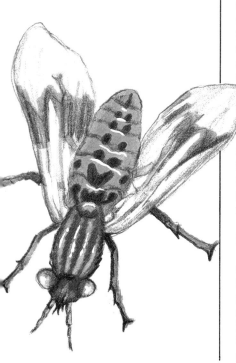

becomes a peculiar howl. In the final stage, the animal's lower jaw becomes paralyzed and hangs down. He then walks with a stagger, and saliva drips from his mouth. About four to eight days after the onset of paralysis, the dog dies.

The second class of symptoms is referred to as "dumb rabies" and is characterized by the dog's walking in a bearlike manner with his head down. The lower jaw is paralyzed and the dog is unable to bite. It appears as if he has a bone caught in his throat.

If a dog is bitten by a rabid animal, he probably can be saved if he is taken to a veterinarian in time for a series of injections. After the signs appear, however, no cure is possible. The local health department must be notified in the case of a rabid dog, for he is a danger to all who come near him. As with the other shots each year, an annual rabies inoculation is very important. In many areas, the administration of rabies vaccines for dogs is required by law.

PARVOVIRUS

This relatively new virus is a contagious disease that has spread in almost epidemic proportions throughout certain sections of the United States. It has also appeared in Australia, Canada, and Europe. Canine parvovirus attacks the intestinal tract, white blood cells, and heart muscle. It is believed to spread through dog-to-dog contact, and the specific course of infection seems to come from fecal matter of infected dogs. Overcoming parvovirus is difficult, for it is capable of existing in the environment for many months under varying conditions and temperatures, and it can be transmitted from place to place on the hair and feet of infected dogs, as well as on the clothes and shoes of people.

Vomiting and severe diarrhea, which will appear within five to seven days after the animal has been exposed to the virus, are the initial signs of this disease. At the onset of illness, feces will be light gray or yellow-gray in color, and the urine might be blood-streaked. Because of the vomiting and severe diarrhea, the dog that has contracted the disease will dehydrate quickly. Depression and loss of appetite, as well as a rise in temperature, can accompany the other symptoms. Death caused by this disease usually occurs within 48 to 72 hours following the appearance of the symptoms. Puppies are hardest hit, and the virus is fatal to 75 percent of puppies that contract it. Death in puppies can be within two days of the onset of the illness.

A series of shots administered by a veterinarian is the best

The stable fly is capable of a painful bite.

preventive measure for canine parvovirus. It is also important to disinfect the area where the dog is housed by using one part sodium hypochlorite solution (household bleach) to thirty parts of water and to keep the dog from coming into contact with the fecal matter of other dogs.

LYME DISEASE

Known as a bacterial infection, Lyme disease is transmitted by ticks infected with a spirochete known as *Borrelia burgdorferi*. The disease is most often

The deer tick is a principal carrier of Lyme disease.

The brown dog tick is the most common tick found on dogs. It is much larger than a deer tick.

acquired by the parasitic bite of an infected deer tick, *Ixodes dammini*. While the range of symptoms is broad, common warning signs include: rash beginning at the bite and soon extending in a bullseye-targetlike fashion; chills, fever, lack of balance, lethargy, and stiffness; swelling and pain, especially in the joints, possibly leading to arthritis or arthritic conditions; heart problems, weak limbs, facial paralysis, and lack of tactile sensation.

Concerned dog owners, especially those living in the United States, should contact a veterinarian to discuss Lyme disease. A vaccination has been developed and is routinely administered to puppies twice before the 16th week, and then annually.

PARAINFLUENZA

Parainfluenza, or infectious canine tracheobronchitis, is commonly known as "kennel cough." It is highly contagious, affects the upper respiratory system, and is spread through direct or indirect contact with already diseased dogs. It will readily infect dogs of all ages that have not been vaccinated or that were previously infected. While this condition is definitely one of the serious diseases in dogs, it is self-limiting, usually lasting only two to four weeks.

The symptoms are high fever and intense, harsh coughing that brings up mucus. As long as your pet sees your veterinarian immediately, the chances for his complete recovery are excellent.

EXTERNAL PARASITES

A parasite is an animal that lives in or on an organism of another species, known as the host, without contributing to the well-being of the host. The majority of dogs' skin problems are parasitic in nature and an estimated 90% of puppies are born with parasites.

Ticks can cause serious problems to dogs where the latter have access to woods, fields, and vegetation in which large numbers of native mammals live. Ticks are usually found clinging to vegetation and attach themselves to animals

Fumigating flea bombs are commonly used to de-flea a home. It is essential to follow the manufacturer's instructions to the letter, as this product's fumes can kill more than just insects.

passing by. They have eight legs and a heavy shield or shell-like covering on their upper surface. Only by keeping dogs away from tick-infested areas can ticks on dogs be prevented.

The flea is the single most common cause of skin and coat problems in dogs. There are 11,000 kinds of fleas which can transmit specific disorders like tapeworm and heartworm or transport smaller parasites onto your dog. The common tapeworm, for example, requires the flea as an intermediate host for completion of its life cycle.

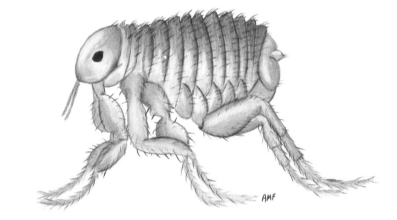

A female flea can lay hundreds of eggs and these will become adults in less than three weeks. Depending on the temperature and the amount of moisture, large numbers of fleas can attack dogs. The ears of dogs, in particular, can play host to hundreds of fleas.

Fleas can lurk in crevices and cracks, carpets, and bedding for months, so frequent cleaning of your dog's environment is absolutely essential. If he is infected by other dogs, then have him bathed and "dipped," which means that he will be put into water containing a chemical that kills fleas. Your veterinarian will advise which dip to use, and your dog must be bathed for at least twenty minutes. These parasites are tenacious and remarkably agile creatures; fleas have existed since prehistoric times and have been found in arctic as well as tropical

Fleas are among the most common external parasites and can be real pests to eliminate from your pet.

climates. Some experts claim that fleas can jump 150 times the length of their bodies; this makes them difficult to catch and kill. Thus, treating your pet for parasites without simultaneously treating the environment is both inefficient and ineffective.

INTERNAL PARASITES

Four common internal parasites that may infect a dog are: roundworms, hookworms, whipworms, and tapeworms. The first three can be diagnosed by laboratory examination of the dog's stool, and tapeworms can be seen in the stool or attached to the hair around the anus. When a veterinarian determines what type of worm or worms are present, he then can advise the best treatment.

Roundworms, the dog's most common intestinal parasite, have a life cycle which permits complete eradication by worming twice, ten days apart. The first worming will remove all adults and the second will destroy all subsequently hatched eggs before they, in turn, can produce more parasites.

A dog in good physical condition is less susceptible to worm infestation than a weak dog. Proper sanitation and a nutritious diet help in preventing worms. One of the best preventive measures is to have clean, dry bedding for the dog, as this diminishes the possibility of reinfection due to flea or tick bites.

Heartworm infestation in dogs is passed by mosquitoes. Dogs with this disease tire easily, have difficulty in breathing, and lose weight despite a hearty appetite. Administration of preventive medicine throughout the spring, summer, and fall months is advised. A veterinarian must first take a blood sample from the dog to test for the presence of the disease, and if the dog is heartworm-free, pills or liquid medicine can be prescribed to protect against any infestation.

CANINE SENIOR CITIZENS

The processes of aging and gradual degenerative changes start far earlier in a dog than often observed, usually at about seven years of age. If we recall that each year of a dog's life roughly corresponds to about seven years in the life of a man,

The fraternity of internal parasites and their eggs: whipworms, hookworms, roundworms and tapeworms.

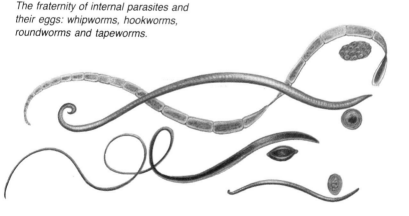

by the age of seven he is well into middle age. Your pet will become less active, will have a poorer appetite with increased thirst, there will be frequent periods of constipation and less than normal passage of urine. His skin and coat might become dull and dry and his hair will become thin and fall out. There is a tendency towards obesity in old age, which should be avoided by maintaining a regular exercise program. Remember, also, that your pet will be less able to cope with extreme heat, cold, fatigue, and change in routine.

There is the possibility of loss or impairment of hearing or eyesight. He may become bad-tempered more often than in the past. Other ailments such as rheumatism, arthritis, kidney infections, heart disease, male prostatism, and hip dysplasia may occur. Of course, all these require a veterinarian's examination and recommendation of suitable treatment. Care of the teeth is

Heartworm life cycle: a carrier mosquito bites a dog and deposits microfilariae, which travel through the dog's bloodstream, lodging in the heart to reproduce. The carrier dog is later bitten by an uninfected mosquito, which becomes infected, and bites and infects another dog . . . .

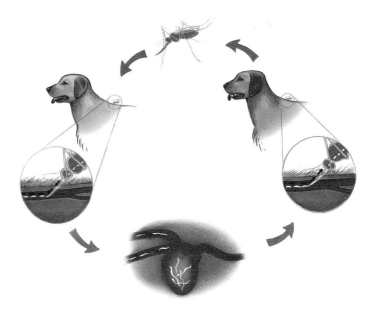

Taking a dog's pulse is useful as it reflects his heartbeat. To do so is quite simple: feel along the inside of your dog's thigh at the juncture where it meets the body. Press with a finger to feel the pulsation. (Do not use your thumb.)

also important in the aging dog. Indeed, the mouth can be a barometer of nutritional health. Degenerating gums, heavy tartar on the teeth, loose teeth, and sore lips are common. The worst of all diseases in old age, however, is neglect. Good care in early life will have its effect on your dog's later years; the nutrition and general health care of his first few years can determine his lifespan and the quality of his life. It is worth bearing in mind that the older, compared to the younger, animal needs more protein of good biological value, more vitamins A, B-complex, D and E, more calcium and iron, and less fat.

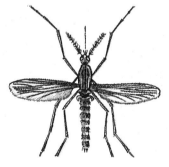

An adult male mosquito. Only female mosquitoes will suck blood from a host animal.

Preventive Dental Care

ALL DOGS NEED TO CHEW

Puppies and young dogs need something with resistance to chew on while their teeth and jaws are developing—to cut the puppy teeth, to induce growth of the permanent teeth under the puppy teeth, to assist in getting rid of the puppy teeth on time, to help the permanent teeth through the gums, to assure normal jaw development and to settle the permanent teeth solidly in the jaws.

The adult dog's desire to chew stems from the instinct for tooth cleaning, gum massage, and jaw exercise—plus the need to vent periodic doggie tensions. . . . A pacifier if you will!

Dental caries, as they affect the teeth of humans, are virtually unknown in dogs; but tartar (calculus) accumulates on the teeth of dogs, particularly at the gum line, more rapidly than on the teeth of humans. These accumulations, if not removed, bring irritation and then infection, which erode the tooth enamel and ultimately destroy the teeth at the roots. It is important that you take your dog to your local veterinarian for periodic dental examinations.

Tooth and jaw development will normally continue until the dog is more than a year old—but sometimes much longer, depending upon the dog, its chewing exercise, rate of calcium utilization and many other factors, known and unknown, which affect the development of individual dogs. Diseases, like distemper for example, may sometimes arrest development of the teeth and jaws, which may resume months or even years later.

An artist's representation of the calculus index, ranging from index rating **4** *(topmost drawing)* through *index rating* **0** *(lowest drawing).*

4 *Buccal crown covered*

3 *⅔ crown covered*

2 *⅓ crown covered*

1 *Only gingival margin covered*

0 *No calculus evident*

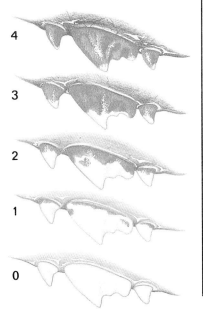

4

3

2

1

0

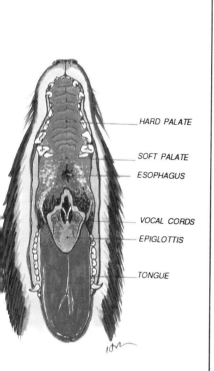

HARD PALATE

SOFT PALATE

ESOPHAGUS

VOCAL CORDS

EPIGLOTTIS

TONGUE

The owner should inspect the dog's mouth regularly to check that all is well.

This is why dogs, especially puppies and young dogs, will often destroy valuable property when their chewing instinct is not diverted from their owners' possessions, particularly during the widely varying critical period for young dogs. Saving your possessions from destruction, assuring proper development of

teeth and jaws, providing for "interim" tooth cleaning and gum massage, and channeling doggie tensions into a non-destructive outlet are, therefore, all dependent upon the dog's having something suitable for chewing readily available when his instinct tells him to chew. If your purposes, and those of your dog, are to be accomplished, what you provide for chewing must be desirable from the doggie viewpoint, have the necessary functional qualities, and, above all, be safe.

It is very important that dogs be prohibited from chewing on anything they can break or indigestible things from which they can bite sizeable chunks. Sharp pieces, such as those from a bone which can be broken by a dog, may pierce the intestinal wall and kill. Indigestible things which can be bitten off in chunks, such as toys made of rubber compound or cheap plastic, may cause an intestinal stoppage; if not regurgitated, they are certain to bring painful death unless surgery is promptly performed.

NATURAL CHEW BONES

Strong natural bones, such as 4- to 8-inch lengths of round shin bone from mature beef—either the kind you can get from your butcher or one of the varieties available commercially in pet stores—may serve your dog's teething needs, if his mouth is large enough to handle them. You may be tempted to give your puppy a smaller bone and he may not be able to break it when you do, but puppies grow rapidly and the power of their jaws constantly increases until maturity. This means that a growing dog may break one of excessive chewing on animal bones. Contrary to popular belief, knuckle bones that can be chewed up and swallowed by the dog provide little, if any, useable calcium or other nutrient. They do, however, disturb the digestion of most dogs and might cause them to vomit the nourishing food they really need.

the smaller bones at any time, swallow the pieces and die painfully before you realize what is wrong.

All hard natural bones are highly abrasive. If your dog is an avid chewer, natural bones may wear away his teeth prematurely; hence, they then should be taken away from your dog when the teething purposes have been served. The badly worn, and usually painful, teeth of many mature dogs can be traced to

Rawhide treats are enjoyed by dogs. Owners should be wary since rawhide can tear off in large pieces and lodge in the dog's throat or cause intestinal blockage.

RAWHIDE CHEWS

The most popular material from which dog chews are made is the hide from cows, horses, and other animals. Most of these chews are made in foreign countries where the quality of the hide is not good enough for making leather. These foreign hides may contain lead, antibiotics, arsenic, or insecticides which might be detrimental to the health of your dog . . . or even your children. It is not impossible that a small child will start chewing on a piece of rawhide meant for the dog! Rawhide chews do not serve the primary chewing functions very well. They are also a bit messy when wet from mouthing, and most dogs chew them up rather rapidly. They have been considered safe for dogs until recently.

Rawhide is flavorful to dogs. They like it. Currently, some veterinarians have been attributing cases of acute constipation to large pieces of incompletely digested rawhide in the intestine. Basically it is good for them to chew on, but dogs think rawhide is food. They do not play with it nor do they use it as a pacifier to relieve doggie tension. They eat it as they would any other food. This is dangerous, for the hide is very difficult for dogs to digest and swallow, and many dogs choke on large particles of rawhide that become stuck in their throats. *Before you offer your dog rawhide chews, consult your veterinarian.* Vets have a lot of experience with canine chewing devices; ask them what they recommend.

Annealed nylon and polyurethane chew toys are recommended by veterinarians as proven-safe and effective canine chew devices.

NYLON CHEW DEVICES

The nylon bones, especially those with natural meat and bone flavor added, are probably the most complete, safe, and economical answer to the chewing need. Dogs cannot break them nor bite off sizeable chunks; hence, they are completely safe. And being longer lasting than other things offered for the purpose, they are very economical.

Hard chewing raises little bristle-like projections on the surface of the nylon bones to provide effective interim tooth

Preventive Dental Care

The Nylafloss® cannot cure tooth decay, but it is an optimum decay-prevention device. Make your dog's playtime a healthy time and invest in your pet's future.

cleaning and vigorous gum massage, much in the same way your toothbrush does it for you. The little projections are raked off and swallowed in the form of thin shavings, but the chemistry of the nylon is such that they break down in the stomach fluids and pass through without effect.

The toughness of the nylon provides the strong chewing resistance needed for important jaw exercise and effective help for the teething functions; however, there is no tooth wear because nylon is non-abrasive. Being inert, nylon does not support the growth of microorganisms, and it can be washed in soap and water or sterilized by boiling or in an autoclave.

There are a great variety of Nylabone® products available that veterinarians recommend as safe and healthy for your dog or puppy to chew on. These Nylabone® Pooch Pacifiers® usually don't splinter, chip, or break off in large chunks; instead, they are frizzled by the dog's chewing action, and this creates a toothbrush-like surface that cleanses the teeth and massages the gums. At the same time, these hard-nylon therapeutic devices channel doggie tension and chewing frustation into constructive rather than destructive behavior. The original nylon bone (Nylabone®) is not a toy and dogs use it only when in need of pacification. Keeping a bone in each of your dog's recreation rooms is the best method of providing the requisite pacification. Unfortunately, many nylon chew products have been copied. These inferior quality copies are sold in supermarkets and other chain stores. The really good products are sold only through veterinarians, pet shops, grooming salons and places where the sales people really know something about dogs. The good products have the flavor impregnated *into* the bone. This makes the taste last longer. The smell is undetectable to humans. The artificial bones which have a strong odor are poor-quality bones with the odor sprayed on to impress the dog owner (not the dog)! These heavily scented dog toys may impart the odor to your carpets or furniture if an odor-sprayed bone lies there wet from a dog's chewing on it.

revolutionary product that is designed to save dogs teeth and keep them healthy. Even though your dogs won't believe you, Nylafloss® is not a toy but rather a most effective agent in removing destructive plaque

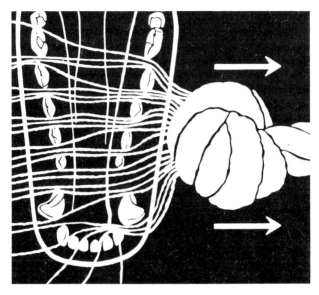

Food particles can be deposited between the teeth, where they can be difficult to remove. Many chew products cannot work to remove these decaying food pieces. For this reason, the Nylafloss® dental device is recommended by professionals as it is the only available mechanism to clean between *the dog's teeth.*

FLOSS OR LOSS!

Most dentists relay that brushing daily is just not enough. In order to prevent unnecessary tooth loss, flossing is essential. For dogs, human dental floss is not the answer—however, canine dental devices are available. The Nylafloss® is a

between the teeth and *beneath* the gum line where gum disease begins. Gentle tugging is all that is necessary to activate the Nylafloss®. These 100% inert nylon products are guaranteed to outlast rawhide chews by ten times and are available for sale at all pet shops.

Preventive Dental Care

THE IMPORTANCE OF PREVENTION

In order to get to the root of canine dentistry problems, it is important for owners to realize that no less than 75% of all canine dental health problems, serious enough to require a vet's assistance, and nearly 98% of all canine teeth lost are attributable to periodontal disease.

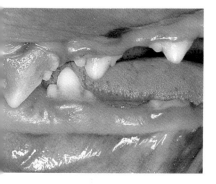

A dog's teeth showing moderate calculus build-up. The moderate calculus build-up on this dog's teeth reflects a certain neglect by the owner. Providing a safe chew item like the Gumabone® can save your dog's teeth.

Periodontal disease not only mars the teeth but also the gums and other buccal tissue in the mouth. Severe cases of periodontal disease involve resultant bacterial toxins which are absorbed into the blood stream and cause permanent damage to the heart and kidneys. In the infected mouth,

teeth are loosened; tartar, unsightly and bad smelling, accumulates heavily; and the dog experiences a complete loss of appetite. Long-standing periodontitis can also manifest itself in simple symptoms such as diarrhea and vomiting.

Periodontal disease deserves the attention of every dog owner—a dog's teeth are extremely important to his ongoing health. The accumulation of plaque, food matter mixed with saliva attaching itself to the tooth surface, is a sure sign of potential bacteria build-up. As toxic material gathers, the bone surrounding the teeth erodes. If plaque and calculus continue to reside without attention, bacteria-fighting cells will form residual pus at the root of the teeth, dividing the gum from the tooth. The debris is toxic and actually kills the buccal tissue. This is a most undesirable situation, as hardened dental calculus is one of the most direct causative agents of periodontitis.

In actuality, the disease is a result of a number of contributing factors. Old age, a diet comprised solely of soft or semi-soft foods, dental tartar, constant chewing of hair and even coprophagy (the eating of stool) are among the most common contributors.

Just as regular dental visits and brushing are necessary for humans, regular hygienic care and veterinary check-ups can help control tooth problems in canines. Involved and expensive routines can be performed on the affected, neglected mouth and teeth if decay has begun eroding the enamel and infecting the gums. Cleaning, polishing, and scaling are routine to remove calculus build-up.

Owners must claim responsibility for their dog's health, and tooth care is no small aspect of the care required. Daily brushing with a salt/baking soda solution is the best answer, but many owners find this tedious or just too difficult to perform. The simpler and more proven effective way to avoid, reduce, and fight periodontal disease and calculus build-up is giving the dog regular access to a thermoplastic polymer chew device. The Gumabone® products are the only scientifically proven line that offers the desired protection from calculus and tartar build-up.

CANINE DENTAL BREAKTHROUGH

The independent research of Dr. Andrew Duke, D.V.M., reveals that 70% of the dogs that regularly use Gumabone® experience a reduction of calculus build-up. This find is a breakthrough for the dog world, since the Gumabone® has already resided in the toy boxes

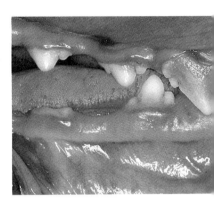

Regular use of the Gumabone® chew products can significantly reduce plaque build-up.

of many dogs as their favorite play item. Little did owners know previously that their dogs were gaining entertainment and unparalleled dental treatment at the same time. Dr. Duke writes: "There is little debate left that dental calculus is an excellent

Teeth of an infected dog showing little to no plaque accumulation after professional cleaning.

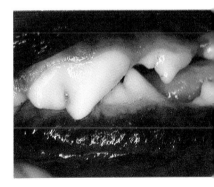

145

indicator of periodontal health in the dog, just as it is in humans. "Calculus does not cause gingivitis and periodontitis, but the plaque and bacteria that cause periodontitis are responsible for the mineral precipitation we know as 'calculus.' All veterinarians who have made a study of dogs' oral health have noticed the middle aged dog who actively chews with excellent gingival health. Many of these dogs that chew hard substances regularly wear the cusps down and even may expose the pulp cavity faster than secondary dentin can be formed. Often these "excellent chewers" are presented with slab fractures of the premolars or apical abcesses.

"The challenge then becomes to find a substance which is effective in removing calculus and plaque but does not wear the enamel excessively. In an attempt to duplicate the chewstuffs enjoyed by dogs in the wild, researchers have used bovine tracheas to demonstrate the inhibition of plaque and gingivitis. Very little else has been done in veterinary medicine

The clean healthy teeth that are desired in dogs should inspire owners to work towards better dental hygiene.

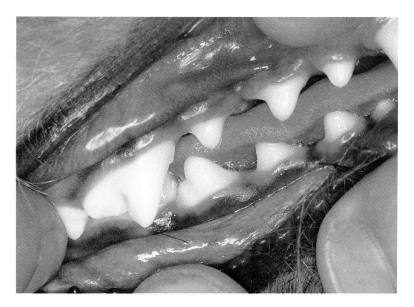

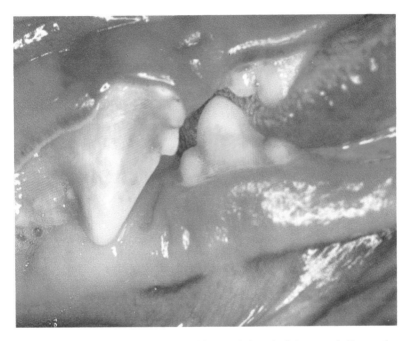

Plaque is formed by the food debris and bacterial deposits left on teeth. Due to the high carbon dioxide and pH levels in the mouth, minerals precipitate quickly on the plaque to form calculus.

to establish a scientific basis for evaluating chewstuffs.

"In the human field it is generally accepted (incorrectly) that fibrous foodstuffs and diet have no effect on oral health. This is a moot point since the practice of brushing is by far a more efficient technique of preventing plaque accumulation, calculus and periodontal disease. Studies in human subjects failed to find any benefits in eating apples, raw carrots, etc. If people are not allowed to brush, it is difficult to conduct clinical trials of more than one week.

"The increased awareness of animals' dental health of recent years has resulted in most veterinary practitioners' recommending some kind of chewstuff to their dog owners. To meet this market demand, there has been a stampede into the market by vendors ready to promote their products. The

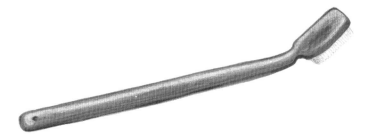

Canine tooth brushes are designed to allow access to the most hard-to-reach places in the canine mouth.

veterinarian is furnished no scientific data, but is asked to promote rawhide, bounce, and squeaky toys. How would our human colleagues handle this situation? Can Listerine® say that it prevents colds, but not support the claim? Can "Tartar Control Crest®" or "Colgate Tartar Control Formula®" be sold if it is not proven that it does in fact reduce tartar? Of course not.

"To this end, the following study was made.

"*Method:* Twenty dogs of different breeds and age were selected from a veterinary

In cases of bad neglect, scaling a dog's teeth can help to save or salvage affected teeth. Your veterinarian will perform this procedure.

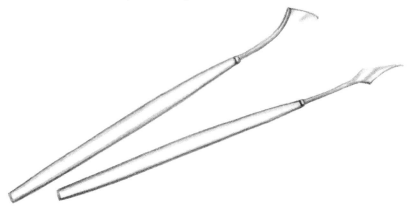

CUMULATIVE CALCULUS INDEX SCORES

Dog	Without Gumabone®	With Gumabone®	Difference
1.	20	9	11
2.	19	23	- 4
3.	49	26	23
4.	21	15	6
5.	34	11	23
6.	36	21	15
7.	44	31	13
8.	25	25	0
9.	34	28	6
10.	44	23	21
11.	22	15	7
12.	23	33	-10
13.	26	23	3
14.	22	14	8
15.	20	20	0
16.	23	13	10
17.	24	14	10
18.	24	17	7
19.	24	31	-7
20.	15	30	-15

As supported by Dr. Duke's study on reducing calculus build-up, the effectiveness of a chewing device can be measured by assigning numerical values to the accumulation when the Gumabone® device is used and not used. Seventy percent of dogs chewing Gumabone® (14 out of 20 dogs) showed a reduction in calculus build-up.

practice's clientele. Although most were from multiple pet households, none were colony dogs. The owners were asked if they would allow their dogs to be anesthetized for two prophylactic cleanings which included root planing, polishing, and gingival debridement necessary to insure good oral hygiene.

"The dogs were divided into two groups of 10. Their teeth were cleaned and their calculus index converted to 0. One group was allowed only their normal dry commercial dog ration for 30 days. The other was allowed to have free choice access to Gumabone® products of the appropriate size.

"After 30 days, photoslides were made of the upper 3rd premolar, upper 4th premolar, and the lower 4th premolar on both sides of the dog's mouth. The dogs were again subjected to a prophylactic cleaning and the group reversed. After the second 30 days, photoslides were again made. A total of six teeth in each mouth were evaluated on each dog. This was 80 slides representing 240 teeth."

Fourteen out of 20 dogs (or 70%) experienced a reduction in calculus build-up by regularly using the Gumabone® product. These products are available in a variety of sizes (for different size dogs) and designed in interesting shapes: bones, balls,

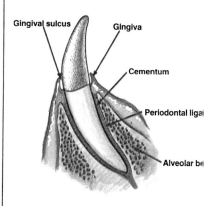

Comparative look at healthy gums (above) *and affected gums* (below) *in a dog's mouth. Instinctively dogs need to massage their gums—and the Gumabone® can satisfy this doggie craving.*

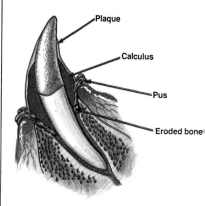

knots and rings (and even a tug toy). The entertainment value of the Gumabone® products is but an added advantage to the fighting of tooth decay and periodontitis. The products are ham-flavored and made of a thermoplastic polymer that is designed to outlast by ten times any rawhide, rubber or vinyl chew product, none of which can promise the proven benefit of the Gumabone®.

If your dog is able to chew apart a Gumabone®, it is probable that you provided him with a bone that is too small for him. Replace it with a larger one and the problem should not re-materialize. Economically, the Gumabone® is a smart choice, even without comparing it to the cost of extensive dental care.

Of course, nothing can *substitute* for periodic professional attention to your dog's teeth and gums, no more than your toothbrush can replace your dentist. Have your dog's teeth cleaned by your veterinarian at least once a year—twice a year is better—and he will be healthier, happier, and a far more pleasant companion.

Gumabones® are available through veterinarians and pet shops.

PERPETUAL WHELPING CHART

Bred—Jan.	1	2	3	4	5	6	7	8	9	10	11	12	13	14	15	16	17	18	19	20	21	22	23	24	25	26	27	28	29	30	31
Due—March	5	6	7	8	9	10	11	12	13	14	15	16	17	18	19	20	21	22	23	24	25	26	27	28	29	30	31	April 1	2	3	4
Bred—Feb.	1	2	3	4	5	6	7	8	9	10	11	12	13	14	15	16	17	18	19	20	21	22	23	24	25	26	27	28			
Due—April	5	6	7	8	9	10	11	12	13	14	15	16	17	18	19	20	21	22	23	24	25	26	27	28	29	30	May 1	2			
Bred—Mar.	1	2	3	4	5	6	7	8	9	10	11	12	13	14	15	16	17	18	19	20	21	22	23	24	25	26	27	28	29	30	31
Due—May	3	4	5	6	7	8	9	10	11	12	13	14	15	16	17	18	19	20	21	22	23	24	25	26	27	28	29	30	31	June 1	2
Bred—Apr.	1	2	3	4	5	6	7	8	9	10	11	12	13	14	15	16	17	18	19	20	21	22	23	24	25	26	27	28	29	30	
Due—June	3	4	5	6	7	8	9	10	11	12	13	14	15	16	17	18	19	20	21	22	23	24	25	26	27	28	29	30	July 1	2	
Bred—May	1	2	3	4	5	6	7	8	9	10	11	12	13	14	15	16	17	18	19	20	21	22	23	24	25	26	27	28	29	30	31
Due—July	3	4	5	6	7	8	9	10	11	12	13	14	15	16	17	18	19	20	21	22	23	24	25	26	27	28	29	30	31	August 1	2
Bred—June	1	2	3	4	5	6	7	8	9	10	11	12	13	14	15	16	17	18	19	20	21	22	23	24	25	26	27	28	29	30	
Due—August	3	4	5	6	7	8	9	10	11	12	13	14	15	16	17	18	19	20	21	22	23	24	25	26	27	28	29	30	31	Sept. 1	
Bred—July	1	2	3	4	5	6	7	8	9	10	11	12	13	14	15	16	17	18	19	20	21	22	23	24	25	26	27	28	29	30	31
Due—September	2	3	4	5	6	7	8	9	10	11	12	13	14	15	16	17	18	19	20	21	22	23	24	25	26	27	28	29	30	Oct. 1	2
Bred—Aug.	1	2	3	4	5	6	7	8	9	10	11	12	13	14	15	16	17	18	19	20	21	22	23	24	25	26	27	28	29	30	31
Due—October	3	4	5	6	7	8	9	10	11	12	13	14	15	16	17	18	19	20	21	22	23	24	25	26	27	28	29	30	31	Nov. 1	2
Bred—Sept.	1	2	3	4	5	6	7	8	9	10	11	12	13	14	15	16	17	18	19	20	21	22	23	24	25	26	27	28	29	30	
Due—November	3	4	5	6	7	8	9	10	11	12	13	14	15	16	17	18	19	20	21	22	23	24	25	26	27	28	29	30	Dec. 1	2	
Bred—Oct.	1	2	3	4	5	6	7	8	9	10	11	12	13	14	15	16	17	18	19	20	21	22	23	24	25	26	27	28	29	30	31
Due—December	3	4	5	6	7	8	9	10	11	12	13	14	15	16	17	18	19	20	21	22	23	24	25	26	27	28	29	30	31	Jan. 1	2
Bred—Nov.	1	2	3	4	5	6	7	8	9	10	11	12	13	14	15	16	17	18	19	20	21	22	23	24	25	26	27	28	29	30	
Due—January	3	4	5	6	7	8	9	10	11	12	13	14	15	16	17	18	19	20	21	22	23	24	25	26	27	28	29	30	31	Feb. 1	
Bred—Dec.	1	2	3	4	5	6	7	8	9	10	11	12	13	14	15	16	17	18	19	20	21	22	23	24	25	26	27	28	29	30	31
Due—February	2	3	4	5	6	7	8	9	10	11	12	13	14	15	16	17	18	19	20	21	22	23	24	25	26	27	28	March 1	2	3	4

Breeding

As the owner of a purebred dog, you may have considered breeding your pet at one time or another. If your dog is a beloved family pet, and not a show dog, you should *not* breed your dog. Breeding is not a hobby for pet owners, but rather a demanding, complicated vocation that is not to be dabbled with. Many people have thought of breeding as an easy-money opportunity: buy two dogs and let them do the work. The rule of thumb is: if you're making money by breeding dogs, you're doing something wrong!

Consider the time and money involved just to get your bitch into breeding condition and then to sustain her throughout pregnancy and afterwards while she tends her young. You will be obligated to house, feed, groom, and housebreak the puppies until good homes can be found for them; and, lest we forget, there will be periodic trips to the vet for check-ups, wormings, and inoculations. Common sense should tell you that it is indeed cruel to bring unwanted or unplanned puppies into an already crowded canine world; only negligent pet owners allow this to happen. Recognizing the number of dogs, purebred and mixed breeds, pet-, show- and breeding-quality, that are put to sleep annually, responsible breeders require that all pet animals be neutered. This condition most often is

incorporated into the selling contract. The motives of good breeders are clear: avoid the manufacturing and mass-producing of average and below-average dogs; control the overblown canine population; concentrate on the improvement of purebred bloodlines. Breeding is a noble calling and unless you can improve the breed, you should not consider breeding your animal. Despite all of the obvious virtues of breeding texts, no book could ever prepare a person for breeding. What a heart-breaking and tragic experience to lose an entire litter because a good-intentioned pet owner wasn't aware of potential genetic complications, didn't recognize a breech birth, or couldn't identify the signals of a struggling bitch! Possibly the dam could be lost as well!

Before you take any step towards mating your bitch, think carefully about why you want her to give birth to a litter of puppies. If you feel she will be deprived in some way if she is not bred, if you think your children will learn from the experience, if you have the mistaken notion that you will make money from this great undertaking, think again. A dog can lead a perfectly happy, healthy, normal life without having been mated; in fact, spaying a female and neutering a male helps them become better, longer-lived pets, as they are not so anxious to search for a mate in an effort to relieve their sexual tensions and have a diminished risk of cancer. As for giving the children a lesson in sex education, this is hardly a valid reason for breeding your dog. And on an economic level, it takes not only years of hard work (researching pedigrees and bloodlines, studying genetics, among other things), but it takes plenty of capital (money, equipment, facilities) to make a decent profit from dog breeding.

Why most dedicated breeders are lucky just to break even. If you have only a casual interest in dog breeding, it is best to leave this pastime to those who are more experienced in such matters, those who consider it a serious hobby and a real vocation. If you have bought a breeder– or show-quality canine, one that may be capable of producing champions, and if you are just starting out with this breeding venture, seek advice from the seller of your dog, from

Breeding dogs requires more than book knowledge. In dogs, breech presentation is not uncommon and the breeder must be prepared to handle this situation and guide the puppy so that neither the pup nor the bitch is injured.

other veteran breeders, and from your veterinarian before you begin.

The following sections on reproduction are intended for academic value only. This is not a "How-to" chapter on breeding, nor a step-by-step approach for the novice for getting started. Hopefully the reader will understand the depth and complexity of breeding as well as the expected ethical and moral obligations of persons who choose to do so—and never attempt it.

THE FEMALE "IN SEASON"

A bitch may come into season (also known as "heat" or estrus) once or several times a year, depending on the particular breed and the individual dog. Her first seasonal period, that is to say, the time when she is capable of being fertilized by a male dog, may occur as early as six months with some breeds. If you own a female and your intention is *not* to breed her, by all means discuss with the vet the possibility of having her spayed: this means before she

Ideally the puppy will be delivered in the normal, head-first position.

Breeding

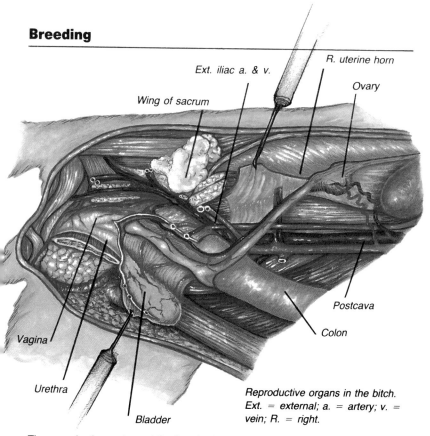

Ext. iliac a. & v.

R. uterine horn

Ovary

Wing of sacrum

Vagina

Urethra

Postcava

Colon

Bladder

Reproductive organs in the bitch.
Ext. = external; a. = artery; v. = vein; R. = right.

The reproductive system of the female dog consists of a highly specialized system of organs situated to the rear of the animal.

reaches sexual maturity.

The first sign of the female's being in season is a thin red discharge, which may increase for about a week; it then changes color to a thin yellowish stain, which lasts about another week. Simultaneously, there is a swelling of the vulva, the exterior portion of the female's reproductive tract; the soft, flabby vulva indicates her readiness to mate. Around this second week or so ovulation occurs, and this is the crucial period for her to be bred, if this is what you have in mind for her. It is during this middle phase of the heat cycle when conception can take place. Just remember that there is great variation from bitch to bitch with regard to how often they come into heat, how long the heat cycles last, how long the period of ovulation lasts, and how much time elapses between heat cycles. Generally, after the third week of heat, the vulval swelling decreases and the estrus period ceases for several months.

It should be mentioned that the female will probably lose her puppy coat, or at least shed part of it, about three months after she has come into season. This is the time when her puppies would have been weaned, had she been mated, and females generally drop coat at this time.

With female dogs, there are few, if any, behavioral changes during estrus. A bitch may dart out of an open door to greet all available male dogs that show an interest in her, and she may occasionally raise her tail and assume a mating stance, particularly if you pet her lower back; but these signs are not as dramatic as those of the sexually mature male. He himself does

Each egg within the female is surrounded by a wall that normally takes many sperm to penetrate. In this way, it is more likely that only the strongest sperm will fertilize the egg. A fertile female in season usually has a number of eggs, known as gametes.

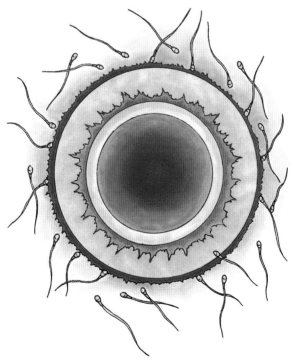

not experience heat cycles; rather, he is attracted to the female during all phases of her seasonal period. He usually becomes more aggressive and tends to fight with other males, especially over females in heat. He tends to mark his territory with urine to attract females and at the same time to warn other competitive males. It is not uncommon to see him mount various objects, and people, in an effort to satisfy his mature sexual urges.

If you are a homeowner and you have an absolutely climb-proof and dig-proof run within your yard, it may be safe to leave your bitch in season there. But then again it may not be a wise idea, as there have been cases of males mating with females right through chain-link fencing! Just to be on the safe side, shut her indoors during her heat periods and don't let her outdoors until you are certain the estrus period is over. Never leave a bitch in heat outdoors, unsupervised, even for a minute so that she can defecate or urinate. If you want to prevent the neighborhood dogs from hanging around your doorstep, as they inevitably will do when they discover your female is in season, take her some distance away from the house before you let her do her business. Otherwise, these canine suitors will be attracted to her by the arousing odor of her urine, and they will know instinctively that she isn't far from her scented "calling card." If you need to walk your bitch, take her in the car to a nearby park or field for a chance to stretch her legs. Remember that after about three weeks, and this varies from dog to dog, you can let her outdoors again with no worry that she can have puppies until the next heat period.

If you are seriously considering breeding your dog, first talk to as many experienced breeders as possible and read up on the subject in specific books and articles. Only when you are fully aware of the demands and responsibilities of breeding should you make your final decision. It must be stated here that there is no shortage of fine dogs in need of good homes, nor is there likely to be in the foreseeable future. So, if your object in breeding is merely to produce more dogs, you are strongly encouraged to reconsider your objective.

WHEN TO BREED

It is usually best to breed a bitch when she comes into her second or third season. Plan in advance the time of year which is best for you, taking into account your own schedule of activities (vacations, business trips, social engagements, and so on). Make sure you will be able to set aside plenty of time to assist with whelping of the newborn pups and caring for the dam and her litter for the next few weeks. At

The male reproductive system includes the penis and testicles. When not excited, the penis is withdrawn into the dog's body.

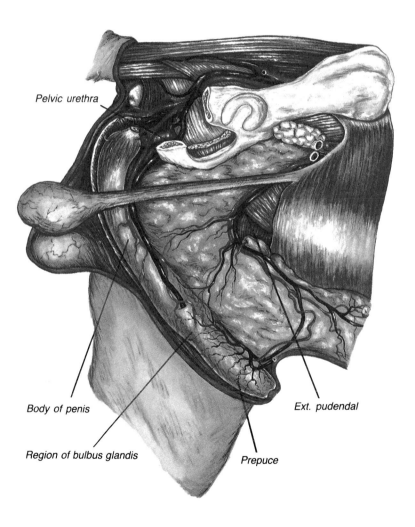

Pelvic urethra

Body of penis

Region of bulbus glandis

Ext. pudendal

Prepuce

the very least, it probably will take an hour or so each day just to feed and clean up after the brood—but undoubtedly you will find it takes much longer if you stop to admire and play with the youngsters periodically! Refrain from selling the litter until it is at least six weeks old, keeping in mind that a litter of pups takes up a fair amount of space by then. It will be your responsibility to provide for them until they have been weaned from their mother, properly socialized, housebroken, and ready to go to new homes (unless you plan to keep them all). Hopefully, as strongly recommended, you will have already lined up buyers for the pups in advance of their arrival into this world.

CHOOSING THE STUD

You can plan to breed your female about six-and-one-half months after the start of her last season, although a variation of a month or two either way is not unusual. Do some research into the various bloodlines within your breed and then choose a stud dog and make arrangements well in advance. If you are breeding for show stock, which will command higher prices than pet-quality animals, a mate should be chosen very carefully. He should complement any deficiencies (bad traits) that your female may have, and he should have a good show record

or be the sire of show winners, if he is old enough to have proven himself. If possible, the bitch and stud should have several ancestors in common within the last two or three generations, as such combinations have been known, generally, to "click" best.

The owner of a stud dog usually charges a stud fee for use of the animal's services. This does not always guarantee a litter, but if she fails to conceive, chances are you may be able to breed your female to that stud again. In some instances the owner of the stud will agree to take a "first pick of the litter" in place of a fee. You should, of course, settle all details beforehand, including the possibility of a single puppy surviving, deciding the age at which the pup is to be taken, and so forth.

If you plan to raise a litter that will be sold exclusively as pets, and if you merely plan to make use of an available male (not a top stud dog), the most important selection point involves temperament. Make sure the dog is friendly, as well as healthy, because a bad disposition can be passed on to his puppies—and this is the worst of all traits in a dog destined to be a pet. If you are breeding pet-quality dogs, a "stud fee puppy," not necessarily the choice of the litter, is the usual payment. Don't

Whelping box prepared with "pig rails," bars on either side of the box to prevent the bitch from rolling on the puppies.

breed indiscriminately; be sure you will be able to find good homes for each of the pups.

PREPARATION FOR BREEDING

Before you breed your female, make sure she is in good health. She should be neither too thin nor too fat. Any skin disease *must* be cured first so that it is not passed on to the puppies. If she has worms, she should be wormed before being bred or within three weeks after the mating. It is generally considered a good idea to revaccinate her against distemper and hepatitis before the puppies are born.

The female will probably be ready to breed twelve days after the first colored discharge appears. You can usually make arrangements to board her with the owner of the stud for a few days, to insure her being there at the proper time; or you can take her to be mated and bring her home the same day if you live near enough to the stud's owner. If the bitch still appears receptive she may be bred again two days later, just to make certain the mating was successful. However, some females never show signs of willingness, so it helps to have an experienced breeder on hand. In fact, you both may have to assist with the mating by holding the animals against each other to ensure the "tie" is not broken, that is, to make certain copulation takes place.

Usually the second day after the discharge changes color is the proper time to mate the bitch, and she may be bred for about three days following this time. For an additional week or so, she may have some discharge and attract other dogs by her odor; but she should not be bred. Once she has been bred, keep her far from all other male dogs, as they have the capacity to impregnate her again and sire some of her puppies. This could prove disastrous with purebred puppies.

THE FEMALE IN WHELP

You can expect the puppies nine weeks from the day of the mating, although sixty-one days is as common as sixty-three. Gestation, that period when the pups are developing inside their mother, varies among individual bitches. During this time the female should receive normal care and exercise. If she was overweight at the start, don't increase her food right away; excess weight at whelping time can be a problem with some dogs. If she is on the thin side, however, supplement her meal or meals with a portion of milk and biscuit at noontime. This will help build her up and put weight on her.

You may want to add a mineral and vitamin supplement to her diet, on the advice of your veterinarian, since she will need an extra supply not only for herself but for the puppies growing inside her. As the mother's appetite increases, feed her more. During the last two weeks of pregnancy, the pups grow enormously and the mother will have little room for food and less of an appetite. She should be tempted with meat, liver, and milk, however.

As the female in whelp grows heavier, cut out violent exercise and jumping from her usual routine. Although a dog used to such activities will often play with the children or run around voluntarily, restrain her for her own sake.

A sign that whelping is imminent is the loss of hair around her breasts. This is nature's way of "clearing a path" so that the puppies will be able to find their source of nourishment. As parturition draws near, the breasts will have swelled with milk and the nipples will have enlarged and darkened to a rosy pink. If the hair in the breast region does not shed for some reason, you can easily cut it short with a pair of scissors or comb it out so that it does not mat and become a hindrance to the suckling pups later on.

PREPARING FOR THE PUPPIES

Prepare a whelping box a few days before the puppies are due, and allow the mother to sleep there overnight or to spend some time in it during the day to become accustomed to it. This way she is less likely to try to have her pups under the front porch or in the middle of your bed. A variety of places will serve, such as the corner of your cellar or garage (provided these

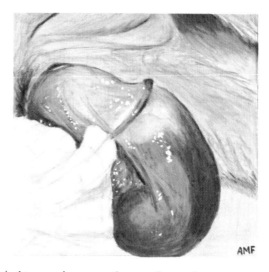

Each puppy is delivered in a separate membranous sac. This sac must be removed by the bitch without delay—if not, the breeder must come immediately to the assistance of the pup.

AMF

places are warm and dry). An unused room, such as a dimly lit spare bedroom, can also serve as the place for delivery. If the weather is warm, a large outdoor dog house will do, as long as it is well protected from rain, drafts, and the cold—and enclosed by fencing or a run. A whelping box serves to separate mother and puppies from visitors and other distractions. The walls should be high enough to restrain the puppies yet low enough to allow the mother to take a short respite from her brood after she has fed them. Four feet square is minimum size (for most dogs) and six-to-eight-inch high walls will keep the pups in until they begin to climb; then side walls should be built up so that the young ones cannot wander away from their nest. As the puppies grow, they really need more room anyway, so double the space with a very low partition down the middle of the box, and soon you will find them naturally housebreaking themselves. Puppies rarely relieve themselves where they sleep. Layers of newspapers spread over the whole area will make excellent bedding and be absorbent enough to keep the surface warm and dry. These should be removed daily and replaced with another thick layer. An old quilt or washable blanket makes better footing for the nursing puppies than slippery newspaper during the first week; this is also softer for the mother to lie on.

Be prepared for the actual whelping several days in advance. Usually the mother will tear up papers, refuse food, and become restless. These may be false alarms; the real test is her temperature, which will drop to below 100°F (38°C) about twelve hours before whelping. Take her temperature with a rectal thermometer, morning and evening, and usher her to her whelping box when her temperature goes down. Keep a close watch on her and make sure she stays safely indoors (or outdoors in a safe enclosure); if she is let outside, unleashed, or allowed to roam freely, she could wander off and start to go into labor. It is possible that she could whelp anywhere, and this could be unfortunate if she needs your assistance.

WHELPING

Usually little help is needed from you, but it is wise to stay close to be sure that the mother's lack of experience (if this is her first time) does not cause an unnecessary complication. Be ready to help when the first puppy arrives, for it could smother if she does not break the amniotic membrane enclosing it. She should tear open the sac and start licking the puppy, drying and stimulating it. Check to see that all fluids have been cleared from the pup's nostrils and mouth after the mother has licked her youngster clean; otherwise the pup may have difficulty breathing. If the mother fails to tear open the sac and stimulate the newborn's breathing, you can do this yourself by tearing the sack with your hands and then gently rubbing the infant with a soft, rough towel. The afterbirth attached to the puppy by the long umbilical cord, should follow the birth of each puppy. Watch to be sure that each afterbirth is expelled, for the retention of this material can cause infection. In her instinct for cleanliness the mother will probably eat the afterbirth after severing the umbilical cord. One or two meals of this will not hurt her; they stimulate her milk supply, as well as labor, for remaining pups. However, eating too many afterbirths can make her lose appetite for the food she needs to feed her pups and regain her strength. So remove the rest of them, along with the wet newspapers, and keep the box dry and clean.

If the mother does not bite the cord or bites it too close to the puppy's body, take over the job to prevent an umbilical hernia. Tearing is recommended, but you can cut the cord, about two inches from the body, with a sawing motion with scissors that have been sterilized in alcohol. Then dip the end of the cut cord in a shallow dish of iodine; the cord will dry up and fall off in a few days.

The puppies should follow

each other at intervals of not more than half an hour. If more time goes past and you are sure there are still pups to come, taking the mother for a brisk walk outside may start labor again. If she is actively straining without producing a puppy, the youngster may be presented backward, a so-called "breech" birth. Careful assistance with a well-lubricated finger to feel for the puppy or to ease it back may help, but never attempt to pull it out by force. This could cause serious damage, so seek the services of an expert—your veterinarian or an experienced breeder.

Even the best planned breeding can bear unexpected problems and complications. Therefore, do not rely solely on textbook knowledge of breeding and genetics. Experienced breeders and veterinarians will generally lend their words of wisdom—take full advantage of their generosity. Mere trial and error is no basis for any responsible breeding program.

If *anything* seems wrong during labor or parturition, waste no time in calling your veterinarian, who will examine the bitch and, if necessary, give her hormones to stimulate the birth of the remaining puppies. You may want his experience in whelping the litter even if all goes well. He will probably prefer to have the puppies born at his

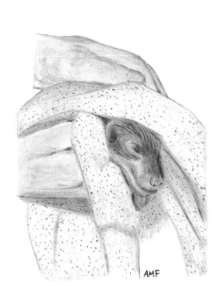

Newborn pups are very susceptible to chills, so the breeder must dry the puppy off thoroughly and place it in a temperature-controlled puppy box.

hospital rather than getting up in the middle of the night to come to your home. The mother would, no doubt, prefer to stay at home; but you can be sure she will get the best of care in a veterinary hospital. If the puppies are born at home, and all goes as it should, watch the mother carefully afterward. Within a day or two of the birth, it is wise to have the veterinarian check her and the pups to ensure that all is well.

Small bowls are helpful in the weaning process. Each pup should have its own bowl so that food intake can be carefully monitored.

Be sure each puppy finds a teat and starts nursing right away, as these first few meals supply colostral antibodies to help him fight disease. As soon as he is dry, hold each puppy to a nipple for a good meal without competition. Then he may join his littermates in the whelping box, out of his mother's way while she continues giving birth. Keep a supply of puppy formula on hand for emergency feedings or later weaning. An alternative formula of evaporated milk, corn syrup, and a little water with egg yolk can be warmed and fed if necessary. A pet nurser kit is also a good thing to have on hand; these are available at local pet shops. A supplementary feeding often helps weak pups

(those that may have difficulty nursing) over the hump. Keep track of birth weights and weekly readings thereafter; this will furnish an accurate record of the pups' growth and health, and the information will be valuable to your veterinarian.

RAISING THE PUPPIES

After all the puppies have been born, take the mother outside for a walk and drink of water, and then return her to take care of her brood. She will probably not want to stay away for more than a minute or two for the first few weeks. Be sure to keep water available at all times and feed her milk or broth frequently, as she needs nourishment to produce milk. Encourage her to eat, with her favorite foods, until she seeks them of her own accord. She will soon develop a ravenous appetite and should have at least two large meals a day, with dry food available in addition. Your veterinarian can guide you on the finer points of nutrition as they apply to nursing dams.

Prepare a warm place to put the puppies after they are born to keep them dry and to help them to a good start in life. An electric heating pad, heat lamp or hot water bottle covered with flannel can be placed in the bottom of a cardboard box and near the mother so that she can see her puppies. She will usually allow you to help her care for the youngsters, but don't take them out of her sight. Let her handle things if your interference seems to make her nervous.

Be sure that all the puppies are getting enough to eat. If the mother sits or stands instead of lying still to nurse, the probable cause is scratching from the puppies' nails. You can remedy this by clipping them, as you would the bitch's, with a pet nail clipper. Manicure scissors also do

furnished with a heating pad and/or heating lamp and some bedding material. Leave half the litter with the mother and the other half in the extra box, changing off at two-hour intervals at first. Later you may exchange them less frequently, leaving them all together except during the day. Try supplementary feedings, too. As soon as their eyes open, at about two weeks, they will lap from a small dish.

"Pooping" the puppies, or rubbing the bowels and genitals to stimulate elimination, may be necessary if the bitch doesn't tend to this herself.

for these tiny claws. Some breeders advise disposing of the smaller or weaker pups in a large litter, as the mother has trouble handling more than six or seven. You can help her out by preparing an extra puppy box or basket

WEANING THE PUPPIES

Normally the puppies should be completely weaned at five weeks, although you can start to feed them at three weeks. They will find it easier to lap semi-solid food than to drink milk at first, so mix baby cereal with whole or evaporated milk, warmed to body temperature, and offer it to the puppies in a saucer. Until they learn to lap it, it is best to feed one or two at a time because they are more likely to walk into it than to eat it. Hold the saucer at their chin level, and let them gather around, keeping paws off the dish. Cleaning with a damp sponge afterward prevents most of the cereal from sticking to the pups if the mother doesn't clean them up. Once they have gotten the idea, broth or babies' meat soup may be alternated with milk, and you can start them on finely chopped meat. At about four weeks, they will eat four meals a day and soon do without their mother entirely. Start them on canned dog food, or leave dry puppy food with them in a dish

for self-feeding. Don't leave the water dish with them all the time; at this age everything is a play toy and they will use it as a wading pool. They can drink all they need if it is offered several times a day, after meals. As the puppies grow up, the mother will go into their "pen" only to nurse them, first sitting up and then standing. To dry up her milk

All puppies are susceptible to worms. Deworming must begin at a very early age with the supervision of a professional.

Bottle-feeding may be necessary with particularly large litters or with a bitch who has become overly stressed or neglectful.

supply completely, keep the mother away for longer periods; after a few days of part-time nursing she can stay away for even longer periods, and then permanently. The little milk left will be resorbed by her body.

The puppies may be put outside during the day, unless it is too cold or rainy, as soon as their eyes are open. They will benefit from the sunlight. A rubber mat or newspapers underneath will protect them from cold or dampness. As they mature, the pups can be let out for longer intervals, although you must provide them with a shelter at night or in bad weather. By now, cleaning up after the

matured youngsters is a man-sized job, so put them out at least during the day and make your task easier. If you enclose them in a run or kennel, remember to clean it *daily*, as various parasites and other infectious organisms may be lurking if the quarters are kept dirty.

You can expect the pups to need at least one worming before they are ready to go to new homes. Before the pups are three weeks old, take a stool sample from each to your veterinarian. The vet can determine, by analyzing the stool, if any of the pups have worms—and if so, what kind of

Breeding

worms are present. If one puppy is infected, then all should be wormed as a preventive measure. Follow the veterinarian's advice; this also applies to vaccinations. You will want to vaccinate the pups at the earliest possible age. This way, the pups destined for new homes will be protected against some of the more debilitating canine diseases.

THE DECISION TO SPAY OR NEUTER

If you decide not to use your male or female for breeding, or if you are obligated to have the animal altered based on an agreement made between you and the seller, make the necessary arrangements with your veterinarian as soon as possible. The surgery involved for both males and females is relatively simple and painless: males will be castrated and females will have their ovaries and uterus removed. In both cases, the operation does not alter their personalities; you will, however, notice that males will be less likely to roam, to get into fights with other male dogs, and to mount objects and people.

Your veterinarian can best determine at what age neutering or spaying should be done. With a young female dog, the operation may be somewhat more involved, and as a result be more costly; however, in the long

The breeder must actively partake in cleaning the pup after feedings. Hands-on contact serves as the initial step in socialization—accustoming the pup to his human family.

PUPPY GROWTH AND BREEDER RESPONSIBILITY	
AGE	**REQUIRED CARE/EXPECTED DEVELOPMENT**
WEEKS 1–2	Helpless; dam must provide constant care; owner must ensure warmth and cleanliness; puppy nurses, crawls, needs stimulation for elimination; sleeps 90% of time.
WEEKS 3–4	Owner sustains optimum environment; puppy is alert, laps from bowl, takes first steps; defecates on its own; baby teeth emerge; barks, wags tail.
WEEKS 4–5	Ambles, growls, and bites; play and interaction increase; human contact limited but essential; learning begins.
WEEKS 5–6	Weaning; human socialization vital; pack order apparent; sex play; explores and sleeps less.
WEEKS 6–8	Two to three daily meals; puppy accustomed to human family; breeder initiates housetraining; first veterinary visit; wary of the unknown.

run you will be glad you made the decision to have this done for your pet. After a night or two at the veterinarian's or an animal hospital, your bitch can be safely returned to your home. Her stitches will heal in a short time, and when they are removed, you will hardly notice her souvenir scar of the routine operation. Once she has been spayed, she no longer will be capable of having a litter of puppies.

Check with your city or town or with the local humane society for special programs that are available for pet owners. In many municipalities you can have your

pet altered for just a small fee; the low price is meant to encourage pet owners to take advantage of this important means of birth control for their dogs. Pet adoption agencies and other animal welfare organizations can house only so many animals at one time, given the money, space, and other resources they have available. This is why pet owners are urged to have their pets altered, so that puppies resulting from accidental breedings won't end up being put to sleep as so many others have that are lost, stray, unwanted, or abandoned.

Dogs and the Law

BY ANMARIE BARRIE

No matter where you live, there will be laws and ordinances restricting the ownership of pets—exotic and wild animals (such as monkeys, pythons, and ocelots) as well as the more traditionally kept domestics (such as dogs and cats). This chapter purports to investigate with brevity the laws which pertain to the ownership and keeping of the domestic canine. Like all other things, laws change and evolve over time, and vary from locale to locale. The information supplied in this chapter is meant as a general guideline for the dog owner. Every owner is strongly encouraged to contact his local authorities to keep abreast on new laws and amendments to existing laws so that he can be the most responsible owner possible.

BUYING AND SELLING

Certain specific laws apply to the purchasing and peddling of pooches. Laws in these areas grow ever more stringent, so the potential buyer and/or seller is well advised to be aware of the laws pertaining to his transactions where dogs are concerned. Dealers and breeders, in most instances, are treated differently from the average dog owner who is trying to sell his first litter. Regardless, a sales contract is in order, a written agreement outlining the various dimensions of the sale. Sales contracts may indicate the quality of the dog, i.e.,

the pet-quality, show-quality, breeder-quality; the sex of the dog; and the breed of the dog. In addition to these basic essentials, the specifics, as registered with the national kennel club, should be included, i.e., the names and registration numbers of the sire and dam; the litter registration number; addresses of all involved, etc. Warranties and conditions of the sale should also be expressly stated, and no implications or unexpressed conditions may apply. For instance, the return policy, the guaranteed pedigree of the dog, the health of the dog (including the possibility of congenital defects in later years) should all be addressed. Replacement warranties are also appropriate to include, should something happen to the purchased puppy. Should a given puppy (of intended show-quality) begin to exhibit faults disqualified in the breed standard, the buyer is able to return the dog. Commonly, if the seller is no longer in the business of selling dogs, the buyer is entitled to half of the agreed-upon price.

GENERAL GUIDELINES FOR DOG OWNERS

"Give to God what is God's, give to Caesar what is Caesar's" is a Gospel quote that has been used and manipulated since it was originally uttered two thousand years ago. The concept of paying taxes has never sat well with humans, nor does it sit well with dogs. Licenses are basically taxes on dogs, though as pet owners we need not stew over the unfairness of "yet another tax." The purpose of licensing dogs is a valid and important one. Licenses serve as a positive means of identifying an animal and afford an owner with a fair chance of regaining his dog if lost or stolen. Licenses also provide a dog additional consideration by authorities and even from strangers, who will respect the fact the owner of this dog cares enough to identify it and affix its ID to its collar.

Many owners resist the call to license their dogs on the premise that their dogs are house dogs or

yard dogs, or never ever walk off their leashes. Nonetheless, accidents and mishaps occur regularly, and it's better to be safe than sorry (why not be safe and law-abiding!?). The threat of impoundment and the treatment which dogs receive as a matter of course from such authorities should be scare tactic enough to persuade an owner to license his dog.

The cost of licenses varies from place to place as well as from dog to dog. Licenses for assistance dogs, such as Seeing Eye dogs, hearing dogs, or any handicap-assistance dogs, may be substan-

Dogs and the Law

tially less than a regular dog. In some areas, assistance dogs receive their licenses gratis, or are covered by their training agency. Recognizing the growing problem of dog over-population, many towns and cities offer reduced license fees for spayed and neutered dogs.

Vaccinations for dogs deserve special mention. Depending on where you live, the vaccination for rabies may or may not be mandatory. In some places, this vaccination is optional. While the chances of your well-kept canine acquiring rabies today may be minuscule, the cases are not so isolated and unheard of that an owner can rest in ultimate confidence. Generally a vaccinated dog can avoid being quarantined in the unfortunate event that it should bite a stranger or would-be assailant. The age for vaccination varies, but most usual is six months old. If a puppy is under the age of six months, it is advisable not to permit it to socialize with unknown dogs on the street. Keep in mind that vaccinations need to be kept updated for both rabies and other diseases.

Among the most common-sense concerns of current-day owners are leash laws. Responsible dog owners marvel with dismay over dogs which run the neighborhood without a collar, supervision, or their owner's concern. Caring dog proprietors are grateful for leash laws as it is the protection of the dog, as well as human passers-by, that is concerned. That a dog is under control at all times remains the premise of leash laws. Dogs that are given the "freedom" to wander the neighborhood or city block are likewise given the "right" to be impounded, snatched and/or injured. Fines are often issued against owners who do not abide by the leash laws of their community.

Running hand in hand, or paw in paw, with leash laws are muzzle ordinances. These laws require that a dog be muzzled at all times when it is in public. Although these laws are less commonplace than leash laws, they do exist in certain communities. Owners are advised to investigate if muzzle laws apply in their area.

Pooper-scooper laws are being enforced in more and more areas these days. "Curb Your Dog" signs have become as common as pedestrian crossings and "Yield signs." For the cleanliness of our communities, these kinds of laws are invented; in order to do our part as responsible dog owners and citizens, we must abide by these clean-up rules. While persons who live in the country have more gripes with these laws, city dwellers fully understand the need to observe these ordinances. Scoops are sold in pet shops, or you can employ simple plastic bags. It is assured that if you are the person walking behind the behind of a 250-pound pooch, you will be grateful for these laws. Some owners use brown paper sheets or newspapers (preferably yesterday's) to assist in the clean-up.

Anti-cruelty laws are geared towards the protection of animals on the whole, sparing dogs from potential, often unintentional, abuse. Laws such as these are sweeping the nations, as an increasing number of people become aware of deleterious situations arising for all animals. While active cruelty to an animal evokes rage in any human being, there are more subtle displays of cruelty which these laws attempt to pinpoint—cruelty in the form of neglect and careless treatment. Persons who are found in violation of anti-cruelty laws are very often subject to fines. All citizens are encouraged to report any cases of cruelty which they witness or suspect to be happening. Commonly, ordinances prohibit the keeping of a dog in a parked car, which can be a cruel, irresponsible practice in most situations. Dogs have been known to suffer from heat prostration, and worse.

Anti-cruelty laws have also seeped into the world of puppy mills, as more and more of these

Dogs and the Law

unethical outfits are being undermined by concerned owners. The cruel treatment of animals in these farms must be combated by increased legislation. Always know the source of your potential new dog. Avoid sellers who cannot give you all the answers you want to know.

As heart-breaking and unimaginable as it seems, our dogs are not permitted in a great number of places. "No Dog" signs are frequently posted in buildings,

parks, restaurants, motels, etc. It seems that dogs are more accepted in Continental countries, where dogs are permitted (even invited) to dine with the family at a fine restaurant. This not being the case in every American state or city of Great Britain, law-abiding citizens must contend with these restrictions.

Ordinances involving the number of dogs which an owner can keep are prevalent in most communities. These laws vary from place to place and from residency to residency. Whether you live in an apartment, condominium, house, or farm, there may be laws regulating the number of pets you are able to keep. Homes that wish to keep more than the maximum number of animals may be forced to apply for a kennel license or be subject to a daily fine and regular inspection.

For sake of neighbors and the general health of your family, it is wise to take these restrictions to heart. No matter how great your love of animals is, it is not humane to the animals involved to subject them to over-crowding and minimal attention. A small suburban apartment can quickly become the haven of 75 stray dogs and cats, should the owner so choose. Laws such as these prohibit these kinds of communes from blossoming all over the nation.

In most well-organized communities, there are organizations that specialize in Lost and Found dogs. For your dog's safety, you must have the dog licensed and vaccinated, as dogs that are protected in this way have a greater chance of finding their way back home, unscathed. If you have lost your dog, do not panic, but do work fast. The more people to whom you speak and angles that you take, the greater your chances of retrieving your lost pet. All local authorities (police, fire company, animal control organizations) and all types of media organizations (radio, newspapers, town crier) should be commissioned to lend a hand, keep out a keen eye and ear for the lost dog. Advertising through posters, newspapers, radio, and community lists will pay off in the end. Written descriptions, accompanied by photographs, can assist in helping people have a better mental image of the dog.

Prevention can never be overstressed. Licensing is a must, and the dog must wear the ID tag. Tattoos are quick becoming very popular. These should be located on the dog's inner thigh, not on its ear, as that appendage can easily be torn off by a thief. Tattoos have

worked for generations on pack dogs, and the same philosophy of identification can work for pet owners too. Often, the dog's kennel club number or other identifying number is tattooed onto the dog.

Impoundment threatens lost dogs and all other dogs running at large, particularly those without collars and licenses. Most animal control authorities maintain the right to impound, sell, and/or destroy any animal that they catch. As an owner's legal prop- erty, a dog cannot be impounded or confiscated without the owner's notice. Of course, if the dog is loose and unidentified, the owner is knowingly waiving his rights, and thereby his chances of seeing that the dog has a fair chance to find its way home. A dog that proves itself a nuisance or dangerous to property and people may be confiscated; the owner may be notified ex post facto. An owner may then be invited to court to defend its dog's right to life.

Pounds, as a rule, are required

to keep a dog for a certain period of time before disposing of it in any permanent way. However, this period rarely exceeds four days in length, so owners must act expediently. The fortunate owner who does find his dog at the pound must have the dog vaccinated and licensed (if not done previously), as well as pay a fine. Unclaimed pets are either destroyed humanely or offered for adoption. Many pounds reserve the right to have the owner spay or neuter his unchained canine.

There are also laws that regard the disposal of a dog's remains. Owners must be aware of restrictions in this area. Under certain legislative bodies, a person is not allowed to bury his dog on his own property. In most cases, contacting your family veterinarian or a humane society to handle the details of burial is the most expeditious approach.

DOGS AS PROPERTY

Let there be no doubt about it: a dog is the personal property of its owner. This fact is well substantiated in the various legal codes and statutes under which we all live our daily lives. For dog owners, the dog's legal-property status can be considered a mixed blessing. On the one hand, the dog's legal status as property necessarily guarantees the owner certain rights under the law, the very same rights which pertain to the possession of other property. Homeowners especially should be familiar with some of these rights. On the other hand, the dog's status as legal property places very considerable responsibility on the shoulders of the dog owner, for he will be held legally accountable for the actions of his dog—

Dogs and the Law

just as the homeowner is legally responsible for any injuries that occur on his property and are the result of, for example, negligence resulting from the owner's maintenance of the property.

For the dog owner to be entitled to the rights of a property owner pertinent to his dog, the dog in question must be licensed by the appropriate authorities, usually the local governing body. However, because of the nature of legal systems in most of the free countries, laws may vary from town to town, county to county, and state to state. Thus the owner is strongly encouraged to investigate the necessary requirements for licensing his dog. At the same time, the owner is encouraged to ascertain the exact nature of the rights of a dog owner under the given laws applicable to the given place of residence.

This varying nature of laws makes it impossible for one to offer details on many of the rights and responsibilities of the dog owner. However, regardless of the place of residence, the dog owner is entitled to due process with regard to the taking of the licensed dog. Due process in this regard refers essentially to the necessary notification of the owner before any further action can be taken by the authorities. In

this way, the owner is offered a chance to act on the behalf of his dog, his legal property.

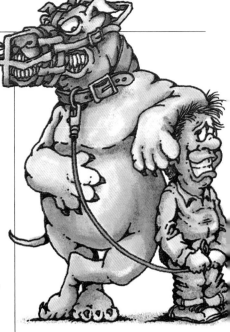

An additional consequence of the legal-property status of the dog is that, as property, the dog cannot be considered a person under the law. One effect of this fact is that the dog therefore cannot be the beneficiary of a will; however, provisions for the care and continued maintenance of the dog can be, and should be, carefully spelled out in the will— just as it would be for the home or any other piece of property.

In summary, the dog is definitely considered property under the law. As such, the dog owner is entitled to given rights and held accountable for given responsibilities. To be granted these rights, the dog owner must license his dog, as well as follow any other guidelines required under the laws of his or her place of residence. Finally, as property, the dog cannot be considered a person, and this fact holds various implications.

Because the dog is the legal property of the dog owner, the dog owner is legally responsible for the behavior of his dog, as well as for the care and maintenance of the animal. However, when the dog is in the possession of a person other than the owner, such as a temporary caretaker, that other person may be held responsible for the dog, depending on the specific circumstances involved

and the specific laws of the jurisdiction in which the action(s) occurs. To offer an example, consider the following scenario: A dog is owned by Mr. Smith, who leaves on vacation and hires an individual to care for his dog. While Mr. Smith is on vacation, the dog caretaker walks the dog without a leash and the dog bites a child. Of course, because the dog is property and not person, someone must be held accountable. Should it be Mr. Smith or the caretaker? In such a case it is likely that the caretaker would be held accountable for the dog's biting of the child, provided of course that Mr. Smith did not leave directions to walk the dog without a leash, etc. As we can

Dogs and the Law

see, many variables can come into play regarding legal responsibility for the dog.

To keep it simple in an attempt to offer the reader as much information as possible without getting weighed down in extraneous details, a few general guidelines will be presented.

First, the dog owner, for all intents and purposes, should raise, train, and keep his dog under the assumption that he is legally responsible for every action and for the entire well-being of his dog, ranging from obeying pooper-scooper laws to anti-cruelty laws to dog-bite statutes. In this way, the owner will act as responsibly as possible and, in the end, avoid possible law suits. Secondly, whenever leaving the dog in the custody of others, whether for a short time or a prolonged period, the dog owner should leave clear, explicit written directions regarding proper and appropriate care of the dog. These directions can be prepared ahead of time and kept on file by the owner for use whenever the need arises. In so doing, the owner protects himself in the case of a lawsuit. Thirdly, a minor can be held legally responsible for the dog as property, and this fact needs to be considered whenever a youngster is in charge of the

dog. Lastly, the dog owner must familiarize himself with the laws that pertain to him as a dog owner, as a resident of his given community. In no other way can the dog owner act responsibly and thus be protected under the law.

Because the dog owner is legally responsible for his dog, he is liable for all damages and personal injuries that result from the dog. Under strict liability, the owner is liable for any damages or injury caused by the dog, even if they are not the "fault" of the owner. Of course, common law doctrines are the products of court decisions, and thus may vary from place to place. Additionally,

liability may be subject to the same circumstantial variables as those which apply to responsibility in general.

Because the owner is liable for the actions of his dog, he can be taken to court and sued. A person injured by a dog will likely receive reimbursement for all medical expenses, as well as a given sum for pain and suffering, depending on the circumstances. The same conditions apply to damages: a person can receive full reimbursement for the loss or damage of any property that was the product of the dog's actions. In serious cases, e.g., those involving blatant negligence, malice or forethought,

Dogs and the Law

the owner of the dog can be sentenced to prison and/or fined.

The subject of vicious dogs abounds in controversy, in part because of the lack of an all-encompassing definition of viciousness as it pertains to the dog and in part because there is a current trend to label entire breeds of dog as inherently vicious. Because of the controversial nature of the vicious-dog subject, the reader is encouraged to do two things: first, read up on the specific laws pertaining to canine viciousness that apply to his locale; and second, to employ utmost common sense in the execution of his dog-owning responsibilities. The first step is by far the easier of the two, for vicious-dog statutes can be found in most libraries and at many municipal buildings. Beginning with inquiries and following up with research ensures the dog owner expedient acquisition of the applicable laws regarding viciousness and his dog. The second step, regarding the application of common sense to all aspects of canine ownership, requires that the dog owner first obey all laws pertinent to his ownership, e.g., leash laws, proper training, housing, restriction, etc.; second be well aware and understand the nature of his charge and adjust its keeping accordingly; and lastly take all steps necessary to ensure that others who may care for the dog be explicitly instructed on how to execute their caretaker task.

By following the two-step process just described to help you guard against a potential vicious-dog law suit, especially in following the application of common sense to your dog ownership, you to a large degree also work to prevent injury, both to yourself and to others. In so doing, you are also necessarily limiting the possibility that you will find yourself beside your dog in court over your dog's injuring another person.

To assist the dog owner in applying common sense to his dog ownership, the following principles are presented: (1) all dogs, meaning each and every dog, no matter how small or large a dog, young or old a dog, has the potential to injure a person; (2) dogs act largely on instinct and perceive the world much differently than people do, i.e., a dog may see a situation as dangerous and react with fear biting even though a person sees the situation as perfectly non-threatening or even pleasant; (3) not all people are dog fanciers, and some people even delight in provoking and taunting an animal, which can easily lead to their being injured; (4) dogs do not treat all people in the same manner as they treat you, their owner and caretaker.

By considering these principles, obeying the laws of dog ownership (which essentially are designed for the protection of you, your dog, and others), and consis-

tently applying common sense in your daily doggie doings, you by and large prevent injury.

In recent years, insurance companies have offered insurance policies to dog owners. Essentially these policies can be grouped into two general categories: canine life insurance and liability insurance. Of course, many different policies from each category are offered, and the cost of the respective policy varies roughly in accordance with the coverage offered. For example, a "life" insurance policy that covered accidental injury as well as providing a death benefit will typically cost more than a policy that offers only a death benefit, provided of course that the death benefits are of equivalent value.

Canine insurance is not for every dog owner, though every dog owner is encouraged to investigate the various policies offered and for themselves make the determination of whether yea or nay they purchase such insurance. Common consensus offers that canine insurance is best suited for two kinds of dog owners, a splitting that roughly corresponds to the two kinds of canine insurance offered. The first kind of owner is the professional breeder

Dogs and the Law

and/or showperson, who has invested large sums of money in his individual dogs and stands to lose much in the case of accidental injury or death. Such a person is strongly encouraged to investigate the canine life insurance available. In short, he is encouraged to protect his investment. The second type of person is the owner of a guard dog or any dog trained or demonstrating the proclivity to attack a person. For this dog owner, investigation of some type of liability insurance is encouraged.

After all is said and done, after all steps and measures towards responsible lawful ownership have been taken, there may still come a

time when the dog owner finds himself in the midst of a controversy. The cause may be a very simple or insignificant one, or it may be a very complex one. The important point to remember is that a controversy must be managed in a legal and responsible way.

If the controversy is a minor one, it might be best to attempt to resolve the the problem between the two parties, in which case a third party (an objective mediator) often proves helpful. If this fails for any reason, e.g., tempers, then going to the authorities is strongly recommended. In no case should anyone attempt to take matters into their own hands, becoming

judge, jury, and executioner all in one. If the controversy involves a serious matter, you are encouraged to seek legal advice as soon as possible. Remember that you are responsible for the actions of your dog, and therefore you can be held liable for any damages or injuries that your dog may inflict. All controversies should be approached in an objective manner; the dog owner must realize that there are at least two sides to the story and that resolution of the conflict will likely involve at least small compromises from each of the parties involved.

CRUELTY

What determines or defines cruelty to animals often excites great controversy in our society.

Anti-cruelty legislation, nonetheless, continues to make headway, as new laws are being enforced with regularity. Avoiding the inhumane treatment of animals, neglect and abuse should be the target of all caring dog owners. The conditions of a breeding facility or animal shelter, cosmetic alterations of puppies (cropping ears and docking tails), protocol for dealing with an injured animal, and impoundment of lost, vicious or destructive dogs are just some of the topics which anti-cruelty laws address. In the United States, ear cropping and tail docking are not prohibited as they are in Great Britain. Britain has for generations deemed such cosmetic alterations unnecessary and unnecessarily cruel.

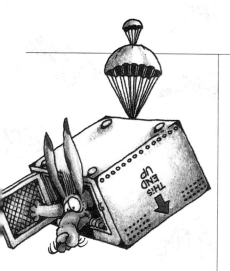

Air travel can be a more difficult matter. Airlines most usually allow dogs to fly on their flights. Small dogs can be carried on, while large ones need to be kept in the baggage area. Of course the appropriate crate is required for any dog traveling by air. Mark the crate: "Live Cargo" or "This End Up" for the safety of your canine luggage. Travel agents are usually well informed and will advise you on such decisions.

LANDLORDS AND DOGS

Regardless of how it may seem, there is no *natural* antipathy between landlords and dogs. Dogs in themselves are no more the natural enemy of landlords

TRAVEL

When traveling with your dog, there are a number of considerations with which to be concerned. The most common method of travel is automobiles, though fewer laws address this mode of transportation. Regarding urban travel, i.e., buses, subways, rails, dogs are usually not permitted on board unless the dog is an assistance dog. Some railways allow dogs to stay in the owner's cabin, while others require that the dog be kept in the baggage compartment (likely there is an area especially equipped for live cargo). Always check with the railway and train station about the regulations regarding your dog. Do this before leaving home! If you intend to travel by sea, less common in today's world of airplanes, it is advised that similar inquiries be made to the ship's station.

than, say, tenants are. Landlords and dogs don't get along for the most part because in many cases dogs and tenants—both dog owners and non-dog owners—don't get along. Landlords often try to outlaw the ownership of dogs by their tenants simply because dogs make trouble. They can be destructive, they can make messes, they can scare people, they can hurt people. To avoid the trouble that dogs can make, landlords write into their leases clauses that prohibit the keeping of dogs by tenants. Landlords in general might not be the nicest people in the world, but you can't blame them for wanting to avoid trouble and expense that tenants' pet dogs may bring them. For example, would you as landlord relish the idea of being sued by some troublemaking yardbird who, while visiting one of your tenants, was bitten by his homicidal cur? And don't ask why he'd be suing the landlord when it wasn't the landlord's dog that bit him—he'd be suing everyone in sight, as the courts encourage that type of madness: wouldn't a reasonably prudent landlord provide 24-hour guard service to make sure that visitors are not attacked in their buildings?

Governmental units at various levels are telling landlords that they can't tell their tenants not to own dogs (or cats), and various courts are starting to tell landlords that either their leases don't say what they plainly do say or that they say it but the courts don't like it and will therefore come up with a reason why it shouldn't be allowed. But the milennium for dog-owning apartment dwellers has not yet arrived; until it does, the best thing a tenant can do is to ask for permission from the owner...and to get it in writing.

Index

Required Reading

Dog Breeding for Professionals
By Dr. Herbert Richards (H-969)

For dog owners who need and actively seek good advice about how to go about breeding their dogs whether for profit or purely because of their attachment to animals. *Please note* that the breeding photography is sexually explicit and some readers may find it offensive.

Hard cover, 5.5 in x 8 in, 224 pages, 105 black and white photos, 62 color photos.
ISBN 0-87666-659-4a

Dog Training
By Lew Burke (H-962)

The elements of dog training are easy to grasp and apply. The author uses the psychological makeup of dogs to his advantage by making them want to be what they should be—substituting the family for the pack.

Hard cover, 5.5 in x 8 in, 255 pages, 64 black and white photos, 23 color photos.
ISBN 0-87666-656-X

The Mini Atlas of Dog Breeds
By Andrew De Prisco & James B. Johnson (H-1106)

An identification handbook giving a concise and thorough look at over 400 of the world's dog breeds. The authors' enthusiastic and knowledgeable approach

brings to life instantly man's oldest friend and companion. A flowing and witty text, further enlivened by 500 full-color photos, successfully maps out the world of dogs; an easy-reference format pinpoints each breed's development, portrait, registry, and

pet attributes. The volume is captioned with specially designed symbols.

Hard cover, 5.5 in x 8.5 in, 544 pages, nearly 700 color photos.
ISBN 0-86622-091-7

Dog Owner's Encyclopedia of Veterinary Medicine
By Allan H. Hart, B.V.Sc. (H-934)

Written by a vet who feels that most dog owners should recognize the symptoms and understand the cures of most diseases of dogs so they can properly communicate with their veterinarian. This book is a necessity for every dog owner, especially those who have more than one dog. *Hard cover, 5.5 in x 8 in, 186 pages, 86 black and white photos. ISBN 0-87666-287-4*

The Proper Care of Dogs
By Christopher Burris (TW-102)
Discusses the basic care of all dogs and highlights the specific needs of every A.K.C.—recog-

nized breed. Ideal for the prospective dog owner, this compact and colorful book lays the groundwork for general canine management and provides an overview of the world of dogs. *Hard cover, 5 in x 7 in, 256 pages, over 200 full-color photos. ISBN 0-86622-402-5*

The Atlas of Dog Breeds of the World
By Bonnie Wilcox, DVM, & Chris Walkowicz (H-1091)

Traces the history and highlights the characteristics, appearance and function of every recognized dog breed in the world. 409 different breeds receive full-color treatment and individual study. Hundreds of breeds in addition to those recognized by the American Kennel Club and the Kennel Club of Great Britain are included—the dogs of the world complete! The ultimate reference work, comprehensive coverage, intelligent and delightful discussions. The perfect gift book. *Hard cover, 9 in x 12 in, 912 pages, 1,106 color photos. ISBN 0-86622-930-2*

The ATLAS of
DOG BREEDS
of the World   t.f.h.

NEW!
THIRD EDITION
With 100 **NEW** color photos

BONNIE WILCOX, DVM,
—and—
CHRIS WALKOWICZ

OVER 1100 FULL-COLOR PHOTOS

The most comprehensive fully illustrated volume on dogs ever published— *EVERY* photo in full color

The Romantic Poets and Their Circle

Published in Great Britain by National Portrait Gallery Publications,
National Portrait Gallery, St Martin's Place, London WC2H 0HE

For a complete catalogue of current publications please write to the
address above, or visit our website at www.npg.org.uk/publications

ISBN 1 85514 355 0

A catalogue record for this book is available from the British Library.

Publishing Manager: Celia Joicey
Editorial Assistant: Kate Phillimore
Design: Pentagram
Production: Ruth Müller-Wirth and Geoff Barlow
Printed and bound in Hong Kong

The publisher would like to thank the copyright holders for granting
permission to reproduce works illustrated in this book. Every effort
has been made to contact the holders of copyright material, and
any omissions will be corrected in future editions if the publisher
is notified in writing.

National Portrait Gallery
Insights
The Romantic Poets and Their Circle
Richard Holmes

Wordsworth

For Eulry with Goodwin
1825

Contents

William Wordsworth
Benjamin Robert
Haydon, 1815

A brooding William
Wordsworth as sketched
by Haydon for his group
portrait *Christ's Entry
into Jerusalem*.

Introduction – Who *were* the Romantic Poets?

The two most popular and widely read poems of the Romantic period (1770–1830) would now surprise us. They were both traditional eighteenth-century pastorals, today almost totally forgotten. The first was James Thomson's *The Seasons*, originally published in 1730 and universally admired and reprinted for over a century. ('That is true fame,' murmured Coleridge, when he found a well-worn copy thrown down in the parlour of a Devonshire inn in 1798.) The second was Robert Bloomfield's *The Farmer's Boy*, a rural idyll in rhyming couplets which sold over 60,000 copies between 1800 and 1810. Yet neither the much-loved Thomson nor the best-selling 'ploughboy poet' Bloomfield (actually a London cobbler) is a name we now associate with Romanticism.

What extraordinary force suddenly buried their reputations and brought about such a seismic shift in popular taste? One answer is simply: the dazzling Lord Byron and the intoxicating idea of the poet as 'Romantic genius'. Byron's portraits give us an unforgettable insight into this explosive notion, which still shapes (or distorts) our concept of inspiration and the creative artist. From now on the Romantic poet was young, solitary, brooding, beautiful and damned.

Byron's incarnation of this image – the dark curly locks, the mocking aristocratic eyes, the voluptuous almost feminine mouth, the chin with its famous dimple and the implicit radiation of sexual danger – became famous throughout Britain after the publication of *Childe Harold's Pilgrimage* (1812). By the time of his death in Greece twelve years later, it had launched an international style. The dark clothes, the white open-necked shirt exposing the masculine throat, the aggressive display of disarray and devilry, these were the visual symbols of one archetype of Romantic genius: the Fallen Angel in rebellion.

Lord Byron
Richard Westall, 1813

'I am like the tyger (in poesy) if I miss my first spring – I go growling back to my jungle'.
(Letter, to his publisher John Murray, 1820)

Lord Byron
after Richard Westall,
1813 or later

**The Meeting of Byron and
Scott at 50 Albemarle Street,
Spring 1815, an imaginary
reconstruction of the scene**
L. Werner, c.1850

The 'geniuses' gather in
John Murray's drawing room,
with Sir Walter Scott and Lord
Byron in discussion at the
window. The portrait over the
fireplace is supposed to be that
of Byron by Thomas Phillips (the
cloak portrait) painted in 1814.

Other versions would – sooner or later – form around his contemporaries, Coleridge, Keats and Shelley. Indeed Coleridge was described by his friend Lamb in 1816 as 'an Archangel a little Damaged'.

Yet if Byron was naturally the *beau ideal* of the Romantic poet, his image was deliberately manufactured and even commercially marketed. He was the most frequently painted poet of his generation: the National Portrait Gallery archives record over forty portraits and miniatures done during his lifetime, as well as several busts, medallions and even 'a wax model from life made by Madame Tussaud in 1816 before his departure for Italy'.

He was also the most self-conscious of subjects. He banned pens or books from his portraits, as being too like 'trade' and not spontaneous enough. His private letters show Byron to have been as anxious about his appearance – his weight, his hair-loss, his club foot, his careful-casual linen – as any modern film star. He was still sending for special tooth powders in the weeks immediately before his death at Missolonghi.

Thomas Phillips's famous portrait of Byron in Albanian soldier's dress (see page 76), complete with turban, jewel and dagger, was a deliberate piece of theatrical staging. Sir David Piper has described it well as 'almost Errol Flynn playing Byron', but it can also be seen as a shrewd commercial publicity shot for the author of *The Giaour*, *Lara* and *The Corsair*. Byron had bought the costume on his travels in Epirus (1809) and commissioned the portrait back in London (1813), paying for it out of his royalties.

The publisher John Murray had a copy made for his 'Poet's Gallery' in Albemarle Street, London, where it was eventually joined by trophy pictures of his other Romantic bards. Murray also skilfully controlled the engraved frontispieces to Byron's best-selling poems (*The Corsair* sold more than 10,000 copies in its first week and 25,000 by the end of 1815).

The plumb-pudding in danger: – or – state epicures taking un petit souper (William Pitt; Napoleon Bonaparte)
James Gillray, 1805

During the Regency period, the depth of feeling against the royal and the political establishment is astonishing. In his cartoons, Gillray produced some of the most biting social satire that Britain has ever known. The protest and mockery are stinging in the satiric poems of Byron and Shelley. But the Napoleonic Wars also revived the idea of patriotism.

Some of these images were immediately 'improved', to conform to the popular expectations of the Romantic genius. In the engraved version of the 1813 portrait opposite, Byron's eyes were raised apocalyptically to heaven, his hair quiffed and tinted, his brow blanched, his throat swollen with passion and even his decorative collar-pin altered from a gentleman's cameo to a large, glassy lover's keepsake.

This powerful idea of individual genius appears early in the history of Romanticism, and with a strong political impulse, inspired by both the American and the French revolutions. In the striking pair of portraits by Peter Vandyke of Coleridge and Southey, commissioned by the young Bristol publisher Joseph Cottle in 1795, the two poets are shown as fiery prophets of a new age (see pages 46 and 50). They are wild, they are provocative, they are androgynous and above all they are *young*. It is no coincidence that they look extraordinarily like the student radicals of the 1960s; or rather that the student radicals – '*Imagination au pouvoir!*' – looked like them. For this was the time of the great dream of Pantisocracy, when Coleridge and Southey planned to abandon their studies and emigrate to the banks of the Susquehanna River in upper-state Pennsylvania to start European civilisation anew in an ideal American community of equal, self-governing men and women.

The poets were giving public lectures on political and moral revolution, and their portraits vividly convey the electricity of their youthful presence to an audience, with their huge eyes and wildly exaggerated hair. This 'vatic static' was much remarked on at the time by local newspaper reports in Bristol. They express a new kind of dangerous, democratic energy and romantic fervour.

When Dorothy Wordsworth first glimpsed Coleridge two years later (characteristically, he jumped over a gate and sprinted across a field to meet her) she quoted

Dove Cottage

Dove Cottage was the home of William Wordsworth from December 1799 to May 1808. Some 80,000 people visit the cottage every year, but it remains much as it was when Wordsworth was living there with his sister Dorothy and wife Mary, when Coleridge was a frequent visitor, and also when Thomas De Quincey moved in as a successor to Wordsworth.

Shakespeare's definition of the inspired poet: 'He is a wonderful man. His conversation teems with soul, mind and spirit … His eye is large and full, not dark but grey … it speaks every emotion of his animated mind; it has more of the "poet's eye in a fine frenzy rolling" than I ever witnessed' (*Letters*, 1797). Remembering Coleridge at the same period, Hazlitt described him as swept off his feet by 'the gusts of genius'.

The circle that formed round Coleridge and Dorothy's brother William Wordsworth over the next decade revolutionised English poetry and reanimated English prose through the highly personalised essays of Charles Lamb, William Hazlitt and Thomas De Quincey. It also began a radical change in the eighteenth-century idea of creativity and originality. The Romantic writer was revealed as essentially an inspired autobiographer, drawing on a unique inner world of experience, frequently going right back into childhood.

Hazlitt, himself trained as a painter and aesthetic philosopher, identified this emergent ideology of genius in his essays. He observed that 'Originality is necessary to genius', and described Wordsworth's genius as 'a pure emanation of the Spirit of the Age'. Keats, also writing of Wordsworth, christened this increasingly epic vision of the self as the 'egotistical Sublime' (Letter, 1818). Thus the portrait became a natural extension of the unique autobiographical self of Romanticism: a visual record of inward energies and originating power.

Yet the 'self' of the Romantic poets was by no means solitary in historical terms. A glance at their individual biographies shows how frequently their paths crossed and how often creative groups formed, as well as how rapidly they dissolved. In this sense there was not one but a whole series of Romantic circles, forever moving outwards. A geographical map of Romanticism would locate a least a dozen sacred gathering places in Britain and in Europe: the Quantock Hills in the 1790s, Grasmere in the 1800s, Lake Geneva in 1816 and Italy after 1818.

In London, such gatherings formed early round the publisher Joseph Johnson at St Paul's Churchyard (a group including Blake, Godwin, Coleridge and Mary Wollstonecraft) and later around the Lambs off Fleet Street, Leigh Hunt in Hampstead and Haydon in his chaotic City studios, each with their inimitable style of hospitality. In 1823 the painter John Doyle celebrated an entirely imaginary banquet of geniuses in *Samuel Rogers at his Breakfast Table*.

In literary terms too, the Romantics were recognised as a group surprisingly soon. In 1826, two years after the death of Lord Byron in Greece, the Parisian publisher Galignani launched a new ten-volume series of contemporary British poets. With their neat octavo covers and lightweight bindings ('Cheapness and Portability'), Galignani's series was designed for the young literary 'Traveller and Economist' abroad. It was cool, smart and unstuffy: a sort of *Lonely Planet* guide to the new territory of Romanticism. All the volumes had a portrait, a life of the author, a critical essay and a specimen of the author's handwriting 'engraved in facsimile intended

Samuel Rogers at his Breakfast Table
Charles Mottram, after John Doyle, 1823

Samuel Rogers (1763–1855), banker, poet, wit and celebrated host, regularly held breakfast parties in St James's Place which assembled men from many walks of life, here including Scott (second left), Wordsworth, Southey, Coleridge (all sitting), Byron (centre, with head on hand) and Turner (second from right).

POETICAL WORKS

COLERIDGE, SHELLEY, AND KEATS.

COMPLETE IN ONE VOLUME.

PARIS
PUBLISHED BY A. AND W. GALIGNANI
N° 18, RUE VIVIENNE
1829

Title page of *The Poetical Works of Coleridge, Shelley and Keats*
Published by Galignani,
1829 edition

George Crabbe
Henry William Pickersgill,
c.1818–19

to emphasise the individual romantic genius of the author' (St Clair, *The Reading Nation*). The series represented the latest in critical taste and youthful fashion, and was the first retrospective attempt to define the Romantic Circle as a group.

Galignani's selection is fascinating. Having already published Burns, his first volumes covered Byron, Scott, Wordsworth and Southey. The historic Volume 9 (1829) grouped together Coleridge, Shelley and Keats. The last volume, 10, though almost an afterthought (1839), shrewdly chose the only woman poet admitted to the series, Felicia Hemans. So a foreign publisher, neatly circumventing copyright laws, established what would remain the canonic poets of British Romanticism until the twentieth century.

There are two notable absentees: William Blake and John Clare. There are also two inclusions that might strike us as odd but are sure indicators of the shift in modern taste. Volume 2 was given up to the songs and lyrics of Tom Moore, Irish author of the best-selling *Lalla Rookh* (1817) but now largely remembered as Byron's witty friend and canny biographer; while Volume 6 presents George Crabbe, author of the haunting verse-tale 'Peter Grimes' (1810) and Jane Austen's favourite poet, but now mainly identified with Benjamin Britten's opera. Both these poets may be due for revival. Finally, Volumes 7 and 8 are sobering reminders of the fickleness of literary fame: group anthologies, they heap together so many forgotten names – Rogers, Campbell, Montgomery, White, Milman, Wilson, Cornwall …

It is significant that Galignani's series was aimed at 'travellers'. For the Romantic poets, in their own restless journeyings, had almost invented certain landscapes. These quickly became the new version of the nineteenth-century Grand Tour, and it is astonishing how faithfully they remain the holiday destinations of many tourists to this day. So the genius

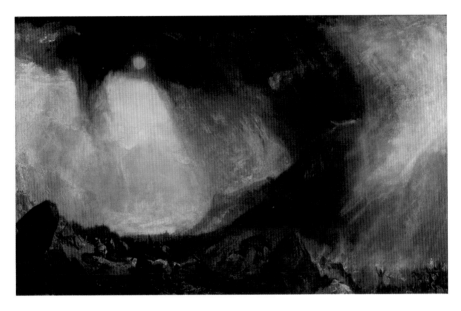

Snow Storm: Hannibal and his Army Crossing the Alps
J.M.W. Turner, exhibited 1812

of Romanticism was also a 'spirit of place', to be found in the English Lake District, the West Country, the Highlands of Scotland, the banks of the Rhine, the Swiss lakes and Alps, the bays of Italy and the islands of Greece. You could say the Romantics had dreamed up the National Parks at home and the Club Mediterranée abroad. It was what Shelley would have called 'a pure anticipated cognition'.

The greatest painter of the age, J.M.W. Turner, progressively visited all these desirable locations (except for Greece), living rough, keeping a journal with his sketchbooks and working as a humble *plein air* artist. He first recorded them as precise topography, but eventually transformed them into places of pure vision and symbolic atmosphere. Engravings from his work later provided many of the illustrations to the poets' *Collected Works* as they were consolidated in the 1830s. A narrative landscape like *Snow Storm: Hannibal Crossing the Alps*, displayed at the Royal Academy in

Keats House

Set in the suburb of Hampstead, London, John Keats lived in this house from 1818 to 1820 and it was where he wrote 'Ode to a Nightingale', and fell in love with Fanny Brawne, the girl next door. It is now a museum.

Illustration from Pierce Egan's
Life in London
George Cruikshank, 1821

Duelling Pistols
*c.*1815

1812, makes a clear historical reference to the Napoleonic campaigns. But it also invokes the whole idea of the Romantic traveller struggling on towards some infinitely distant destination. The Romantic self is dwarfed by the sublime terrors and energies of Nature, but also baptised by them, like Wordsworth in *The Prelude*, Coleridge in 'The Ancient Mariner' or Shelley in his ode 'To the West Wind'.

A modern extension of Romantic travel has been to make the Romantics' own houses (or at least their temporary lodgings upon earth) the sites of literary pilgrimage. This is a peculiarly British phenomenon, combining the notion of museum heritage with that of modern hagiography. Here are places of meditation and remembrance. They have become secular shrines, many administered in a priest-like way by private foundations or the National Trust. They include, most famously, Wordsworth's Dove Cottage in Grasmere, Coleridge's cottage in Nether Stowey and the Keats House in Hampstead. Further afield can be found the Keats–Shelley Museum in Rome, Shelley's Casa Magni near Lerici, Tuscany, and Byron's Palazzo Mocenigo in Venice. More recherché locations might include Clare's lunatic asylum in Northampton, Mary Tighe's tomb in Ireland and Trelawny's cave on Mount Olympus.

At home, the Britain of the Romantics presents the kind of social paradox with which we are still familiar. It was, said Coleridge, 'an Age in which Extremes Meet'. Here was a world which somehow produced both Jane Austen and John Clare, both J.M.W. Turner and James Gillray. Here was an immensely elegant society, which was also singularly drunken and dissolute. Here was a cool and self-confident society, which was also turbulent, violent and highly unstable just beneath the surface. Here was the most civilised society in Europe (the proponent of the waltz, the flushing water-closet and the seaside watercolour),

**Horatio Nelson, Viscount
Nelson**
Lemuel Francis Abbott, 1797

**Dido, in despair!
(Emma Hamilton)**
James Gillray, 1801

A buxom Lady Hamilton
dissolves into tears as Nelson
sails away, and Sir William
sleeps. The title refers to the
desertion of Dido, Queen of
Carthage, by her lover, Aeneas.

which also widely condoned the pistol duel, the bare-knuckle prize fight and the teenage prostitute in the park (probably Regent's Park).

It was also what Coleridge called 'emphatically, the Age of Personality' (*The Friend*, 1818). It was an age of personal display, of style, of singularity. Portraiture began to flourish during the Regency, the last generation before the daguerreotype photograph. There was a growing hunger for glamorous, humourous or erotic images. Boxers, balloonists, opera singers, dragoons and actresses reappeared as tinted pin-ups for the gentleman's folding wash-screen. It was not surprising that successful writers had their profiles engraved as frontispieces to their works. National figures achieved the apotheosis of being elevated to huge wooden pub signs, or received the fatal accolade of a cartoon by Gillray, Cruikshank or Rowlandson. Thanks to new print technology, these were reproduced by the thousand. Ironically, such notoriety, then as now, was prized even by its victims. The Prince of Wales paid vast sums to collect the originals of Gillray's cartoons of himself.

The Romantic idea of genius produced a celebrity culture of heroes and villains (often rapidly interchangeable) which is also startlingly familiar to us. The patriotic fame of Nelson was a new phenomenon and was characteristically celebrated by a fine, all-action biography by the poet Southey (1813); but he and Emma Hamilton were also pilloried by Gillray. Cult love-hate figures like Pitt and Napoleon dominated the political stage and appeared ceaselessly in the poetry, journalism, painting and caricatures of the day. In 1822 a national subscription (ladies-only) paid for the erection of a naked statue of Achilles in honour of the Duke of Wellington at Hyde Park Corner. It's still there, like Nelson's Column in Trafalgar Square (1842); and there are still more 'Wellington' and 'Nelson' pub signs than any other in England.

James Belcher
Unknown artist, c.1800

Theatrical mendicants, relieved (Sarah Siddons; Charles Kemble; John Philip Kemble; Hugh Percy, 2nd Duke of Northumberland)
James Gillray, 1809

Similarly in the sporting world, fencers, jockeys, swimmers and long-distance runners began to gain national recognition (and often nicknames). Bare-knuckle boxers like Tom Cribb and Jem Belcher attracted huge personal followings (and wagers), and gained a new kind of glamour. Hazlitt attended a prize fight near Newbury in 1821 in which Bill Neate fought Tom 'The Gasman' Hickman for a combined purse of £200,000. The young, handsome and gentlemanly Belcher was idolised by Hazlitt and Byron, and had a lively fan club among the senior members of the Royal Academy. Renowned for his courage, his cravats and (like Nelson) his lost eye, Belcher has been described as 'a Romantic poet among pugilists'. He died at the age of thirty-two.

The influence of Romantic genius was most apparent in the London theatre. Driven by the rivalry between the houses of Drury Lane and Covent Garden, late eighteenth-century productions had been dominated by the actor-manager John Philip Kemble and his sister, the great tragic actress Sarah Siddons. Their style was solemn, ornate and strictly classical, and their approach businesslike and highly respectable. (Mrs Siddons would not visit Mary Wollstonecraft after her affair with Godwin.) But with the burning down of their Covent Garden theatre in 1808 and the breaking of their monopoly, a new kind of intensely charismatic and emotional actor began to appear.

With Edmund Kean and Dorothy Jordan private lives and public theatre overlapped, often scandalously, and produced a new expressive style of acting, and a new sense of Romantic authenticity. This was especially true in their reinterpretations of Shakespeare's plays, with Kean revolutionising the notion of the tragic villain and outsider, while Jordan brought back to life the wit and tenderness of the Shakespearean heroine. Keats's play *Otto the Great* was specifically written for Kean. The Shakespeare lectures of both Coleridge and Hazlitt drew directly on the spontaneous psychology of these actors, and effectively transformed Shakespeare himself into a Romantic author. Coleridge's great essay 'Shakespeare's Judgement Equal to his Genius' (1808) became a central statement of Romantic doctrine.

What is far less well known is that the world of science also produced Romantic figures, whose discoveries were seen as great adventures of the mind. William Herschel, with his discovery of the seventh planet Uranus in 1781 and his theories of galaxies outside the Milky Way, made astronomy the most popular science of the age and a field in which theological problems of the Creation, and extraterrestrial life, could be imaginatively discussed. The chemist Humphry Davy proved one of the most brilliant public lecturers of the day, drawing huge audiences to the Royal Institution in Albemarle Street (opposite Byron's publisher Murray), as well as inventing the miners' safety lamp. Mary Shelley partly based the ambitions of Dr Frankenstein on what she had heard in Davy's lectures on the future of chemistry and electrical power. Eccentric explorers and zoologists like Charles Waterton (1782–1865), who travelled for years alone in South America and the West Indies, also opened up the horizons of Romantic knowledge and brought a new sense of a global environment with his autobiographical *Wanderings* (1825).

Embracing all these figures, Romantic portrait painting concentrated on a new, quiet psychological penetration of character. It required the artistic rendering of inner landscapes, of interiority. This was not the world of the great flamboyant society painters of the day: Reynolds, Hoppner and Lawrence. It was the domain of small-time professionals and often of amateurs. One of the most successful practitioners was

Charles Waterton
Charles Wilson Peale, 1824

James Northcote
Self-portrait, 1784

John Opie
Self-portrait, 1785

James Northcote, RA (1746–1831), who painted plain but noble studio portraits of Godwin and Coleridge, and numerous self-portraits. Significantly he posed himself with paintbrushes in one hand and the other pointing pensively to his brow, to indicate the inward source of all artistic power. Hazlitt wrote an entire book about him, *Boswell Redivus: or, Conversations of James Northcote* (1827), constructed from a series of personal interviews, which is itself a Romantic form, seeking for autobiographical revelations and confessions (or at least good gossip).

Thomas Phillips, RA (1770–1845), also based much of his career on commissioned portraiture, producing notable studies of Blake, Byron, Coleridge and Davy. He was particularly admired for the 'noble gloom' with which he revealed the Romantic intensity of his sitters. In 1818 it was he whom John Murray commissioned to produce a whole gallery of literary portraits in Albemarle Street.

It is one of the features of the Romantic Circle that so many of their portraits were painted by personal friends, like Haydon, John Opie, Amelia Curran, William Hazlitt, Washington Allston and Joseph Severn. Opie's tender portraits of his wife Amelia and of her friend Mary Wollstonecraft are masterpieces (see pages 54 and 32). These paintings have a strong biographical element, a sense of shared intimacy and conversational directness. They have the tender feel of treasured souvenirs. At the same time, they powerfully suggest the intense solitary inner life of the sitters, an extraordinary haunting quality of self-reflection and self-awareness. This is particularly true of the many portraits and sketches of Keats, nearly all of them amateur. For the painters, the problem of rendering the inward quality of Romantic genius, the workings of the imagination as an interior force (no longer represented by external Muses), had become the new touchstone of Romantic authenticity.

The American painter Washington Allston (1779–1843), when trying to capture the fluctuating genius of his friend Coleridge in middle age (see page 49), remarked on the supreme difficulty of rendering this essential, inward, fleeting quality of the poet's mysterious power:

> So far as I can judge the likeness is a true one. But it is Coleridge in repose, and though not unstirred by the perpetual groundswell of his everworking intellect … it is not Coleridge in his highest mood – the poetic state. When in that state no face I ever saw was like his, it seemed almost spirit made visible, without a shadow of the physical upon it. But it was beyond the reach of my art.
> (*Life and Letters*, 1893)

The notion of Romantic genius as fleeting and ephemeral, doomed to die young or remain unrecognised by the general public (a subject of obsessive meditation by Haydon in his *Journals*), gradually modulated the pictorial style. Several painters, like Hilton, Severn and Curran, unsatisfied with their first attempts, returned to their canvases after the sitter's death. Their portraiture thus takes on a memorial quality, the immediate 'likeness' becoming subtly overlaid with retrospective feelings of tragic loss, of 'intimations of mortality' and the haunting sense of historical grandeur not fully recognised in the sitter's own lifetime. Thus some of the most famous images of Keats and Shelley are in fact true 'icons': not made from life but composed from sacred memory, an attempt to go beyond death.

Indeed the idea of early death seems inseparable from Romanticism, and it was painfully true of Keats (twenty-five), Shelley (twenty-nine), Byron (thirty-six), Mary Wollstonecraft (thirty-eight) and Burns (thirty-eight), not to mention Jem Belcher (thirty-two), where the sense of 'unfulfilled renown' is overwhelming.

Joseph Severn
Self-portrait, c.1820

But bearing in mind that the average lifespan in the English Regency was not much more than fifty (an age achieved by Hazlitt, Davy and Mary Shelley), it is less often remarked how many of the Romantic group achieved a comparatively ripe old age. Wordsworth, Godwin and Herschel lived into their eighties; Turner, Hunt, De Quincey, Clare and Blake into their seventies. Nonetheless, the individual biographies reveal what a high proportion of all their lives, long or short, was disrupted or ended by poverty, insanity, drug addiction, alcoholism or suicide (actual or attempted). And as Virginia Woolf observed, 'The true length of a person's life, whatever the *DNB* may say, is always a matter of dispute' (*Orlando*, 1928).

John Keats
Joseph Severn, 1819

The question of literary recognition, or neglect, is harder to assess. It touches on complex issue of changing tastes and shifting reputations. Burns, Byron, Scott and Felicia Hemans (all identified by Galignani) achieved huge popular success in their lifetimes and immediately afterwards. But Hemans was forgotten after the First World War and Walter Scott is currently unfashionable (until perhaps rediscovered by tartan Hollywood). Within a generation Wordsworth had become a national institution and Coleridge a national scandal, positions they have both magnificently maintained. Shelley's reputation was upheld by pirate publications, and the saintly (almost fatal) dedication of his wife and the Shelley Society, until successfully radicalised again by twentieth-century scholarship.

By contrast, William Blake was completely forgotten outside a tiny circle by the time of his death, and his works remained out of print for a generation, until unexpectedly revived by Gilchrist's brilliant Victorian biography of 1863. The research so exhausted its author that he died before publication, leaving the biography to be finished by his wife. Similarly, Keats was not widely read until Monckton Milnes's biography of 1848, and his subsequent championing by the Pre-Raphaelite painters and editors. John Clare had to wait until the late twentieth century to be fully published and rediscovered, and placed in context by Jonathan Bate's biography of 2003. For Leigh Hunt that process is just beginning (see Select bibliography).

The position of women writers within the Romantic Circle is particularly anomalous. Jane Austen is now a cult figure, but was not widely admired until Austen Leigh's *Memoir* of 1870. By contrast, Mary Wollstonecraft was apparently doomed to a century of obscurity by the noble, well-intentioned *Memoirs* of her husband in 1798. Mary Robinson, one of the most glamorous figures of her entire generation, sank into complete oblivion until suddenly recovered by two simultaneous biographies in 2004. Many other women poets, like Mary Tighe and Laetitia Landon, remain unjustly forgotten – at least up to the present date (see pages 104–5).

So what Coleridge called 'true fame' is still fickle and uncertain. Yet the genius of the Romantic poets seems infinitely renewable. Their wonderful circle of creative energy still pulses out towards us, always challenging, always surprising, always expanding. One mark of genius, said Goethe, is posthumous productivity.

John Keats, plaster cast of death-mask
Unknown artist, 1821

William Blake, life-mask
James S. Deville, 1823

William Wordsworth, plaster cast of life-mask
Benjamin Robert Haydon, 1815

Romantic genius always ready for renewal and reawakening.

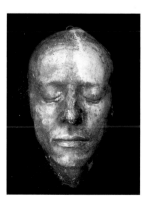

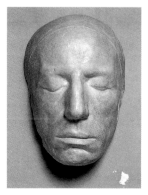

Biographies

The Unknown Romantics

In 1796 the Bristol bookseller Joseph Cottle began
commissioning pencil drawings of a number of
unknown young poets whose work he thought
might have a future. Over the next two years he
published four of them with engravings of their
portraits by Robert Hancock as the frontispieces
to their books.

Cottle's selection was astonishingly prescient.
All four of his poets were in their twenties, without
literary recognition of any kind, and with
undistinguished backgrounds and very chequered
early careers. Yet these curiously stiff and vulnerable
little profiles, which seem almost like naive

photo-booth images, can be seen now as their passport pictures to future fame.

William Wordsworth (1770–1850) was from Cumberland and, after graduating from Cambridge, had lived for some time in revolutionary France, where he had fathered an illegitimate child by his lover Annette Vallon.

Samuel Taylor Coleridge (1772–1834) was from Devon, had left Cambridge without a degree and, under the pseudonym Silas Tomkyn Comberbache, temporarily joined the 15th Light Dragoons, from which he was discharged as 'insane'.

Robert Southey (1774–1843) was from Bristol, had graduated from Oxford and was planning to establish a utopian community in America ('Pantisocracy') and to lecture with Coleridge on revolutionary politics.

Charles Lamb (1775–1834) was born in London, had attended Christ's Hospital School with Coleridge and, after his sister Mary had gone briefly but spectacularly mad (she murdered their mother), had joined the East India Company as an office clerk.

Their early collaborative works included a verse-play, *The Fall of Robespierre* (1794, Southey and Coleridge); a selection of the early *Poems* (1797, Coleridge and Lamb); and the first great collection of the English Romantic movement, *Lyrical Ballads* (1798, Wordsworth and Coleridge).

The *Lyrical Ballads* astonished the reading public with its directness of style and challenging subject matter in such poems as 'The Ancient Mariner', 'The Mad Mother', 'The Idiot Boy', 'The Thorn' and 'Tintern Abbey'. The first Romantic Circle had been formed and would be soon followed by many others.

Clockwise from top left:
William Wordsworth
Robert Hancock, 1798

Samuel Taylor Coleridge
Robert Hancock, 1796

Robert Southey
Robert Hancock, 1796

Charles Lamb
Robert Hancock, 1798

William Blake (1757–1827)

Poet, painter and engraver, William Blake grew up in London 'conversing with angels' and retained a visionary view of the world throughout his long, hard-working and poverty-stricken career. His *Songs of Innocence and of Experience* (1794) – which contained such lyric masterpieces as 'The Sick Rose', 'The Tyger' and 'London' – sold fewer than thirty copies in his lifetime.

Powerfully influenced by the revolutions in America and France, and an idiosyncratic form of Swedenborgian mysticism, he created a series of illuminated 'prophetic books', including *Visions of the Daughters of Albion* (1793), *The Four Zoas* (1804), *Milton* (1808) and *Jerusalem* (1820). Well known in the radical circle of Mary Wollstonecraft, Tom Paine and William Godwin, he retained a fierce, eccentric independence and was arrested on a charge of treason at Chichester in 1803, though found not guilty. His antinomian views are memorably expressed in 'The Proverbs of Hell' (1790) with aphoristic force: 'The tigers of wrath are wiser than the horses of instruction.'

Blake's marriage to the beautiful Catherine Boucher, daughter of a London market gardener, with whom he sunbathed naked in his garden at Lambeth, was childless but intensely happy. Towards the end of his life his poetry was recognised by Coleridge, Wordsworth and Southey, and he was extensively interviewed on his beliefs by the journalist Henry Crabb Robinson. He attracted a circle of young followers, including the painters John Linnell and Samuel Palmer, who called themselves 'The Ancients' in his honour. He died singing at Fountain Court, off the Strand. His beautiful poem from Milton, known as 'Jerusalem', has become adopted as the 'alternative' British national anthem: 'And did those feet in ancient time/Walk upon England's mountains green?'

William Blake
Thomas Phillips, 1807

William Blake
Bronze cast, 1953, of a life-mask
by James S. Deville of 1823

This bronze head was cast from
the plaster life-mask executed
by the sculptor and phrenologist
James Deville in 1823 to
illustrate the 'Faculty of
Imagination'. The cannonball
skull and closed eyes vividly
suggest the power and
inwardness of Blake's visions.

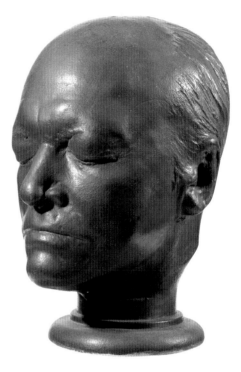

His disciple Frederick Tatham described Blake as
short, stocky and energetic, with strange prominent
blue eyes and a habit of constantly rolling a pencil,
paintbrush or engraver's burin between his fingers.
'My fingers Emit sparks of fire with Expectation of
my future labours,' wrote Blake. 'I have very little of
Mr Blake's company,' said Catherine once, 'he is
always in Paradise.'

Thomas Phillips's portrait was commissioned by
the publisher R.H. Cromek and shows Blake sitting
uneasily in the corner of a mahogany bench,
uncharacteristically wearing a smart white waistcoat
and cravat, and a gold seal on a red ribbon, the outfit
of a successful small businessman. The tense position,
upward glance and poised right hand holding a

William Blake
John Linnell, 1861

pencil suggest Blake's mind is on higher things and he is impatient to get back to work. Phillips later recalled that during the sitting Blake described a vision of the Archangel Gabriel ascending through his studio ceiling.

A disturbing hint of the gargoyle animates John Linnell's penetrating study of Blake in old age. The drawing is based on one of Linnell's own ivory miniatures (1821; Fitzwilliam Museum, Cambridge) and was copied by the artist in 1861 for Gilchrist's biography (1863). For this later version Linnell allowed himself a freer retrospective interpretation of Blake's visionary power.

Robert Burns (1759–96)

Scottish national poet, exquisite love-song writer and incorrigible philanderer, Burns grew up on his father's poverty-stricken farm in Ayrshire and could genuinely be described as a ploughboy poet. He said his first poems were inspired at fifteen by 'a bewitching, bonnie, sweet, sonsie lass' working beside him in the fields at harvest time – 'thus with me began Love and Poesy' (autobiographical letter, August 1787). Volatile and seductive, a fine dancer and fiddle-player, Burns was also a passionate student of English, Scottish and French poetry, and soon developed a sophisticated knowledge of Highland folklore. The failure of a farming project with his long-suffering brother Gilbert, together with a chaotic series of tangled love affairs (resulting in two illegitimate children), determined Burns to 'quit his native country forever' and emigrate to Jamaica. But the unexpected literary success of his *Poems, Chiefly in the Scottish Dialect* (1786) led to fame and lionisation in Edinburgh. His early pieces included the bawdy 'Cotter's Saturday Night', the caustic 'Holy Willie's Prayer' and the infinitely touching 'To a Mouse, on Turning Her Up in Her Nest with the Plough', which begins 'Wee, sleekit, cow'rin, tim'rous beastie …'. In 1788 Burns married and attempted to settle down, obtaining work as an excise officer in Dumfriesshire, while contributing over two hundred songs to James Johnson's classic folk anthology *The Scots Musical Museum*, quixotically refusing all payment. These wonderful vernacular lyrics included 'Auld Lang Syne', 'O my Luv's like a red, red Rose', 'Scots wha hae' (a battle song), 'The Banks o' Doon', 'Highland Mary', 'John Anderson, my Jo', the heartbreaking 'Ae Fond Kiss' and the revolutionary refrain 'A Man's a man, for a' That'.

After producing nine legitimate children, Burns 'fell asleep upon the snow' (Lockhart, 1830), on his way home from a festive tavern dinner in February 1796, and died shortly thereafter from rheumatic heart disease. The celebration of Burns Night (25 January) by Scottish patriotic clubs began almost immediately in 1801, and eventually spread around the globe. Wordsworth delighted in the rumbustious tale of 'Tam O'Shanter' (1791) and soberly praised Burns as an archetypal Romantic figure: the poet 'who walked in glory and in joy/Following his plough along the mountainside' ('Resolution and Independence', 1802). Lamb declared that in his youth 'Burns was the god of my idolatry', while Hazlitt remarked that 'he would rather have written one song of Burns's than all the epics of Walter Scott' (*Select British Poets*, 1824) – a very English compliment.

Robert Burns
Alexander Nasmyth, *c*.1821–2

Walter Scott described the poet's eye as remarkably large, dark and glowing – 'I say it literally glowed … I never saw such another eye in a human head'. Byron loved Burns's 'antithetical mind – tenderness, roughness – delicacy, coarseness – sentiment, sensuality – soaring and groveling – dirt and deity – all mixed up in that one compound of inspired clay!' (*Journal*, 1813).

Mary Wollstonecraft (1759–97)

An inspiration for the British feminist mo
Mary Wollstonecraft was also the author of .el
books, short stories, novels and influential works on
children's education. Half-Irish by birth, tempestuous
and articulate by nature, she started a school in
Newington Green with her great friend Fanny Blood,
travelled in Portugal and settled in London in 1787,
working as a journalist and translator for the radical
publisher Joseph Johnson. There she met Tom Paine,
William Blake and William Godwin, and in 1792
published *A Vindication of the Rights of Woman*.

She lived in Paris during the French Revolution
and had a child by the American Gilbert Imlay. In
1795 she travelled in Scandinavia, published *A Short
Residence in Sweden, Norway and Denmark* and, abandoned
by Imlay, tried to commit suicide by throwing herself
into the River Thames. She fell in love with Godwin,
conceived a second daughter – the future Mary
Shelley – but died in childbirth at the age of thirty-
eight. Godwin wrote her biography in 1798, which
caused great scandal, and Shelley put her into his
revolutionary poem *The Revolt of Islam* (1817).

Handsome and dashing, with an unruly mass
of auburn hair, she was frequently painted by her
contemporaries. The novelist Amelia Alderson,
who had been her rival in love for William Godwin,
once remarked: 'Everything I ever saw for the first
time always disappointed me, except for Mary
Wollstonecraft and the Cumberland Lakes.'

John Opie's portrait (*c*.1797) was painted in
London, when Mary Wollstonecraft was pregnant with
her second child, and Godwin kept the picture above
the desk in his study for the rest of his life.

Mary Wollstonecraft
John Opie, *c*.1797

In *Memoirs* (1798), William
Godwin gave his impression
of Mary Wollstonecraft in love:

'Her whole character seemed
to change with her change of
fortune. Her sorrows, the
depression of spirits, were
forgotten, and she assumed
all the simplicity and vivacity
of a youthful mind … . She
was playful, full of confidence,
kindness and sympathy. Her
eyes assumed new lustre, and
her cheeks new colour and
smoothness. Her voice became
cheerful; her temper overflowing
with universal kindness; and that
smile of bewitching tenderness
from day to day illuminated her
countenance, which all who
knew her will so well recollect.'

William Godwin (1756–1836)

With his concepts of social justice, equality and fearless self-expression, the political philosopher and popular novelist William Godwin had a profound effect on many of the Romantics in their idealistic youth, including Coleridge, Wordsworth, Hazlitt and Shelley. Born in the misty fenlands of East Anglia, Godwin was educated at Hoxton Academy, London, in preparation for the Dissenting ministry, but his wide reading in the French *philosophes* such as Voltaire and Condorcet converted him to atheistic and anarchist views tending towards revolutionary Jacobinism.

Godwin's great work *An Enquiry Concerning Political Justice* (1793) proposed republican and communitarian ideas, and attacked many institutions such as private property, marriage and the established Church, and became notorious for its defence of 'free love'. He defended a number of leading working-class radicals, including John Thelwall, in the famous Treason Trials of 1794. 'Wherever liberty, truth, justice was the theme, his name was not far off' (Hazlitt, 1825).

A shy, modest and intensely intellectual man, he was transformed by his marriage to Mary Wollstonecraft and devastated by her early death in childbirth. Their daughter, Mary, subsequently ran away with his most devoted young disciple, Shelley. In later life he was harried by debts and the organising capacities of his second wife, Mrs Clairmont. He ran a bookshop from his house in Skinner Street, Holborn, and tried to make a living from a series of thriller novels, including *Caleb Williams* (1794), *Fleetwood* (1805) and *Mandeville* (1817).

Godwin's face – 'fine, with an expression of placid temper and recondite thought' (Hazlitt) – with its high intellectual forehead usually surmounted by a twinkling pair of round gold spectacles, entirely belied his reputation as a political firebrand. Shelley's first

William Godwin
James Northcote, 1802

35

William Godwin
William Brockedon, 1832

The former political firebrand ended his days as Yeoman Usher in the House of Commons, with a state pension and all his fiction re-issued in Bentley's Standard Novels.

wife, Harriet, described Godwin after she had seen him in his study in 1812, shortly before Shelley had the fatal meeting with his daughter: 'His manners are so soft and pleasing that I defy even an enemy to be displeased with him … . Have you ever seen a bust of Socrates, for his head is very much like that?' Even so, Godwin's name always remained associated with a Romantic idea of social progress. 'Truth is omnipotent … Man is perfectible, or in other words susceptible of perpetual improvement' (*Political Justice*).

In 1825 Hazlitt observed how Godwin had mellowed:

> In private, the author of Political Justice, at one time reminded those who knew him of the Metaphysician grafted on the Dissenting Minister. There was a dictatorial, captious, quibbling pettiness of manner. He lost this with the first blush and awkwardness of popularity … . He is, at present, as easy as an old glove … . There is a very admirable likeness of him by Mr Northcote. (*The Spirit of the Age*, 1825)

Benjamin Robert Haydon (1786–1846)

Passionately (but wrongly) convinced of his own destiny as a great history painter, Haydon put his true genius into five volumes of anguished and exuberant *Journals* (1804–46), which recount his heroic struggles with incomparable gusto. Both intimate and operatic, they dramatise the Romantic artist's life in London: his moments of candlelit inspiration, his stormy friendships, his erotic dreams, his Napoleonic fantasies (he painted more than twenty-five versions of *Napoleon Musing at St Helena*), and his frequent imprisonments for debt.

Charismatic, self-opinionated and deeply religious, Haydon attracted to his chaotic studio rooms the inner circle of Romantic writers, including at various times Lamb, Coleridge, Scott, Hazlitt, Wordsworth, Hunt, Shelley and Keats. His wonderful accounts include Hazlitt driven mad by love, Shelley hot-gospeling atheism and Mrs Siddons terrifying the servants with her sepulchral rendition of Lady Macbeth. In December 1817 he hosted the 'Immortal Dinner' when Wordsworth told jokes, Lamb got drunk and Keats proposed the toast: 'Newton's health, and confusion to Mathematics!' The heads of Wordsworth,

Benjamin Robert Haydon
Sir David Wilkie, 1815

The chalk study of Haydon asleep in his studio apparently shows a contented man dreaming of fame. Yet, for most of his life, Haydon was tortured by his inability to fulfil his overwhelming ambition to 'paint like Titian and draw like Raphael'. 'Poor Haydon', exclaimed Elizabeth Barrett Browning, 'Think what an agony life was to him, so constituted! - his own genius a clinging curse!'

Christ's Entry into Jerusalem
Benjamin Robert Haydon,
1814–20

Grouped in the top right hand
corner are Newton (extreme
right), Wordsworth (monkishly
looking down) and Keats (in
profile, immediately above) in
animated discussion with his
friend the painter William
Bewick. Haydon's study of
Wordsworth for the painting is
illustrated on page 4.

Opposite:
Benjamin Robert Haydon
Georgiana Margaretta Zornlin,
1825

Newton and Keats appear in his enormous canvas
Christ's Entry into Jerusalem, which took six years to
complete (1814–20) and a further three years to sell
(at a loss). Later monumental paintings include
The Raising of Lazarus (1820–23), *The Reform Banquet*
(1832–4) and *The Anti-Slavery Society Convention*
(1840–41). But his masterpiece was a rapidly executed
portrait, *Wordsworth on Helvellyn* (1842; see page 45),
which, as Hazlitt observed brilliantly, caught the
ageing poet's 'drooping weight of thought and
expression'. Despite his *Lectures on Painting*, his
successful pupils (including Sir Edwin Landseer) and
his quixotic support of the Elgin Marbles, Haydon was
never elected to the Royal Academy and eventually
committed suicide in his studio, in front of an
unfinished canvas. 'The solitary grandeur of Historical
Painting is gone,' he wrote. 'There was something
grand, something poetical, something mysterious, in
pacing your quiet Painting Room after midnight, with
a great work lifted up on a gigantic easel' (*Journal*,
2 October 1844).

James Gillray (1757–1815)

James Gillray
Self-portrait, *c*.1800

No form of art could be considered less Romantic and more ephemeral than the personal caricature. Yet the graphic work of Gillray, a caricaturist of relentless ferocity and seething imagination, permanently stamped the sensibility of his age. The natural heir to Hogarth, a superb draughtsman and engraver, Gillray added a unique element of satirical malevolence, directed against power, beauty or celebrity. His victims included many of the leading political, literary and aristocratic figures of the day (who were often, like the Prince Regent, his most assiduous collectors); but he was especially merciless to the royal family and their scandalous excesses.

Born in London of strict Moravian parents (who forbade all games and entertainments), Gillray lived at home till the age of thirty-six and never married. Trained in the Royal Academy Schools (like Blake), but unable to support himself by conventional illustration, he suddenly found his vein producing topical caricatures for the publisher Hannah Humphrey in 1791. He was assigned rooms above her fashionable printshop at 18 Old Bond Street, and began pouring forth a weekly flood of reckless, uncensored etchings. Wraith-like French Jacobins are depicted lynching the portly English Club men of St James's in *The Promis'd horrors of the French invasion* (1796). Radical young poets such as Coleridge, Southey and Charles Lamb appear as grotesque animals in the *New morality* (1798). The scientist Humphry Davy is shown sniggering at the farts produced by *Scientific researches! – new discoveries in pneumaticks!* at the Royal Institution (1802, see page 75). Pitt and Napoleon voraciously carve up the globe with cutlasses in *The plumb-pudding in danger* (1805, see page 9). Even national heroes like Nelson do not escape Gillray's lash, especially when attached to a

Promis'd Horrors of the French INVASION, — or — Forcible Reasons for negociating a Regicide PEACE. Vide . The Authority of Edmund Burke.

**The Promis'd horrors of
the French invasion,
– or – forcible reasons for
negotiating a regicide peace**
James Gillray, 1796

French revolutionary troops
storm down St James's, while
Charles James Fox flagellates
the Prime Minister William Pitt,
Tory members of White's Club
are lynched from their balcony,
and Whig members of Brooke's
Club mount a pro-French
guillotine.

buxom mistress like Emma Hamilton (*Dido, in despair!*,
1801, see page 15). 'No one would guess this gaunt,
bespectacled figure, this dry man, was a great artist,'
wrote the German journalist Huttner. The
government tried to curb him with a £200 pension,
but Gillray began drinking heavily, and from 1807 his
work became increasingly nightmarish. Confined to
his rooms at Mrs Humphrey's, he tried to throw
himself from an upper window but became stuck in
the iron bars. He was officially diagnosed as insane in
1811, and when the young illustrator George
Cruikshank called upon his hero, he was dismayed to
be told: 'My name is not Gillray, but Rubens.'

William Wordsworth (1770–1850)

The greatest poet of his age, who can be properly compared to Shakespeare and Milton for his noble conception of mankind in nature, William Wordsworth dedicated his whole life to poetry and only came slowly into his powers. His two major poems were largely composed in his thirties and forties: his verse autobiography, *The Prelude* (1805, revised 1850), and his philosophic epic, *The Excursion* (1814). He was the son of a Cumberland attorney, born at Cockermouth and educated at Hawkshead Grammar School in the Lake District. After Cambridge, Wordsworth travelled and lived in France, where he witnessed the early stages of the Revolution.

Wordsworth settled near Coleridge at Alfoxden in the Quantock Hills and together they published *Lyrical Ballads* (1798). After a period in Germany, Wordsworth finally returned to Grasmere in 1799, where he remained until his death. His passionate friendship with his younger sister Dorothy, whose famous *Journal* (1798–1803) describes their life together at Alfoxden and Grasmere in exquisite natural detail, shaped and sustained his entire career. (Ironically, Dorothy avoided having her own portrait painted and only a paper silhouette is known; see page 44.)

The shorter lyrics published in *Poems in Two Volumes* (1807), including the mysterious 'Lucy' poems, 'Daffodils' and his 'Ode: On the Intimations of Immortality from Recollections of Early Childhood', slowly established his reputation among a generation of younger admirers (such as Thomas De Quincey). Happy in his marriage to Mary Hutchinson and increasingly conservative in his views, he was appointed Stamp Distributor for Westmorland in 1813, wrote a *Guide to the Lakes* in 1822 and was appointed Poet Laureate in 1843.

Tall, taciturn and weatherbeaten, with a deep

William Wordsworth
Benjamin Robert Haydon, 1818

Dorothy Wordsworth
Unknown artist, 1806

Opposite:
William Wordsworth
Benjamin Robert Haydon, 1842

Cumberland voice and commanding presence, he impressed everyone he met with a sense of inner power. His appearance in 1798 was described by Hazlitt as 'gaunt and Don Quixote-like', with eccentric touches:

> He was quaintly dressed (accordingly to the costume of that unconstrained period) in a brown fustian jacket and striped pantaloons. There was something of a roll, a lounge in his gait, not unlike his own Peter Bell. There was a severe, worn pressure of thought about his temples, a fire in his eye (as if he saw something in objects more than the outward appearance), an intense high narrow forehead, a Roman nose, cheeks furrowed by strong purpose and feeling, and a convulsive inclination to laughter about the mouth, a good deal at variance with the solemn, stately expression of the rest of the face.
> (*My First Acquaintance with Poets*, 1823)

The painter Haydon was fascinated by him and executed the chalk drawing on page 42 in 1818 as a gift for Wordsworth's wife, Mary: 'He sat like a Poet and Philosopher, calm, quiet, amiable. I succeeded in a capital likeness of him.' Wordsworth later called the drawing 'The Brigand'.

Wordsworth remained an active fell-walker into old age and climbed Helvellyn to celebrate his seventieth birthday. Haydon marked this feat with the full-length picture illustrated opposite, which was actually executed from sittings in his London studio but with the symbolic setting of Helvellyn at sunset painted in afterwards from memory. With its intense, brooding inwardness, it is one of the great successes of Romantic portraiture.

Samuel Taylor Coleridge (1772–1834)

'Poet and philosopher-in a-mist' (according to his own description), fell-walker, lecturer and opium addict, Coleridge is the great inspirational figure of English Romanticism. Wordsworth called him 'the only wonderful man I ever knew'. Born at Ottery St Mary, Devon, the son of a clergyman, he attended Cambridge University, volunteered for the Dragoons, collaborated with Wordsworth on the *Lyrical Ballads* (1798), studied in Germany and settled for four years at Keswick in the Lake District. This period saw the writing of his most famous poems, 'Kubla Khan', 'The Ancient Mariner', 'Christabel', 'Frost at Midnight' and 'Dejection: an Ode'.

Thereafter, his marriage broken by a disastrous love affair (see the 'Asra' poems) and health wrecked by opium, he travelled restlessly in the Mediterranean, lectured on poetry in London and Bristol, and in 1816 finally settled at Highgate in the care of the surgeon James Gillman, where he wrote his *Aids to Reflection*, and many late poems such as 'Limbo' and 'Alice Du Clos'. His *Biographia Literaria* (1817), his collected essays in *The Friend* (1818) and his superb *Notebooks* (1794–1834) all give a vivid impression of his troubled genius.

Coleridge was a marvellous talker and autobiographer, as shown in his self-mocking description in a letter written shortly after the Vandyke portrait was painted for his publisher, Cottle, in 1795. This was not so much modesty as a Romantic sense of his own peculiarities, in which chaotic inner energy was bodied forth as weakness and eccentricity:

My face, unless when animated by immediate eloquence, expresses great Sloth, & great, indeed almost idiotic good-nature. 'Tis a mere carcass of a face, fat flabby and expressive chiefly of

Samuel Taylor Coleridge
Peter Vandyke, 1795

47

Samuel Taylor Coleridge
James Northcote, 1804

inexpression. My gait is awkward, & the walk, &
the Whole man indicates indolence capable of
energies … . I have read almost everything – a
library-cormorant – I am deep in all out of the
way books … . Metaphysics, & Poetry, & 'Facts of
Mind' … . I cannot breathe thro' my nose – so my
mouth, with sensual thick lips, is almost always
open. In conversation I am impassioned … .
(Letter to John Thelwall, 1796)

The American painter Washington Allston had
first met Coleridge in Italy, where they became lifelong
friends, and his portrait of 1814 (done in Bristol when

Samuel Taylor Coleridge
Washington Allston, 1814

Coleridge was forty-two) presents a large, powerful, suffering man who seems immobilised in his own dreamy meditations. The plump, round, silver face above the severe, black clerical garb curiously suggests the full moon on a dark night, one of Coleridge's enduring images from 'The Ancient Mariner'. Coleridge wrote: 'Whatever is impressive is part fugitive, part existent only in the imaginations of persons impressed strongly with my conversation. The face itself is a FEEBLE, unmanly face ...'. (*Letters*, 1814). Allston's own perceptive comments are given in the Introduction (page 19).

Robert Southey (1774–1843)

History has not been kind to Southey, choosing to forget almost everything he wrote except the famous children's story of *The Three Bears*. Widely admired in his lifetime as a prolific poet, essayist and historian, he was appointed Poet Laureate in 1813, and for thirty years was the most feared and influential critic on the Tory *Quarterly Review*.

Born in Bristol (a lonely child looked after by a rich and eccentric aunt), Southey was educated at Oxford, dreamed of Pantisocracy with Coleridge and wrote revolutionary verse-dramas such as *Wat Tyler* (1794, published 1817), *The Fall of Robespierre* (1794) and *Joan of Arc* (1796), which came back to haunt him in respectable middle age. He spent a formative year in Lisbon, learned Spanish and Portuguese, and returned to marry and settle at Keswick (1803), where he established a huge private library and heroically supported his own and Coleridge's large extended family with regular journalism, translation and reviewing, written to a ferocious daily timetable, with a silver pocket-watch on his desk. In Edward Nash's watercolour of 1820 (page 53) the metamorphosis is complete: revolutionary bard into *Quarterly* reviewer.

The exotic and splendidly titled verse-epics, over which he slaved with such devotion – *Thalaba the Destroyer* (1801), *The Curse of Kehama* (1810), *Roderick: The Last of the Goths* (1814) – were ridiculed by the younger generation. He also had the misfortune to attack both Byron and Shelley in print for their bad poetry and worse morals. Southey retreated into vast histories of Brazil and the Peninsular War, while his sister-in-law hanged herself, and his wife eventually went mad. His best writing is biographical – in remarkably assured lives of Nelson (1813), the preacher John Wesley (1820) and the melancholy poet Cowper (1837) – and in shrewd, funny and

Robert Southey
Henry Edridge, 1804

Opposite:
Robert Southey
Edward Nash, 1820

refreshingly outspoken letters about his famous friends, especially Lamb, Coleridge, Wordsworth, De Quincey and Walter Scott.

Southey's fine, equine, almost arrogantly handsome face was set on a gangling, long-legged body, giving him something of the appearance of a highly strung, thoroughbred racehorse. Hazlitt recalled him in his youth, before political disillusion and domesticity had curbed him:

> Mr Southey, as we formerly remember to have seen him, had a hectic flush upon his cheek, a roving fire in his eye, a falcon glance, a look at once aspiring and dejected … . He wooed Liberty as a youthful lover, but it was perhaps more as a mistress than a bride; and he has since wedded with an elderly and not very reputable lady, called Legitimacy.
> (*The Spirit of the Age*, 1825)

Many painters called to take his likeness at Keswick, especially after the Laureateship, but Southey disliked most of the results, describing one portrait by Thomas Phillips as giving his eyes 'an expression which I conceive to be more like two oysters in love than anything else'. The drawing by Henry Edridge done in Southey's study in 1804, with Derwentwater and the fells projected like a picturesque backcloth, catches better than most the domesticated bard, well brushed and buttoned up, clever and a touch sarcastic, with elegant socks and shoes that never tramped a hillside. Thomas Carlyle remembered him, 'all legs; in shape and stature like a pair of tongs' (*Reminiscences*, 1881).

Amelia Opie (1769–1853)

Poet and novelist Amelia Opie (née Alderson) was one of the great beauties of the Romantic generation, entrancing the Godwin circle with her high spirits and revolutionary ardour. The clever daughter of a leading Norwich doctor, well read in French and musically talented, she published her early poems in local papers and sang her own ballads at private receptions.

In 1794 she came to London and attended the treason trials of John Thelwall, Horne Tooke and Thomas Holcroft at the Old Bailey. When Horne Tooke was acquitted, she is said to have walked across the top of the barristers' table to kiss him. She was courted by Holcroft and then Godwin, much to Mary Wollstonecraft's annoyance, but finally married the painter John Opie in 1798. They visited Paris in 1802, after the publication of her *Poems*, which ran to six editions. In 1804 she published her most famous work, *Adeline Mowbray, or The Mother and the Daughter*, a novel about contemporary marriage based partly on the lives of Godwin and Mary Wollstonecraft.

After John Opie's early death in 1807, she returned to Norwich to keep house for her beloved father and became a Quaker, dedicating her life to visiting prisons, hospitals and workhouses. In 1818, however, she said she was still writing for eight hours a day and lamented: 'Shall I ever cease to enjoy the pleasures of this world? I fear not.' Other novels included *Father and Daughter* (1801), *Madeline* (1822) and the unfinished *The Painter and His Wife*. She kept up a wide circle of friends in both London and Paris, including Byron, Scott, Wordsworth, Madame de Staël and Lafayette. When she died a street was named after her in Norwich.

With her large brown eyes, clear bold features and voluptuous figure, Mrs Opie always attracted clever men and alarmed clever women. Crabb Robinson noted that 'her becoming a Quakeress gave her a sort of éclat' (*Diary*, 1824); Mrs Inchbald called her 'cleverer than her books'; while Miss Sedgwick cattily observed that her 'elaborate simplicity and the fashionable little train to her pretty satin gown indicated how much easier it is to adopt a theory than to change one's habits' (*Letters from Abroad*, 1840).

John Opie's portrait is a tender tribute to his wife, painted in the year of their marriage. Its intimacy is emphasised by the direct unflinching gaze (with its hint of mischief), the fullness of the mouth and the casual placing of the formal hat with its riding veil on her knee. The beautifully braided hair subtly suggests a laurel wreath, symbol of literary renown.

Amelia Opie
John Opie, 1798

William Hazlitt (1778–1830)

Political journalist and superb all-round critic of the arts, Hazlitt became the radical conscience of Romanticism. Famed equally for the gusto of his prose and the bitterness of his quarrels, he was a lifelong republican. The son of a Unitarian preacher from Ireland, Hazlitt first trained for the Dissenting ministry and then as a portrait-painter, but, inspired by a meeting with Coleridge and Wordsworth in the Quantocks in 1798, he gradually took up freelance writing. This experience is memorably described in one of his greatest essays, *My First Acquaintance with Poets* (1823).

Hazlitt could write with equal brilliance on theatre, painting, boxing, politics, poetry and long-distance walking. Keats said that 'the depth of Hazlitt's taste' was one of the three glories of the age (the other two being Wordsworth's poetry and Haydon's pictures). His major essays were collected in *The Characters of Shakespeare's Plays* (1817), *Political Essays* (1819), *Lectures on The English Comic Writers* (1819) and *Winterslow* (1831), named after his writing retreat on the edge of Salisbury Plain. He produced a vivid and often devastating assessment of his contemporaries in a gallery of twenty-five pen portraits (including Coleridge, Wordsworth, Southey, Godwin, Byron and Scott) collected as *The Spirit of the Age* (1825).

Lonely and mercurial, he was twice married (both times unhappily), and in 1823 published *Liber Amoris*, the agonised account of his unrequited passion for Sarah Walker, a teenage servant girl. His conversations with the painter James Northcote, an interesting experiment in biography, were collected as *Boswell Redivivus* (1827). Hazlitt ended his days in tragic isolation and poverty, working on a four-volume life of his hero, Napoleon, and sending a last letter to the editor of the *Edinburgh Review* from his Soho lodgings: 'Dear Sir, I am dying; can you send me £10, and so consummate your many kindnesses to me?' (*Letters*, 1830). Hazlitt's extraordinary mixture of shyness and aggression was not easily captured on canvas. The Bewick sketch was done during his second honeymoon at Melrose in Scotland, and his wife remarked: 'Oh, it is exactly your own hair, my dear' (T. Landseer, *Life of Bewick*, 1871). Some years later, his friend George Patmore recalled him as 'a pale anatomy of a man … the forehead was magnificent, the nose strong, light and elegant, the mouth greatly resembled Edmund Kean's, the eyes grey (furtive), sometimes sinister, never brilliant, the head nobly formed with a profusion of coal-black curls' (*My Friends and Acquaintances*, 1854).

William Hazlitt (detail)
William Bewick, 1825

Coleridge, whom Hazlitt both praised and mocked, gave this memorable verbal portrait of Hazlitt at twenty-four: 'William Hazlitt is a thinking, observant, original man … . His manners are to 99 in 100 singularly repulsive – brow-hanging, shoe-contemplative, strange… he is, I verily believe, kindly-natured … but he is jealous, gloomy, & of an irritable Pride – & addicted to women, as objects of sexual Indulgence. With all this there is much good in him … he says things that are his own in a way of his own … he sends well-headed & well-feathered Thoughts straight forwards to the mark with a Twang of the Bow-string' (*Letters*, 1802).

Charles Lamb (1775–1834)

The most kind and lovable of men, Lamb set out to be a poet but found his true identity as an essayist and whimsical autobiographer. He created the persona of 'Elia', who could enliven any subject under the sun, from reading Shakespeare to eating roast pig for supper. The son of a lawyer's clerk of the Inner Temple, Lamb attended Christ's Hospital School with Coleridge, and then worked for forty years as a clerk in the East India Company in the City.

Almost all Lamb's work is a celebration of London and the metropolitan sensibility, just as his closest friends celebrated the Lake District and wild nature. One of his most penetrating early essays was *On the Genius and Character of Hogarth* (1811). His occasional poems, tender and elegiac, include 'The Old Familiar Faces' (1798), the ballad 'Hester' (1803), and the infinitely touching 'On an Infant Dying as Soon as Born' (1827).

Insanity dogged Lamb's family: Lamb himself spent six weeks in Hoxton Lunatic Asylum in 1795, and the following year his beloved elder sister Mary was incarcerated there for five months after fatally stabbing their mother during a paranoid episode. Lamb dedicated the rest of his life to looking after Mary, and together they published *Tales from Shakespeare* (1807) and *Adventures of Ulysses* (1808) for children. His rooms near the Strand became the late-night meeting place for his many friends, including Coleridge, Wordsworth, Southey, Hazlitt, Haydon and Leigh Hunt. Here Lamb presided in a celestial cloud of tobacco smoke, port fumes and precipitate puns, brought to earth with his inimitable stutter. The first collected volume of the *Essays of Elia*, dedicated to Coleridge, appeared in 1823, and the second in 1833. When he died Wordsworth mourned him in a poem as 'Lamb, the frolic and the gentle'.

Charles Lamb
William Hazlitt, 1804

Charles Lamb with his sister Mary Lamb
Francis Stephen Cary, 1834

Lamb's affectionate guardianship of his beloved sister often included the terrible duty of temporarily re-committing her to the asylum.

Small, animated, deeply eccentric and often rather drunk, no painter ever captured Lamb's pixie-like and mischievous charm. He had one brown eye and one grey. His reply to Coleridge's loving epithet, 'my gentle-hearted Charles' (in the poem 'This Lime-Tree Bower My Prison'), was characteristic: 'call me rather drunken-dog, ragged head, seldom-shaven, odd-ey'd, stuttering, or any other epithet which truly and properly belongs' (*Letters*, 1797). He got his own back twenty years later by calling Coleridge, in a superb phrase, 'an Archangel a little Damaged' (*Letters*, 1816). Leigh Hunt wrote: 'Charles Lamb had a head worthy of Aristotle, with as fine a heart as ever beat in a human bosom, and limbs very fragile to sustain it … . There never was a true portrait of Lamb' (*Autobiography*, 1850).

The best attempt is Hazlitt's curiously solemn picture of 1804, one of the last he ever painted before taking up writing, which Crabb Robinson drily described as 'certainly the only painting by Hazlitt that I ever saw with pleasure' (*Diary*, 1812). The seventeenth-century Spanish costume was not the result of Lamb dressing up (like Byron in Albanian draperies) for theatrical effect as an Iberian Elia. It was instead a typical act of lambent friendship: Hazlitt wanted to do a copy of Velázquez's *Philip IV*, and Lamb had humbly agreed to act as his clothes-horse. One can only imagine the philippic puns that accompanied the sitting.

Mary Robinson (1758–1800)

Mary Robinson
Sir Joshua Reynolds, 1783–4

Poet, actress, novelist and adventuress, Mary 'Perdita' Robinson was one of the most glamorous and talented women of her generation, embodying the early spirit of Romanticism in her life as much as her work. She played many of Shakespeare's heroines in the London theatres between 1778 and 1790, and in the last decade of her career published seven novels and three volumes of poetry. She knew Godwin and befriended the young Coleridge, hearing him recite 'Kubla Khan' sixteen years before the poem was published. She was poetry editor of *The Morning Post*, and probably influenced the narrative style of the *Lyrical Ballads* (1798).

Mary Robinson
by or after Sir Joshua Reynolds,
c.1782

Married at sixteen to a feckless husband (with whom she spent ten months in prison for debt), Mary Robinson took to the stage and caught the eye of the teenage Prince of Wales while playing Perdita in *The Winter's Tale* at Covent Garden in 1779. After a heady year as the royal mistress (from whence her nickname), she moved into the bed of the great Opposition statesman Charles James Fox, who arranged for her to receive a state pension of £500 per annum, a considerable sum giving her complete independence, and then formed a passionate but fraught alliance with a distinguished military historian and MP, the roving Colonel Tarleton, which lasted on and off till the end of her life.

In 1792 she visited revolutionary France, in the middle of a lover's quarrel. But a near-fatal miscarriage left her increasingly paralysed with an agonising form of arthritis and, in her remarkable *Memoirs* (published posthumously in 1801), she describes how she took opium against the pain and wrote under its influence in a way very similar to Coleridge. While her novels are sentimental, her poetry has unexpected dash and clarity. Very much in her own voice, it is sometimes racily satirical, but always stylish.

Like the other Romantics, she made poetry out of the incidents of her own life, but also identified very early on the subjects that would attract her male contemporaries. Her *Poems* (1791) include an 'Ode to Melancholy' and an 'Ode to the Nightingale', as well as 'Monody to the Memory of Chatterton' and 'Sonnet: the Mariner'. In the year of her death, Coleridge wrote her a touching poem of greeting and farewell, 'A Stranger Minstrel', praising her 'witching melody'.

Famous for her imperious beauty (as well as her dramatic hats), Mary Robinson was frequently painted by Romney, Gainsborough, Reynolds and Zoffany.

Mary Robinson
George Dance, 1793

MARY ROBINSON

But for them she was primarily an actress on display.
George Dance's intimate, rather melancholy drawing,
done in later life (1793), shows her instead as a writer
more at home in her private study, wrapped up in a
plain day dress with her hair pulled back in a practical
– but typically flamboyant – silk scarf with its
seductive bow.

Almost her last publication was a spirited essay in
support of Mary Wollstonecraft, *A Letter to the Women of
England on the Injustice of Mental Subordination*, (1799), in
which she recommended the foundation of a
University for Women.

Edmund Kean (1787–1833)

A tragic actor of unnerving power, Kean brought a new sense of psychological depth to the English stage. Small, dark and intense, he could instantly dominate an audience with his brilliant eyes, and became famous for his reinterpretation of Shakespeare's villains and outsiders. Hazlitt wrote that he destroyed for ever 'the Kemble religion' of classical acting.

Born in London, unstable and probably illegitimate (his Jewish father flung himself off a roof), Kean learned his craft in travelling circuses and fairground booths, often playing Hamlet and Harlequin on the same night. His debut as Shylock at the Drury Lane Theatre in January 1814 took London by storm. It was followed over the next decade by redefining performances of King Lear, Richard III, Othello, Iago, Hamlet and King Lear. His brooding, volatile manner on stage, combined with his radical politics and disreputable private life ('Give me bread and cheese and a couple of whores!' he shouted at his manager, Elliston), earned him a Mephistophelean reputation. Byron (a member of the Drury Lane Committee) said approvingly that Kean was like his own Corsair and had 'a laughing devil in his sneer'.

Kean undertook two successful American tours (there were riots in Boston and New York) and was made an honorary Huron chieftain. Back in London he sometimes received guests in feathers and warpaint. He purchased a large house in Piccadilly and an island estate in Scotland, and triumphantly sent his son to Eton. But venereal disease, alcohol and a scandalous trial for adultery forced him into early retirement in Richmond (after three 'final' benefit nights). Walter Scott drily observed that Kean was 'rendered mad by conceit and success', but for Coleridge Kean's stage performances were 'like reading Shakespeare by flashes of lightning' (*Shakespearean Criticism*, 1840).

Above:
Edmund Kean as Richard III
J. Prynn, *c*.1814–33

Opposite:
Edmund Kean as Shylock
Henry Hoppner Meyer;
W.H. Watts, 1814

Dorothy Jordan (1761–1816)

Exuberant Yorkshire actress and singer renowned for her unruly mop of auburn curls, Dora Jordan began her career in Dublin playing Miss Lucy in Fielding's comedy *The Virgin Unmasked* and ended it in London playing royal mistress to the Duke of Clarence, later William IV. Mrs Jordan (the stage name she adopted because she had successfully 'crossed over the waters') became the most celebrated romantic comedy actress of her generation and was painted by Hoppner for the Royal Academy as *The Comic Muse* (1786).

Her seductive cross-dressing parts, which included Viola in *Twelfth Night*, Rosalind in *As You Like It* and Priscilla Tomboy in *The Romp*, brought her a huge following, including Lamb, Hazlitt, Hunt, Coleridge, Fanny Burney and even Jane Austen (who was 'highly amused' watching her at Covent Garden in 1814). At the height of 'Jordo-mania', Beechey painted her in skin-tight yellow knee breeches (1789) and Hoppner in the peacock uniform of a Spanish hussar (1791). Her tender, flirtatious acting style brought a new Romantic poignancy to Shakespeare's heroines, especially Juliet, Miranda and Ophelia, and made the classical solemnity of Sarah Siddons suddenly old-fashioned.

Lamb described her succinctly as 'Shakespeare's woman'. From 1791 she was also the Duke's mistress and bore him no fewer than ten children, skilfully alternating pregnancies with stage appearances. Their domestic ménage became the subject of endlessly suggestive cartoons by Gillray, many punning on her stage name ('jordan' being Regency slang for 'chamberpot'). Comedy finally turned to tragedy when the Duke cast her off in 1811, making an allowance with the cruel proviso that she could not act again. She fled to France as 'Mrs James', where she died at Saint-Cloud, heartbroken and penniless. But she was never forgotten by her true Romantic devotees.

M.ʳˢ Jordan as Viola .

Above:
Dorothy Jordan as Viola
Unknown artist, late eighteenth century

Opposite:
Dorothy Jordan
John Hoppner, exhibited 1791

According to Hazlitt: 'her face, her tears, her manners were irresistible … . She was all gaiety, openness and good nature. She rioted in fine animal spirits, and gave more pleasure than any other actress, because she had the greatest spirit of enjoyment in herself' (*View of the English Stage,* 1818).

Thomas De Quincey (1785–1859)

The strangest and most exotic of the Romantics, De Quincey made his name at the age of thirty-seven with his *Confessions of an English Opium Eater* (1821), written in a garret off Covent Garden and originally published the previous year in two instalments by the *London Magazine.* Scholarly, fantastical, deeply read in German and Oriental literature, De Quincey was a gentleman bohemian who supported himself, a large family and his lifelong drug-addiction by a huge output of journalism. He became the master of a baroque form of autobiographical dream-prose and a critic of peculiar psychological insights. His taste for the grotesque and his combination of arcane learning with black humour are brilliantly displayed in his essays *On Murder Considered as One of the Fine Arts* (1827) and *On the Knocking on the Gate in Macbeth* (1823)

The son of a wealthy linen merchant, eccentric in his habits and diminutive in stature (he was barely five feet tall), De Quincey absconded first from Manchester Grammar School and then from Oxford, drifting through Wales and London, reading the poetry of Wordsworth and Coleridge, taking opium and living with a teenage prostitute whom he tenderly describes in his *Confessions* as 'Ann of Oxford Street'. In 1808 he settled in the Lake District near his idol Wordsworth, taking over Dove Cottage and filling it with fifty-six tea chests of books.

De Quincey's memories of this time, shrewd and mischievous, later appeared as *Recollections of the Lake Poets* (1834–9) with memorable portraits of William and Dorothy Wordsworth, Coleridge and Southey. He lived with the daughter of a local farmer, whom he finally married in 1817, producing eight children. Thereafter he drifted between London and Edinburgh, writing irregular but brilliant essays in his 'impassioned prose', including an unfinished study of

Thomas De Quincey
Sir John Watson-Gordon, *c*.1845

his opium-dreams, *Suspiria de Profundis* (1845, *Sighs from the Deep*), and the thrilling, moonlit vision of disaster entitled *The English Mail Coach* (1849). His work made an immediate impact in France, second only to Byron's, and was translated by Baudelaire in *Les Paradis Artificiels*, and praised by Gautier.

When De Quincey first came to Grasmere, Dorothy Wordsworth was entranced by his ability to play with the children and he always retained an impish, changeling quality, as if his whole life was some fantastic, labyrinthian game. 'We feel often as if he were one of the Family – he is loving, gentle and happy – a very good scholar, and an acute Logician ... . His person is unfortunately *diminutive*, but there is a sweetness in his looks, especially about the eyes, which soon overcomes the oddness in your first feeling at the sight of so very little a Man' (*Letters*, 1808).

In later life, when opium and poverty had taken their toll, Crabb Robinson observed a pale, wizened creature whose strangeness was nonetheless still attractive: 'In London he could not possibly maintain himself. I saw him occasionally there as a shiftless man. He had a wretchedly invalid countenance: his skin looked like mother-of-pearl. He had a very delicate hand & voice more soft than a woman's, but his conversation was highly intelligent and interesting' (*Reminiscences*, 1843). Sir John Watson-Gordon's portrait was done at about this time (*c*.1845). The large, heavy, handsome overcoat with its furred collar and sleeves seems deliberately designed to disguise the shrunken, penniless, haunted Opium Eater within.

Sir William Herschel (1738–1822)

Astronomer and cosmologist of visionary genius, Herschel revolutionised Romantic ideas about the size and nature of the physical universe.

Born into a family of German musicians, he emigrated to England and in 1767 settled in Bath, where he was employed as an organist and music teacher. Increasingly drawn by the music of the spheres, he built a series of reflector telescopes in his back garden, hand-grinding their enormous mirrors and spending entire nights mapping the constellations. In March 1781 he observed a strange comet in Gemini, which turned out to be the seventh planet in

William Herschel
James Godby, published 1814

William Herschel
Lemuel Francis Abbott, 1785

the solar system, Uranus, the first to be discovered since the time of Ptolemy. For this he was knighted, appointed royal astronomer and later celebrated by Keats in his sonnet 'On First Looking into Chapman's Homer' (1816).

Herschel established a giant forty-foot telescope near Windsor and began to formulate startling new theories about evolving galaxies *beyond* the Milky Way ('On the Construction of the Heavens', 1785) and the existence of 'deep time'. He was also romantic enough to believe that the moon was inhabited.

Shelley discussed his cosmology in the 'Notes' to *Queen Mab* (1811); Byron reflected gloomily that 'Night was a more religious concern' when observed through Herschel's telescope (*Detached Thoughts*, 1821), while Fanny Burney exclaimed wildly that Herschel had discovered 'fifteen hundred universes! How many more he may find who can conjecture?' (*Diary*, December 1786).

He told the poet Thomas Campbell: 'I have looked further into space than ever human being did before me. I have observed stars of which the light, it can be proved, must take two million years to reach the earth.' In response, Campbell remarked that '... anything you ask he labours to explain with a sort of boyish earnestness ... . I really and unfeignedly felt at the moment as if I had been conversing with a supernatural intelligence.' (Letter, September 1815)

Caroline Herschel, his beloved younger sister, discovered several new comets. She went on to become the first woman scientist elected to the Astronomical Society and receive a royal stipend. It was she who chose Herschel's epitaph: 'He burst the bounds of Heaven.'

Sir Humphry Davy (1778–1829)

The greatest British scientist of his day and President of the Royal Society, Davy was also an intimate friend of Coleridge and Wordsworth, knew Scott and Byron, and was a gifted minor poet in his own right. He published a delightful volume of piscatorial reflections (in dialogue form), *Salmonia, or Days of Fly-Fishing* (1828), and a moving book of meditations, *Consolations in Travel, or the Last Days of a Philosopher* (1830). His brilliant career shows no evidence of the modern split between the 'two cultures', and his ability to explain and popularise his experimental work in books and lectures (which

Sir Humphry Davy
Thomas Phillips, 1821

particularly influenced Coleridge) suggests that there was once such a thing as Romantic science. He wrote: 'Whilst chemical pursuits exalt the understanding, they do not depress the imagination or weaken genuine feeling.'

A Cornishman by birth, Davy studied at the famous Bristol Pneumatic Institution under Dr Thomas Beddos (where Coleridge joined him in experiments with laughing gas) and oversaw the proof corrections to the *Lyrical Ballads*. In 1803 he was appointed Professor of Chemistry at the newly founded Royal Institution in London, and began his celebrated Bakerian Lectures at the Royal Society, demonstrating the electrical affinity of chemical elements and isolating sodium and potassium. Like a true Romantic, he had an instinctive appreciation of fire and combustion, inventing in 1813 the famous Davy Safety Lamp, an 'insulated light' which did not ignite the lethal hydrogen or methane gases in deep-pit mine shafts. Another of his more hazardous experiments was to launch Coleridge as a lecturer at the Royal Institution in 1808.

In 1812 he was knighted for his work, and received many other honours both in London and in Paris. However, his marriage of the same year to a fashionable Scottish blue-stocking, Jane Apreece, was childless and increasingly discordant. By the time he was appointed President of the Royal Society (1820), he had become an isolated and tragically embittered man, cut off from his friends, gloomy and introspective, and suffering from progressive heart disease. His great protégé, Michael Faraday, found him cold and remote. Davy travelled much on the Continent, drinking and writing (like Coleridge and Shelley he produced a long poem on 'Mont Blanc'), and died in a hotel room in Geneva aged fifty. But he left the Romantics with a noble and dynamic view of the physical universe as a constant flux of energies and mysterious forms.

An attractive, rather boyish figure with dark Celtic

Scientific Researches! — New Discoveries in PNEUMATICKS! — or — an Experimental Lecture on the Powers of Air —

Scientific researches! – new discoveries in pneumaticks!
James Gillray, 1802

A mixed audience at the Royal Institution observes the startling effects of inhaling nitrous oxide, or laughing gas, administered by Professor Young and a leering Humphry Davy (with bellows).

features and a commanding nose, Davy burst into life on the lecture platform and had the gift of enchanting his audiences. 'He is now about thirty-three,' wrote George Ticknor in 1815, 'but with all the freshness and bloom of five-and-twenty, and one of the handsomest men I have seen in England' (*Life and Letters*, 1876). Phillips's portrait was executed after a miners' banquet held in Davy's honour at Newcastle and shows the elegant shape of the Davy Lamp, which saved so many of their lives, placed proudly at his elbow.

Lord Byron (1788–1824)

With Lord Byron, English Romanticism developed
into an international style. A charismatic figure of
devastating charm and vanity, Byron became the *beau
ideal* of the Romantic writer while pretending to do
nothing so unspeakably vulgar. His poems were
effortless best-sellers, his letters are among the finest
and funniest in the language, and his stormy private
life inspired over two hundred biographies and
memoirs. His masterpiece is *Don Juan*, an
autobiographical poem in five cantos begun in 1818,
which reflects his lifelong travels through Europe and
the Levant, and is written in his wonderful world-
weary style of mocking colloquialisms and lyric irony.

His father, 'Mad Jack' Byron, died when he was
only three and Byron grew up at Newstead Abbey,
a dilapidated gothic pile in Nottinghamshire, a clever,
lonely and passionate child who was always haunted
by a secret 'mark of Cain', his club foot. At
Cambridge he formed a brilliant circle of dandyish
friends (one of them, Scrope Davies, noted that he
slept in paper curlers) and in 1809 he set the literary
establishment on fire with his satire 'English Bards and
Scotch Reviewers'.

He came back from two years' wanderings in
Spain, Malta, Greece and Turkey to publish the first
two cantos of *Childe Harold's Pilgrimage* (1812) and
'awoke to find myself famous'. These were followed by
several Oriental verse-tales (*The Corsair* was written in
ten days) and a glorious period of social lionising,
including his scandalous affair with the volatile Lady
Caroline Lamb (1785–1828), who sometimes dressed
for him as a pageboy.

Lady Caroline Lamb subsequently published a
gothic novel of her passionate entanglement with
Byron, *Glenarvon* (1816), and died insane twelve
years later.

Lady Caroline Lamb
Henry Hoppner Meyer,
published 1819

Edward John Trelawny
Joseph Severn, 1838

Byron worked for the Drury Lane Theatre Committee, made lasting alliances with Walter Scott and the poet Tom Moore (a future biographer, 1830) and encouraged Coleridge to publish 'Christabel'. But the liaison with his half-sister, Augusta Leigh, and the collapse of his marriage to Arabella Millbank drove him abroad again in 1816, to settle in Italy with his menagerie of Venetian mistresses and exotic animals, brilliantly evoked in his poem 'Beppo' (1818). In 1821 he moved to the Palazzo Lanfranchi, Pisa, with the Countess Teresa Guiccioli, a bulldog and a billiard table.

His magnetic presence attracted Shelley and his wife, Mary (whose half-sister Claire Clairmont became another mistress), and innumerable raffish admirers and hangers-on. Among these were the young Scottish physician John William Polidori (1795–1821), author of *The Vampyre* (1819), who later committed suicide. Most striking was Edward John Trelawny (1792–1881), a bearded Cornish adventurer and inspired teller of tall stories who cast himself as a natural Byronic hero and in 1822 accompanied Byron to the Greek War of Independence. His *Records of Shelley, Byron and the Author* (1858) is a vividly convincing and totally unreliable work of Romantic biography.

Byron's final commitment to the Philhellene cause in Greece electrified the youth of Europe and hundreds rushed to join him. His private disillusion in the brutal chaos of the war, witnessed in his last letters and poems ('Tis time this heart should be unmoved', dated Missolonghi, 22 January 1824), was offset by extraordinary courage and generosity, and an unflinching dedication to 'Freedom's battle'. Stylish and self-mocking to the end (he sported a plumed helmet but lamented the grey hairs beneath), his death from fever at Missolonghi in April 1824 was mourned throughout Europe and signalled the apotheosis of

Lord Byron
E.H. Bailey, 1826

John William Polidori
F.G. Gainsford, *c*.1816

Romanticism. In Lincolnshire, on hearing the news, a young poet called Tennyson carved 'Byron is Dead' upon a rock.

Byron's fine aristocratic beauty was admired equally by men and women, and inspired dozens of pictures, sketches, busts and medallions both during his lifetime and after. The large head with its dark curls, mocking eyes and voluptuous mouth, distracted from the stocky body that was always tending to overweight and the distinctive limp with its hint of the cloven hoof. He was Apollo combined with Mephistopheles.

'Lord Byron's head,' wrote John Gibson Lockhart, 'is without doubt the finest in our time – I think it better on the whole, than either Napoleon's, or Goethe's, or Canova's, or Wordsworth's' (*Letters*, 1819). Byron himself was typically droll on the matter: 'my personal charms have by no means increased – my hair is half grey – and the Crow's foot has been rather lavish of its indelible steps – my hair though not gone is going – and my teeth remain by way of courtesy – but I suppose they will follow' (*Letters*, 1819). But Coleridge recalled that being in Byron's presence was like seeing the sun (*Letters*, 1816).

Sir Walter Scott (1771–1832)

Sir Walter Scott
Sir Edwin Landseer, 1830–31

Now remembered as a great historical novelist, Scott first made his name as a poet and prolific writer of Romantic verse-tales. He had no reputation a novelist until his mid-forties, and his work was seen primarily as a rival to Southey's and Byron's. Fascinated by the Border ballads of his native Lowlands and a skilful translator of German gothic ballads by Bürger and Goethe (which also attracted Coleridge and Wordsworth), he published *Minstrelsy of the Scottish Borders* in 1802–3.

Scott popularised a form of highly musical, melodramatic, 'antiquarian' verse-tales of the Highlands – battles, hauntings, castles, lakes and star-crossed lovers – whose titles still hold an ineffable misty romance: *The Lay of the Last Minstrel* (1805), *The Lady of the Lake* (1810), *The Bridal of Triermain* (1813) and *The Lord of the Isles* (1815). It was only when his audience was finally captured by Byron that he turned to prose and the vast resources of Scottish clan history. Among his outstanding achievements were the original *Waverley* (1814), *Old Mortality* (1816), *Rob Roy* (1817), *The Heart of Midlothian* (1817), *Ivanhoe* (1819), *Quentin Durward* (1823) and *Castle Dangerous* (1831).

As the author of such wild and aboriginal romances, Scott's solid, genial and meticulous nature presents a curious paradox. He was educated at Edinburgh University, successfully trained for the Scottish bar, became a partner in Ballantyne's publishing house, helped found the *Quarterly Review* and took immense pride in his manse at Abbotsford on the Tweed, which he purchased in 1811. He was Sheriff-depute of Selkirkshire and was knighted in 1820. It was wholly characteristic that he refused the Poet Laureateship (in Southey's favour) in 1813, and when Ballantyne's went bankrupt in 1826 he shouldered the huge debt of £114, 000 and gradually

Sir Walter Scott
Sir Edwin Landseer, c.1824

Landseer went up to paint this
portrait at Abbotsford in 1824,
while Scott was working on
Redgauntlet. 'He has painted
every dog in the house,'
remarked Scott, 'and ended up
with the owner' (*Letters*, 1824).

paid it off from the profits of his pen – a heroic effort
which undoubtedly shortened his life. The one shadow
in his career was that he was accused, with some
reason, of plagiarising Coleridge's 'Christabel' in his
early work, but this could be taken as a compliment.

Gruff, witty, hospitable, hard-working and hard-
drinking – every inch a Scotsman – Scott was often
painted in his lair at Abbotsford. 'There was more
benevolence expressed in Scott's face,' said his friend
the painter C.R. Leslie, 'than is given in any portrait
of him' (*Autobiographical Recollections*, 1865). But the fine
florid, distinguished features – with hair prematurely
silver – and tall, powerful body all spoke clearly of his
inner strength and creative force.

Percy Bysshe Shelley (1792–1822)

As reckless and brilliant in his poetry as in his life, Shelley poured out the great body of his major work in less than a decade, and drowned (with two friends) off the coast of Tuscany at the age of twenty-nine, while trying to race a summer storm back to Lerici in his small yacht and pressing on with full sail. He is still popularly remembered as a love poet ('Lines Written in the Bay of Lerici'), a master of plangent lyrics ('To a Skylark'), of superb odes ('To the West Wind') and moving elegies ('Adonais', on the death of Keats). But he was also a philosophical and political essayist, and a gifted poetic translator from German, Italian, Greek, Spanish and Arabic.

Many of Shelley's radical and revolutionary ideas, powerfully influenced by his father-in-law William Godwin, were expressed in his great dramatic poem *Prometheus Unbound* (1820). He wrote wonderful letters about his travels in Italy, describing it as 'the Paradise of Exiles', and a historic *Defence of Poetry* (1821). Wordsworth called him 'one of the best artists of us all; I mean in workmanship of style'.

The rebellious son of a Sussex baronet, Shelley was educated at Eton and Oxford (from which he was sent down for atheism), and was twice married. His first wife, Harriet Westbrook, committed suicide in the Serpentine; his second wife, Mary Godwin, wrote *Frankenstein*; and two of his children died in Italy. His complex relationship with Byron is described in one of his finest, plainest and most haunting poems, 'Julian and Maddalo' (1818). At the time of his death, while living at his remote beach-house, the Casa Magni in San Terenzo, Shelley was working on a long poem in *terza rima* based on Dante's *Inferno*, the visionary 'Triumph of Life'. Parts of this manuscript are written on the back of drawings of the sailing rig for his yacht, the *Don Juan*.

Percy Bysshe Shelley
Amelia Curran, 1819

Thomas Love Peacock
Roger Jean, c.1805

Opposite:
Memorial to the drowned Shelley in Christchurch Priory, Dorset
Horatio Weekes, 1854

Another angelic myth: the body of the atheist Shelley, cradled by his mourning wife Mary, is transformed into a Romantic *pieta*.

His friend Thomas Love Peacock (1785–1866) affectionately satirised him – along with Byron and Coleridge – as the unworldly idealist Scythrop Glowry in the novel *Nightmare Abbey* (1818). Thin, wide-eyed and intense, Shelley was an expert pistol shot, a good horse-rider, an athletic walker and a convinced vegetarian. Impetuous by temperament and much troubled by physical seizures (probably kidney stones) and psychic manifestations, he lived with an unsettling urgency that affected all those around him. His sensible banker friend Horace Smith called him 'a psychological curiosity, infinitely more curious than Coleridge's Kubla Khan'. (Letter, 1816)

The only authentic portrait of Shelley was painted by Amelia Curran in her studio near the Spanish Steps in Rome, at the time he was finishing *Prometheus Unbound* in 1819. Curran later told Mary Shelley that she had almost burned the picture, because it was 'so ill done' and had failed to capture his restless spirit. Leigh Hunt, who saw Shelley in the port of Livorno a few days before he drowned, left a memorable description:

> His figure was tall and slight, and his constitution consumptive. He was subject to violent spasmodic pains … his shoulders were bent a little, owing to premature thought and trouble … . Like the Stagyrite's, his voice was high and weak. His eyes were large and animated, with a dash of wildness in them … . He had brown hair, which, though tinged with grey, surmounted his face well, being in considerable quantity, and tending to curl… when fronting and looking at you attentively his aspect had a certain seraphical character that would have suited a portrait of John the Baptist, or the angel whom Milton describes as holding a reed 'tipt' with fire.
> (*Autobiography*, 1850)

Mary Shelley (1797–1851)

Celebrated as the author of one unforgettable book, *Frankenstein, or The Modern Prometheus*, which was published when she was twenty-one, Mary Shelley was actually a professional *femme de lettres* of many talents and striking versatility. She wrote six major novels, over forty short stories, a travel book (based on her Continental adventures with Shelley) and numerous essays and short biographies. She also produced an autobiographical novella of her mental breakdown in Italy, *Mathilda* (1819), and a confessional poem about her life after Shelley's death, 'The Choice' (1822) – both unpublished until the twentieth century – as well as the moving biographical 'Notes' to the 1839 edition of Shelley's *Collected Poems*.

The beautiful only child of William Godwin and Mary Wollstonecraft (who died in childbirth), she was her father's darling and was privately educated to a standard far higher than usually achieved at Oxford or at Cambridge (Girton, the first college for women, was not founded until 1869). After her elopement with Shelley in 1814 (which shattered Godwin as much as her mother's death had sixteen years previously), she published her first book anonymously, *History of a Six Weeks Tour* (1817), in collaboration with Shelley.

Frankenstein, also anonymous, followed in 1818, on the eve of their departure for Italy. Inspired by a ghost-story competition with Byron and Polidori at the Villa Diodati, Lake Geneva, in the summer of 1816, it broke the conventions of the eighteenth-century gothic novel to become the first recognisable work of modern science fiction. Its celebrated 'eight foot' monster (subsequently the star of a score of modern films, of which the best by far was Kenneth Branagh's in 1994) is as much a Romantic outcast, a sort of Adam after the Fall, as a Hammer House horror figure with a bolt through his neck. Much of Mary's

Mary Shelley
Richard Rothwell, exhibited 1840

own scientific reading about electrical phenomena and anatomy, as well as her own terrible experiences in childbirth, went into the book; and it has been convincingly argued that Dr Frankenstein is a composite portrait of both her father and her husband. After the trauma of Shelley's death, Mary returned to London in 1823 (where *Frankenstein* was already being staged) to look after her father and her surviving son, Percy Florence.

Though much courted (by women as well as men), she never remarried but lived quietly in retirement, steadily publishing her later novels: *Valperga* (1823), *The Last Man* (1826, also a science fiction novel set in a republican England in the twenty-first century), *The Fortunes of Perkin Warbeck* (1830, a historical romance), *Lodore* (1835), *Falkner* (1837) and a distinguished biographical collection, *Lives of the Most Eminent Literary and Scientific Men of France* (1837). She sent her son to Harrow, like Byron, and dedicated the remainder of her life to seeing him conventionally educated, happily married and safely settled on his country estate at Boscombe Down, Sussex, to be as much unlike his father as possible.

Brilliantly clever, shy, pale and painfully unexpressive in company, Mary Shelley hid a passionate nature that probably very few people except Godwin, Shelley and her friend Jane Williams (whose husband was also drowned in the yacht disaster) ever really saw. Her half-sister, Claire Clairmont, called her 'a mixture of vanity and good nature'.

Her elusive character is oddly reflected in the history of her portraits. An early picture by Amelia Curran done in Rome (1819) was lent to Trelawny for safe-keeping and subsequently lost in his wanderings. Drawings by Edward Williams done at Pisa for Shelley's birthday (1821) disappeared after the shipwreck. A striking portrait of 'an unknown woman'

**Frontispiece to *Frankenstein*,
(3rd edition)**
W. Chevalier after T. Holst, 1831

by John Stump (National Portrait Gallery, 1831), said to be Mary surrounded by her books and holding up a lover's locket assumed to contain Shelley's hair, has been consistently dismissed by modern art historians as unauthenticated, even though it corresponds closely to a contemporary description by Elizabeth Rennie:

> If not a beauty, she was a most lovable-looking woman; with skin exquisitely fair, and expressive gray eyes; features delicate, yet of the style and proportion that have won the term 'aristocratic'; hair of light but bright brown, mostly silky in texture and luxuriant in profusion, which hung in long drooping ringlets over her colourless cheek, and gathered in a cluster behind, fell waveringly over her shoulders; a large, open forehead; white and well-moulded arms and hands. She was a degree under the middle height, and rather enclining to embonpoint.
> (*Traits of Character*, Vol. 1, 1860)

Richard Rothwell's portrait, showing Mary as a much-subdued and evidently suffering older woman, was probably completed in 1840. Though the eyes are still full of tender intelligence, the great 'alabaster' shoulders suggest that she is turning into a monument. The curious 'flame-like' drapery in the background, revealed during cleaning at the turn of the century, was said to represent Shelley's unappeased spirit awaiting their reunion.

Leigh Hunt (1784–1859)

James Henry Leigh Hunt
Samuel Laurence, c.1837

This portrait captures Hunt's boyish resilience and sense of mischief, even at the age of fifty-three. 'He was rather tall,' wrote his son Thornton admiringly, 'as straight as an arrow, and looked slenderer than he really was ... His eyes were black and shining, his general complexion dark' (Preface to *Autobiography*).

Literary journalist, essayist and gifted verse-writer, Hunt proved himself a brilliant and courageous campaigning editor of the *The Examiner* (1808–21). With his brother John as business manager, he made it the outstanding liberal Sunday newspaper of the Romantic period, renowned for its new poetry, its generous reviewing and its reformist politics.

Imprisoned from 1813 to 1815 for seditious libel against the Prince Regent ('this fat Adonis'), Hunt characteristically transformed his grim prison cell into a dilettante's 'bower of bliss', complete with grand piano, classical busts, rose-patterned wallpaper and painted sky-blue ceiling. Here he became the object of literary pilgrimage, visited by Byron, Moore, Hazlitt, Haydon and Lamb. In December 1816 he began the celebrated 'Young Poets' series, which launched the careers of Keats and Shelley. Mocked as patron of the 'Cockney School of Poetry' (Lockhart, *Blackwood's Magazine*, 1817), he still had considerable success with his own decorative and beguiling verse, *The Story of Rimini* (1816), based on Dante's erotic tale of Paolo and Francesca. In 1821 he sailed to Italy to launch *The Liberal*, but was devastated when he quickly lost its main contributors, Shelley (drowned) and Byron (struck down by fever in Greece), though he published work by Hazlitt and Mary Shelley. Hunt returned to edit further magazines (*The Companion*, *The Tatler*) and pleasing anthologies (*The Book of Gems*), but was doomed to live in the posthumous shadow of his more famous friends, publishing a provocative memoir, *Lord Byron and Some of his Contemporaries*, in 1828 and much later his shrewd and revealing *Autobiography* (1850), which contains a moving portrait of Shelley (page 84).

Hunt's 'feckless' personality was later caricatured as Skimpole in Dickens's *Bleak House*. His family had black Caribbean roots and all his life he felt an outsider in England, his sunny bohemian temperament and sprightly verse-writing – 'Abou Ben Adhem, may his tribe increase' (1834), 'Jenny kissed me' (1838) – bravely masking depressions, debts, much domestic unhappiness (chiefly involving his sister-in-law) and permanent discomfort in the cold English climate.

But he was a warm-hearted and generous man who loved pranks, parties and nicknames, and always referred to Keats as 'Junkets'. Byron in turn referred to Leigh Hunt as 'Leontius', the freedom fighter, in humorous recognition of his independence as an editor.

John Keats (1795–1821)

Though he became the epitome of the young, beautiful, doomed poet of late English Romanticism, Keats struck everyone who knew him with his tremendous energy, his robust good humour and his zest for living. The son of a stables manager from the East End of London, he was built rather like a flyweight boxer: short, stocky, with disproportionate broad shoulders and a strong, open face with a powerful, bony nose. Sensuous and highly intelligent, a lover of good claret and good company, he said poetry should be 'felt on the pulses'.

Apprenticed for four years to an apothecary, he applied in 1815 to study surgery at Guy's Hospital, where he walked the wards and attended medical lectures, while reading widely in seventeenth- and eighteenth-century English literature.

In 1816 he had the good fortune to meet Leigh Hunt, who published his sonnet 'On First Looking into Chapman's Homer' in *The Examiner*. Valuable friendships with Hazlitt, B.R. Haydon, Lamb, the young poet John Hamilton Reynolds and Shelley (not altogether easy) quickly followed and helped Keats's work to develop with astonishing speed and confidence. He published a first volume of *Poems* in 1817 and his first extended work, *Endymion*, in 1818. Though scathingly attacked in *Blackwood's Magazine*, as the adolescent member of the 'Cockney School', he went on undaunted with his verse-epic *Hyperion*. During these hectic and exciting years he wrote a series of superb letters on poetry, many to his brothers George and Tom and his sister Fanny, which contain his most influential ideas: imagination as 'Negative Capability' (partly drawn from Coleridge), art as 'disinterested', style as 'fine excess' and life as 'a vale of Soul-making'. When Tom died of consumption, Keats moved to his friend Charles Armitage Brown's house

John Keats
William Hilton after Joseph
Severn, c.1822

John Keats
Joseph Severn, 1821–3

on the edge of Hampstead Heath; their next-door neighbour was the eighteen-year-old Fanny Brawne, with whom he fell passionately in love.

In the twelve months from September 1818, Keats produced an outpouring of major poetry which is unmatched in English: 'The Eve of St Agnes', 'Ode to a Nightingale', 'Ode on Melancholy', 'Ode to Psyche', 'Ode on a Grecian Urn', 'La Belle Dame sanse Merci' (again partly inspired by Coleridge), 'Lamia' and the quintessential poem of Keatsian ripeness, 'To Autumn'. They were all published in July 1820 and Keats's future seemed assured. But that spring he had begun spitting up arterial blood (which, as a medical student, he instantly recognised as the symptom of consumption), and in September he sailed for Italy with his friend Joseph Severn, hoping the southern climate might bring a remission from the fatal illness. Keats wrote no more poetry and died in a tiny apartment above the Spanish Steps in Rome in February 1821. Listening to the plashing Bernini fountain in the piazza below his window, he framed his own epitaph: 'Here lies one whose name was writ in water.' His poetry has flowed out to generations of readers ever since.

Keats was often sketched by his friends Severn, Brown and Haydon (who also made a life mask), and was perceptively observed by Hunt:

> His shoulders were very broad for his size; he had a face in which energy and sensibility were remarkably mixed up, and eager power checked and made patient by ill-health. Every feature was at once strongly cut and delicately alive. If there was any faulty expression it was in the mouth which was not without something of a character of pugnacity. The face was rather long than otherwise … the chin was bold, the cheeks sunken; the eyes

John Keats
Charles Armitage Brown, 1819

mellow and glowing, large dark and sensitive.
(*Lord Byron and Some of His Contemporaries*, 1828)

William Hilton's famous picture of Keats brooding over his manuscript book of poems, and perhaps foreseeing his own death, turns out to be posthumous. It is a careful amalgamation of several visual sources: Severn's ivory miniature (1819), Hilton's own chalk drawing, also done from life (1820), and the death mask made in Rome (1821). It was actually painted as a souvenir for Keats's friend Richard Woodhouse, probably in 1822 (see page 92).

Joseph Severn also went to enormous pains to reconstruct a remembered image of Keats in the study at Wentworth Place, Hampstead, when he had just completed the 'Ode to a Nightingale' in spring 1819. Severn actually began it in Rome in autumn 1821, several months after Keats's death, and over two years added meticulous authenticating details: 'the room, the open window, the carpet and chairs are all exact portraits, even to the mezzotint portrait of Shakespeare given him by his old landlady in the Isle of Wight' (*Letters*, 1859). In these works, Romantic portraiture has taken on a new emotional impulse, a conscious tribute to lost genius, a secular form of sacred iconography. They appear to be vividly realistic 'likenesses', but they are really pious memorials.

John Clare (1793–1864)

The last in a long line of eighteenth-century 'ploughboy' poets, Clare arrived in London from Northamptonshire in 1820 with the straw still clinging to his worsted jacket. He was the son of a farm labourer from the village of Helpstone, near Peterborough, and had taught himself to write poetry while working as a hedge-setter and lime-burner. Influenced by Crabbe and Goldsmith rather than Wordsworth, he brought a late flowering of the Romantic sensibility to a realistic knowledge of agricultural work and farming landscapes.

Clare's first book, *Poems Descriptive of Rural Life and Scenery* (1820), was published by Keats's bookseller, Taylor and Hessey of Fleet Street, with an advance of £100. It sold out within two months and Clare became the darling of the London literary season, meeting Hazlitt, Hunt, Lamb and Coleridge. It was followed by *The Village Minstrel* (1821), *The Shepherd's Calendar* (1827) and *The Rural Muse* (1835). Clare's poetry, with exquisite and earthy observations of the natural world (dung as well as dew-drops), is suffused by a sense of loss and an awareness of hardships and the unfeeling cruelty of the great landlords. His life became increasingly disturbed and unhappy as the vogue for his poetry declined, and in 1837 he was admitted to an insane asylum at Epping. Though married to a faithful wife, Martha Turner, he came to believe he was living with his first, abandoned love, Mary Joyce. After escaping to rejoin Mary in 1841, he spent the rest of his life in Northampton General Asylum, continuing to pour out poetry that remained largely unpublished for many years. The full text of his Romantic satire, *The Parish*, was only published from a manuscript in Peterborough Museum in 1985.

When Clare first came to London at the age of twenty-seven, he was a thin, wiry figure with long

John Clare
William Hilton, 1820

Hilton's moving portrait, which captures Clare's extraordinary mixture of innocence and painful anxiety, was commissioned by his publisher, Taylor, in the first flush of his perilous London celebrity of 1820.

sideburns and a fine country bloom upon his cheeks. But his deep-set eyes and prominent cheekbones already told of suffering and inner turmoils. The society writers gushed over his acute, natural sensitivity: 'What life in the eyes! What ardent thirst for excellence, and what flexibility and susceptibility to outward impression in the quivering lips!' (T.G. Wainewright, *The London Magazine*, 1821).

The editor Thomas Hood met him at a smart dinner party, nervously sipping a tankard of ale and shining 'verdantly' amidst the urban literati: 'in his bright grass-coloured coat and yellow waistcoat (there are greenish stalks, too, under the table) he looks a very cowslip' (*The London Magazine*, 1823).

Jane Austen (1775–1817)

Jane Austen
Cassandra Austen, c.1810

It still seems paradoxical that the outstanding English novelist of the turbulent Romantic age should be the decorous, unmarried daughter of a Hampshire clergyman. Jane Austen cheerfully announced that 'three or four families in a Country Village is the very thing to work on' (*Letters*, 1814), and modestly declared that her books were ladylike miniatures, 'the little bit (two Inches wide) of Ivory on which I work with so fine a brush, as produces little effect after much labour' (*Letters*, 1816). Yet her subtle, often scathing comedies of courtship and cross-purposes have a

Jane Austen
Unknown artist, c.1810–15

universal human resonance. She was passionately dedicated to her art, wrote and rewrote relentlessly, and called her novels her 'darlings'. Growing up at the bustling Steventon rectory (two of her brothers became admirals), she had produced a romantic novella *Love and Friendship* by the age of fourteen (her two heroines 'fainted alternately on a sofa'); and an illustrated *History of England* at fifteen ('by a partial, prejudiced and ignorant Historian'). Early drafts of her first three novels – which eventually became *Sense and Sensibility* (1811), *Pride and Prejudice* (1813), and *Northanger Abbey* (1818) - were already completed before the age of twenty-five. She accepted a proposal of marriage one evening in December 1802, but after overnight consultation with her sister Cassandra, changed her mind the following morning. Cassandra remained Jane's closest confidante and produced the famous watercolour sketch (*c.*1810), though her niece Anna said the round, pert, sarcastic face was 'hideously unlike' her aunt. Cassandra called Jane 'the sun of my life, the soother of every sorrow' (*Letters*, 1817), and subsequently destroyed much of their correspondence. After a long, distracting interlude at Bath, they returned with their elderly mother to Hampshire (Chawton Cottage), where Austen rapidly completed her six major novels – now including *Mansfield Park* (1814), *Emma* (1816) and *Persuasion* (1818) – in an extraordinary burst of creative energy before her death, aged forty-two, from Addison's disease. The great historical novelist Walter Scott wrote: 'That young lady had a talent for describing the involvements and feelings and characters of ordinary life, which is the most wonderful I ever met with. The big Bow-Wow strain I can do myself like any now going, but [her] exquisite touch … is denied me' (*Journal*, 1826).

Felicia Hemans (1793–1835)

Felicia Dorothea Browne is now remembered as 'Mrs Hemans', famous for her patriotic recitation piece 'Casabianca' (1826), based on an incident during the Battle of the Nile: 'The boy stood on the burning deck/Whence all but he had fled …'. She was the most successful 'parlour poet' of her age, the darling of the new illustrated women's annuals such as *The Keepsake*, and from the 1820's outsold every other poet including Byron and Scott. She caught the stirring, recessional mood of late Romanticism in a number of hymn-like lyrics, celebrating death, domesticity and imperial duty: 'The Homes of England', 'The Graves of a Household' and 'The Palm Tree'. Her own domestic life was chaotic: abandoned by her father, who emigrated to Quebec, and later by her husband, who absconded to Italy, Felicia gallantly supported herself and her five sons with a prodigious outpouring of more than twenty books of travel, poetry and plays. Her outstanding work, *Records of Women* (1828) is a landmark collection of exclusively female voices. Its startling, bitter dramatic poems and monologues include 'The Indian Woman's Death Song', 'Arabella Stuart', 'Joan of Arc', 'The American Forest Girl' and 'Properzia Rossi' (a forgotten Renaissance sculptress).

Tall, beautiful and alarmingly business-like, Felicia befriended a number of struggling women writers such as Mary Tighe, Laetitia Landon and Joanna Baillie. On her early death aged forty-two, Wordsworth put her into his literary pantheon, his 'Extemporary Elegy' (1836), the only woman poet alongside Coleridge, Lamb, Crabbe and Scott. But her later popularity among Victorians, and some clever parodies by Noël Coward ('The Stately Homes of England'), reduced her reputation to a few well-worn classroom favourites (often assumed to be written by Kipling) until she was recently rediscovered by modern feminists.

Above:
Felicia Hemans
Angus Fletcher, 1829

'Imagine my dismay on visiting Mr Fletcher's sculpture-room,' she wrote ironically to a friend, 'on beholding at least six Mrs Hemans, placed as if to greet me in every direction. There is something frightful in this multiplication of oneself to *infinity*.' (Letter, July 1830).

Left:
Mrs Felicia Hemans
Edward Smith after Edward Robertson, published 1837

J.M.W. Turner (1775–1851)

J.M.W. Turner
George Dance, 1800

Landscape, seascape and history painter of revolutionary force, Turner gloriously reinvented the appearances of light, wind and water. He memorably embodied the mysterious, energised universe of the Romantic poets, and triumphantly anticipated French Impressionism. His contemporary, John Constable described his work as 'airey visions, painted with tinted steam'. Much of it was done on a series of annual sketching tours, at first to 'picturesque' regions of Britain (Wales, the Lake District, the Highlands) and later abroad to France, the Swiss lakes, Italy and Germany. He kept extensive travel journals, filled over three hundred sketchbooks and scribbled a mass of poetry to caption his pictures.

Turner exhibited his first painting at the Royal Academy at the age of fifteen, was appointed Associate RA at twenty-four, and elected Professor of Perspective at thirty-two (1807). He achieved early popular success with atmospheric Wordsworthian scenes like *Buttermere Lake* (1798), dramatic views of Nelson's sea battles like *Trafalgar as seen from the Mizzen Shroud of the Victory* (1806), and his epic 'narrative landscapes' including *Snow Storm: Hannibal and his Army Crossing the Alps* (1812), reflecting Napoleon's doomed ambitions. In the 1830s he became the favoured artist to illustrate the *Collected Poetical Works* of Byron, Scott, Rogers and Campbell. In John Doyle's imaginary conversation piece *Samuel Rogers at his Breakfast Table* in 1815 (1823), Turner's small alert figure appears standing behind Byron (see page 11).

He always kept several secret studios in London (including a houseboat on the Thames), and cultivated a certain gruff misanthropy which, like his incongruous stovepipe hats, was designed to protect. He was generous to his students, slept with a series of pretty housekeepers, and probably fathered at least two children (Evalina and Georgiana), to whom he was greatly attached. He never stopped pushing the boundaries of vision, and produced his late Romantic masterpiece *Rain, Steam and Speed: The Great Western Railway* in 1844. His work puzzled and impressed Hazlitt: 'they are pictures of the elements … the artist delights to go back to the first chaos of the world … pictures of nothing, and very like' (*On Imitation*, 1817). Later he was championed by Ruskin in *Modern Painters* (1843). He died at his studios in Chelsea, where he was living incognito with his latest landlady, Sophia Booth, and known familiarly by riverside locals as 'good old Admiral Booth'.

J.M.W. Turner
John Linnell, 1838

The Forgotten Romantics

It is safe to say that not one person in a thousand will have heard of the beautiful Mary Blachford (1772–1810), read a line of her poetry or previously seen her entrancing picture (which is actually a miniature on ivory, no bigger than a beer mat). At seventeen she fell in love with the Anglo-Irish MP Henry Tighe, but their subsequent marriage was unhappy and childless, her one novel was never completed and she died from consumption at the age of thirty-eight.

Yet in 1811 a major Romantic poem in six cantos, *Psyche, or The Legend of Love*, was published posthumously 'by the late Mrs Henry Tighe' and went through five English and American editions. She was praised by Thomas Moore, eagerly discussed by Shelley and admired by Keats when he was writing *Endymion* in 1817, though he later felt he had grown out of her: 'Mrs Tighe and James Beattie once delighted me – now I see through them and can find nothing in them … yet how many they will still delight!' (*Letters*, 1819). The Tighe family erected a flamboyant tomb to her memory in Ireland, designed by John Flaxman (1815), in which the figure of a winged Psyche archly meditates upon her poetic

Clockwise from top left:
Mary Tighe
attributed to John Comerford
after George Romney, 1794–5

Mary Tighe Memorial
John Flaxman, 1815

Elizabeth Inchbald
George Dance, 1794

Laetitia Elizabeth Landon
Daniel Maclise, c.1830–35

Ann Yearsley
Henry R. Cook, 1814

slumbers. Felicia Hemans made a special pilgrimage there, and published an immensely popular and lachrymose poem in her honour, 'The Grave of a Poetess', in 1827.

The irony of Mary Tighe's subsequent slide into literary oblivion suggests what has become the most notable absence from the Romantic circle as we now look back on it. So many of the gifted women writers of the period, once praised and celebrated by their contemporaries, are now virtually unknown to modern readers. They have also become cruelly invisible, as even the archives of the National Portrait Gallery retain scant visual records, because so few portraits were commissioned or bequeathed by their friends, family, lovers, husbands or publishers.

There is one drawing of the Jacobin novelist and playwright Elizabeth Inchbald (1753–1821), who was spurned in love by William Godwin; one engraving of the poet and novelist Laetitia Landon (1802–38) who committed suicide at a remote slave-trade outpost in West Africa; one mezzotint of the self-educated poet Ann Yearsley (1756–1806), who supported herself with a daily milk-round in Bristol; one stipple engraving of the poet Charlotte Smith (1749–1806) of whom Wordsworth calmly wrote: 'A Lady to whom English verse is under greater obligations than are likely to be either acknowledged or remembered' (*Letters*, 1835).

There is no known portrait at all of the working-class poet from Kendal in the Lake District, Isabella Lickbarrow (even her dates are uncertain). She was the orphan of a Quaker schoolmaster, and roamed the hills of Cumberland, as she wrote in her *Poetical Effusions* of 1814:

> I, like the wild flowers of the mountains,
> That unknown unheeded lie,
> Like them shall leave a name unhonour'd
> And like them forgotten lie.

Select bibliography

1. Contemporary Sources
Samuel Taylor Coleridge, *Notebooks: A Selection*, ed. Seamus Perry (Oxford University Press, Oxford, 2002)
Thomas De Quincey, *Recollections of the Lakes and the Lake Poets*, 1839, ed. David Wright (Penguin, Harmondsworth, 1970)
Joseph Farington, *Diaries*, ed. Kenneth Garlick, 17 vols (Yale University Press, New Haven, 1998)
William Gilpin, *Three Essays: On Picturesque Beauty; On Picturesque Travel; On Sketching Landscape* (London, 1792)
Benjamin Robert Haydon, *Autobiography and Journals* (London, 1853)
William Hazlitt, *The Spirit of the Age* (London, 1825)
—— *Conversations of James Northcote* (London, 1827)
—— *Essays on the Fine Arts* (London, 1873)
Richard Payne Knight, *An Analytical Enquiry Into the Principles of Taste* (London, 1805)
John Opie, with a Memoir by Amelia Opie, *Lectures on Painting* (London, 1809)
Sir Joshua Reynolds, *Discourses on Art*, 1790, ed. R.R. Wark (Yale University Press, New Haven and London, 1975)
J.G. Lockhart, *The Life of Robert Burns* (Edinburgh, 1828)
Memoirs of the life of Sir Walter Scott, 7 vols (Galignani, Paris, 1838)
Leigh Hunt, *Autobiography* (Smith, Elder and Co, London, 1850)
Henry Crabb Robinson, *On Books and their Writers*, ed. Edith Morley, 3 vols (J.H. Dent and Sons Ltd, London, 1938)
Mary 'Perdita' Robinson: *Memoirs of the Late Mrs Robinson, Written by herself*, edited by her daughter Mary Elizabeth Robinson, 4 vols (London, 1801)
William Godwin: *Memoirs of the Author of A Vindication of The Rights of Woman*, 1798, ed. Richard Holmes, (Penguin Classics, London, 1987)
Joseph Severn: *Letters and Memoirs*, edited by Grant F. Scott (Ashgate Books, Aldershot, 2005)
Edward John Trelawny, *Records of Shelley, Byron and the Author* (1858, revised 1878)
Dorothy Wordsworth, *Journals 1798-1803*, ed. Mary Moorman (Oxford University Press, Oxford, 1978)

2. Select Modern Biographies (alphabetically by subject)
Jane Austen: A Life, **Claire Tomalin** (Penguin Books, London, 1998)
Blake, **Peter Ackroyd** (Minerva, London, 1996)
Robert Burns: A Life, **Ian McIntyre** (Penguin Books, London, 2001)
Byron: Life and Legend, **Fiona MacCarthy** (Faber & Faber, London, 2002)
Coleridge: A Critical Biography, **Rosemary Ashton** (Blackwell, Oxford, 1996)
Coleridge: Early Visions and *Coleridge: Darker Reflections*, **Richard Holmes**, 2 vols (Harper Perennial, London, 2005)
John Clare, **Jonathan Bate** (Picador, London, 2003)
George Crabbe: An English Life 1754–1832, **Neil Powell** (Pimlico, London, 2004)
Humphry Davy: Science and Power, **David Knight** (Blackwell, Oxford, 1992)
Thomas De Quincey: The Opium Eater, **Grevel Lindop** (Dent, London, 1981)
The Godwins and the Shelleys, **William St Clair** (Faber & Faber, London, 1989)
The Day-Star of Liberty: William Hazlitt's Radical Style, **Tom Paulin** (Faber & Faber, London, 1998)
Hazlitt in Love, **Jon Cook** (Short Books, London, 2006)
Felicia Hemans: Selected Poems, Letters, Reception Materials, **Susan J.Wolfson** (Princeton University Press, New Jersey and Oxford University Press, Oxford, 2000)
The Herschel Chronicle, **Constance Lubbock** (Cambridge University Press, Cambridge, 1933)
Fiery Heart: The First Life of Leigh Hunt, **Nicholas Roe** (Pimlico, London, 2005)

Mrs Jordan's Profession, **Claire Tomalin** (Viking, London, 1994)
Edmund Kean: Fire from Heaven, **Raymund Fitzsimons** (Hamish Hamilton, London, 1976)
John Keats, **Andrew Motion** (Faber & Faber, London, 1997)
John Keats, **Robert Gittings** (Penguin Books, London, 2001)
Perdita: The Life of Mary Robinson, **Paula Byrne** (HarperCollins, London, 2004)
Perdita: Royal Mistress, Writer, Romantic, **Sarah Gristwood** (Bantam Press, London, 2005)
Robert Southey, **Mark Storey** (Oxford University Press, Oxford, 1997)
Mary Shelley, **Miranda Seymour** (John Murray, London, 2000)
Shelley: The Pursuit, **Richard Holmes** (Harper Perennial, London, 2005)
Turner: A Life, **James Hamilton** (Hodder & Stoughton, London, 1997)
The Life and Death of Mary Wollstonecraft, **Claire Tomalin** (Penguin Books, London, 1992)
Mary Wollstonecraft: A Revolutionary Life, **Janet Todd** (Weidenfeld & Nicholson, London, 2000)
Mary Wollstonecraft: A New Genus, **Lyndall Gordon** (Little Brown, London, 2005)
William Wordsworth: A Life, **Stephen Gill** (Oxford Paperbacks, Oxford 1990)
William Wordsworth, **Hunter Davies** (Sutton Publishing, Stroud, 1997)

3. Specialist Studies

Frances Blanshard, *Portraits of Wordsworth* (George Allen & Unwin, London, 1959)
Anthony Burton and John Murdoch, *Byron*, exhibition catalogue (Victoria and Albert Museum, London, 1974)
Richard Godfrey, *James Gillray: The Art of Caricature*, exhibition catalogue (Tate Publishing, London, 2001)
Richard Holmes and David Crane, *Romantics and Revolutionaries*, exhibition catalogue (National Portrait Gallery, London, 2002)
Geoffrey Keynes, *The Complete Portraiture of William and Catherine Blake* (Trianon Press for William Blake Trust, London, 1977)
Iain McCalman (ed), *An Oxford Companion to the Romantic Age: British Culture 1776-1832* (Oxford University Press, Oxford, 1999)
Richard Ormond, *Early Victorian Portraits*, 2 vols (The Stationary Office Books, London, 1973)
Morton D. Paley, *Portraits of Coleridge* (Oxford University Press, Oxford, 1999)
Donald Parson, *Portraits of Keats* (Cleveland World Pub. Co, New York, 1954)
David Piper, *The Image of the Poet: British Poets and their Portraits* (Clarendon Press, Oxford, 1982)
Desmond Shawe-Taylor, *Genial Company: the Theme of Genius in Eighteenth-Century British Portraiture*, exhibition catalogue (Nottingham University Art Gallery, Nottingham, and Scottish National Portrait Gallery, Edinburgh, 1987)
Jacob Simon, *The Art of the Picture Frame* (National Portrait Gallery, London, 1996)
William St Clair, *The Reading Nation in the Romantic Period* (Cambridge University Press, Cambridge, 2004)
Richard Walker, *Regency Portraits*, 2 vols (National Portrait Gallery, London, 1985)
Richard Wendorf, *The Elements of Life: Biography and Portraiture in Stuart and Georgian England* (Clarendon Press, Oxford, 1990)
Richard Wendorf, *Sir Joshua Reynolds: the Painter in Society* (National Portrait Gallery, London, 1996)
Carol Wilson and Joel Hafner (eds), *Re-visioning Romanticism: British Women Writers 1776-1837* (University of Pennsylvania Press, Philadelphia, 1994)
Robert Woof and Stephen Hebron, *Romantic Icons*, exhibition catalogue (The Wordsworth Trust, Dove Cottage, Grasmere, 1999)
Jonathan Wordsworth and Stephen Hebron, *Romantic Women Writers*, exhibition catalogue (The Wordsworth Trust, Dove Cottage, Grasmere, 1994)
Jonathan and Jessica Wordsworth (eds), *The New Penguin Book of Romantic Poetry* (Penguin Books, London, 2001)

List of illustrations

Introduction

p.4 **William Wordsworth**, Benjamin Robert Haydon, 1825. Pencil and chalk, 445 x 311mm (17⅛ x 2¼") © The Wordsworth Trust, Dove Cottage; p.6 **George Gordon Byron**, **Lord Byron**, Richard Westall, 1813. Oil on canvas, 914 x 711mm (36 x 28") © National Portrait Gallery, London (NPG 4243); p.8 **George Gordon Byron**, **Lord Byron**, after Richard Westall, 1813. Oil on canvas, 762 x 635mm (30 x 25") © National Portrait Gallery, London (NPG 1047); p.8 **The Meeting of Byron and Scott at Albermarle Street, Spring 1815**, L. Werner, *c*.1850. Watercolour, 318 x 400mm (12½ x 15¾") Courtesy of the John Murray Archives; p.9 **The plumb-pudding in danger: – or – state epicures taking un petit souper**, James Gillray. Published by Hannah Humphrey, 26 February 1805. Hand-coloured etching 261 x 362mm (10¼ x 14¼") © National Portrait Gallery, London (NPG D12840); p.10 **Dove Cottage** © The Wordsworth Trust, Dove Cottage; p.11 **Sam Rogers at his Breakfast Table**, engraved by Charles Mottram after John Doyle, *c*.1823. Engraving and mezzotint on paper, 580 x 866mm (23 x 34") © Tate, London 2005; p.12 Title page of *The Poetical Works of Coleridge, Shelley and Keats* © Private Collection; p.12 **George Crabbe**, Henry William Pickersgill, *c*.1818–19. Oil on canvas, 759 x 635 mm (29⅞ x 25") © National Portrait Gallery, London (NPG 1495); p.13 **Snow Storm: Hannibal and His Army Crossing the Alps**, J.M.W. Turner, exhibited 1812. Oil on canvas, 1460 x 2375 mm (57½ x 93½") © Tate, London 2005; p.14 **Keats House** © Joint Archive Service/Corporation of London; p.14 **An Introduction: Gay moments of Logic, from 'Life in London' by Pierce Egan**, Robert I. Cruikshank, 1821. Coloured aquatint © Private Collection, The Stapleton Collection / Bridgeman Art Library; p.14 **Duelling Pistols**, *c*.1815 © Museum of London; p.15 **Horatio Nelson**, **Viscount Nelson**, Lemuel Francis Abbott, 1797. Oil on canvas 749 x 622 (29½ x 24½") © National Portrait Gallery, London (NPG 334); p.15 **Dido, in despair!**, James Gillray. Published by Hannah Humphrey, 6 February 1801. Hand-coloured etching and stipple, 267 x 376 mm (10½ x 14¾") (NPG D13034); p.16 **James Belcher**, Unknown artist, *c*.1800. Oil on canvas 762 x 638 (30 x 25⅛") © National Portrait Gallery, London (NPG 5214); p.16 **Theatrical mendicants, relieved**, James Gillray. Published by Hannah Humphrey, 15 January 1809. Hand-coloured etching and aquatint, 264 x 359 mm (10⅜ x 14⅛") © (NPG D12915); p.17 **Charles Waterton**, Charles Wilson Peale, 1824. Oil on canvas, 613 x 514 mm (24⅛ x 20¼") © National Portrait Gallery, London (NPG 2014); p.18 **James Northcote**, Self-portrait, 1784. Oil on canvas, 737 x 610mm (29 x 24") © National Portrait Gallery, London (NPG 3253); p.18 **John Opie**, Self-portrait, 1785. Oil on canvas, 743 x 622 mm (29¼ x 24½") © National Portrait Gallery, London (NPG 47); p.19 **Joseph Severn**, Self-portrait, *c*.1820. Drawing, 254 x 178mm (10 x 7") © National Portrait Gallery, London (NPG 3091); p.20 **John Keats**, Joseph Severn, 1819. Oil on ivory, 108 x 79mm (4¼ x 3⅛") © National Portrait Gallery, London (NPG 1605); p.21 **John Keats**, Cast of death-mask, 1821. Plaster, height 235mm, reproduced by permission of the Provost and Fellows of Eton College/National Portrait Gallery, London (NPG 4031); p.21 **William Blake**, James S. Deville, published 1823. Sculpture, height 292mm (11½") © National Portrait Gallery, London (NPG 1809); p.21 **William Wordsworth**, Benjamin Robert Haydon,1815. Plaster cast of life-mask, height 241 mm (9½") © National Portrait Gallery, London (NPG 2020)

Biographies

p.24 **William Wordsworth**, Robert Hancock, 1798. Pencil and chalk, 165 x 140mm (6½ x 5½") © National Portrait Gallery, London (NPG 450); p.24 **Samuel Taylor Coleridge**, Robert Hancock, 1796. Pencil and chalk, 178 x 156mm (7 x 6⅛") © National Portrait Gallery, London (NPG 452); p.24 **Robert Southey**, Robert Hancock, 1796. Pencil and chalk, 171 x 146mm (6¾ x 5¾") © National Portrait Gallery, London (NPG 451); p.24 **Charles Lamb**, Robert Hancock, 1798. Pencil and chalk, 171x146mm (6¾ x 5¾") © National Portrait Gallery, London (NPG 449)

p.26 **William Blake**, Thomas Phillips, 1807. Oil on canvas, 921x720mm (36¼ x 28⅜") © National Portrait Gallery, London (NPG 212); p.28 **W. Blake**, after James S. Deville, 1953 (1823). Bronze cast of a plaster life mask, height 292mm (11½") © National Portrait Gallery, London (NPG 1809a); p.29 **W. Blake**, John Linnell, 1861. Watercolour, 229 x 178mm (9 x 7") © National Portrait Gallery, London (NPG 2146) p.30 **Robert Burns**, replica by Alexander Nasmyth, c.1821–2 (1787). Oil on canvas, 406 x 292 mm (16 x 11½") © National Portrait Gallery, London (NPG 46)

p.32 **Mary Wollstonecraft**, John Opie, c.1797. Oil on canvas, 768 x 641mm (30¼ x 25¼") © National Portrait Gallery, London (NPG 1237)

p.34 **William Godwin**, James Northcote, 1802. Oil on canvas, 749 x 622mm (29½ x 24½") © National Portrait Gallery, London (NPG 1236); p.35 **W. Godwin**, William Brockedon, 1832. Pencil and red and white chalk, 371 x 269mm (14⅝ x 10⅝") © National Portrait Gallery, London (NPG 2515(29))

p.37 **Benjamin Robert Haydon**, Sir David Wilkie, 1815. Black and white chalk, 127 x 197mm (5 x 7¾") © National Portrait Gallery, London (NPG 1505); p.38 **Christ's Entry into Jerusalem**, B.R. Haydon, 1814–20. Oil on canvas, 3960 x 4570mm (156 x 180") Photograph by Matt Lee by permission of the Athenaeum of Ohio; p.39 **B.R. Haydon**, Georgiana Margaretta Zomlin, 1825. Oil on canvas, 686 x 572mm (27 x 22½") © National Portrait Gallery, London (NPG 510)

p.40 **James Gillray**, Self-portrait, c.1800. Watercolour on ivory, 76 x 64 mm (3 x 2½") © National Portrait Gallery, London (NPG 83); p.41 **Promis'd horrors of the French invasion, – or – forcible reasons for negotiating a regicide peace**, J. Gillray, Published by Hannah Humphrey, 20 October 1796. Hand-coloured etching and aquatint, 325 x 437mm (12¾ x 17¼") © National Portrait Gallery, London (NPG D12579)

p.42 **William Wordsworth**, Benjamin Robert Haydon, 1818. Chalk, 546 x 419mm (21½ x 16½") © National Portrait Gallery, London (NPG 3687); p.44 **Dorothy Wordsworth**, unknown artist, 1806. Silhouette, 76 x 58mm (3 x 2¼") © The Wordsworth Trust, Dove Cottage; p.45 **W. Wordsworth**, Benjamin Robert Haydon, 1842. Oil on canvas, 1245 x 991mm (49 x 39") © National Portrait Gallery, London (NPG 1857)

p.46 **Samuel Taylor Coleridge**, Peter Vandyke, 1795. Oil on canvas, 559 x 457mm (22 x 18") © National Portrait Gallery, London (NPG 192); p.48 **S.T. Coleridge**, James Northcote, 1804. Oil on canvas, 559 x 457mm (30 x 25") © The Wordsworth Trust, Dove Cottage; p.49 **S.T. Coleridge**, Washington Allston, 1814. Oil on canvas, 1143 x 876mm (45 x 34½") © National Portrait Gallery, London (NPG 184)

p.50 **Robert Southey**, Peter Vandyke, 1795. Oil on canvas, 546 x 445mm (21½ x 17½") © National Portrait Gallery, London (NPG 193); p.52 **R. Southey**, Henry Edridge, 1804. Pencil, chalk and wash, 282 x 225mm (11⅛ x 8⅞") © National Portrait Gallery, London (NPG 119); p.53 **R. Southey**, Edward Nash, 1820. Miniature on ivory, 136 x 102mm (5⅜ x 4") © National Portrait Gallery, London (NPG 4028)

p.54 **Amelia Opie**, John Opie, 1798. Oil on canvas, 743 x 622mm (29¼ x 24½") © National Portrait Gallery, London (NPG 765)

p.56 **William Hazlitt**, William Bewick, 1825. Chalk, 575 x 375mm (22⅝ x 14¾") © National Portrait Gallery, London (NPG 2697)

p.58 **Charles Lamb**, William Hazlitt, 1804. Oil on canvas, 762 x 622mm (30 x 24½") © National Portrait Gallery, London (NPG 507); p.60 **Mary and Charles Lamb**, Francis Stephen Cary,1834. Oil on canvas, 1130 x 851mm (44½ x 33½") © National Portrait Gallery, London (NPG 1019)

p.61 **Mary Robinson**, Sir Joshua Reynolds, 1783–4. Oil on canvas, 770 x 640mm (30⅜ x 25¼") © Wallace Collection, London; p.62 **M. Robinson**, by or after Sir Joshua Reynolds, c.1782. Pen and brown ink over pencil 254 x 203mm (10 x 8") © National Portrait Gallery, London (NPG 5264); p.63 **M. Robinson**, George Dance, c.1793. Pencil, 260 x 210 mm (40¼ x 8¼") © National Portrait Gallery, London (NPG 1254)

p.64 **Edmund Kean as Shylock**, Henry Hoppner Meyer after W.H. Watts, 1814. Mezzotint, 327 x 243mm (12⅞ x 9⅝") © National Portrait Gallery, London (NPG D3451); p.65 **E. Kean as Richard III**, J.Prynn, c.1814–33. Etching and stipple engraving, 327 x 243mm (12⅞ x 9⅝") © National Portrait Gallery, London (NPG D 3452)

p.66 **Dorothea Jordan**, John Hoppner, exhibited 1791. Oil on canvas, 749 x 622mm (29½ x 24¼") © Tate; on loan to the National Portrait Gallery. London (NPG L174); p.67 **D. Jordan as Viola in 'Twelfth night'**, Unknown artist, late eighteenth century. Hand-coloured line engraving, 187 x 122mm (7⅜ x 4¼") © National Portrait Gallery, London (NPG D20567)

p.68 **Thomas De Quincey**, Sir John Watson-Gordon, c.1845. Oil on canvas, 1273 x 1013mm (50⅛ x 39⅞") © National Portrait Gallery, London (NPG 189) p.71 **William Herschel**, James Godby, published 1814. Stipple engraving, 320 x 230mm (12⅝ x 9") © National Portrait Gallery, London (NPG D9004); p.72 **W. Herschel**, Lemuel Francis Abbott, 1785. Oil on canvas, 762 x 635mm (30 x 25") © National Portrait Gallery, London (NPG 98)

p.73 **Sir Humphry Davy**, Thomas Phillips, 1821. Oil on canvas, 914 x 711mm (36 x 28") © National Portrait Gallery, London (NPG 2546); p.75 **Scientific researches! – new discoveries in pneumaticks! – or – an experimental lecture on the powers of air**, James Gillray, Published by Hannah Humphrey, 23 May 1802. Hand-coloured etching 253 x 352mm (10 x 13⅞") © National Portrait Gallery, London (NPG D13036)

p.76 **George Gordon Byron, Lord Byron**, Thomas Phillips, c.1835, after the portrait of 1813. Oil on canvas, 765 x 639mm (30⅛ x 25⅛") © National Portrait Gallery, London (NPG 142); p.78 **Lady Caroline Lamb**, Henry Hoppner Meyer, published by Henry Colburn, 1 May 1819. Stipple engraving, 181 x 119mm (7⅛ x 4¾") © National Portrait Gallery, London (NPG D15947); p.78 **John William Polidori**, F.G. Gainsford, c.1816. Oil on canvas, 584 x 480mm (23 x 18⅞") © National Portrait Gallery, London (NPG 991); p.78 **Edward John Trelawny**, John Severn, 1838. Pen and ink, 152 x 152mm (6 x 6") © National Portrait Gallery, London (NPG 2132); p.79 **Lord Byron**, E.H. Bailey, 1824. Marble, height 760mm. Reproduced with permission of the Keepers and Governors of Harrow School. National Portrait Gallery (RN29636)

p.80 **Sir Walter Scott, 1st Bt**, Augustin Edouart, 1830–31. Silhouette 241 x 114mm (9½ x 4½") © National Portrait Gallery, London (NPG 1638); p.81 **W. Scott**, Sir Edwin Landseer, c.1824. Oil on Panel, 292 x 241mm (11½ x 9½") © National Portrait Gallery, London (NPG 391)

p.82 **Percy Bysshe Shelley**, Amelia Curran, 1819. Oil on canvas, 597 x 476mm (23½ x 18¾") © National Portrait Gallery, London (NPG 1234); p.84 **Thomas Love Peacock**, Roger Jean, c.1805. Miniature on ivory, oval 76 x 60mm (3 x 2⅜") © National Portrait Gallery, London (NPG 3994); p.85 **Memorial to the drowned Shelley in Christchurch Priory**, Horatio Weekes, 1854. © Roger Bamber

p.86 **Mary Wollstonecraft Shelley**, Richard Rothwell, exhibited 1840. Oil on canvas, 737 x 610mm (29 x 24") © National Portrait Gallery, London (NPG 1235); p.89 **Frontispiece to *Frankenstein* (3rd edition)**, W. Chevalier after T. Holst, 1831. © National Portrait Gallery (NPG Archives)

p.90 **James Henry Leigh Hunt**, Samuel Laurence, c.1837. Oil on canvas, 1118 x 905mm (44 x 35⅝") © National Portrait Gallery, London (NPG 2508)

p.92 **John Keats**, William Hilton after Joseph Severn, c.1822. Oil on canvas, 762 x 635mm (30 x 25") © National Portrait Gallery, London (NPG 194); p.94 **J. Keats**, Joseph Severn, 1821–3. Oil on canvas, 565 x 419mm (22¼ x 16½") © National Portrait Gallery, London (NPG 58); p.95 **J. Keats**, Charles Armitage Brown, 1819. Pencil, 229 x 216mm (9 x 8½") © National Portrait Gallery, London (NPG 1963)

p.97 **John Clare**, William Hilton, 1820. Oil on canvas, 762 x 635mm (30 x 25") © National Portrait Gallery, London (NPG 1469)

p.98 **Jane Austen**, Cassandra Austen, c.1810. Pencil and watercolour, 114 x 80mm (4½ x 3⅛") © National Portrait Gallery, London (NPG 3630); p.99 **J. Austen**, unknown artist, c.1810–15. Hollow-cut silhouette, 102 x 80mm (4 x 3⅛") © National Portrait Gallery, London (NPG 3181)

p.100 **Felicia Hemans**, Edward Smith after Edward Robertson, published 1837. Engraving © National Portrait Gallery, London (NPG Archives); p.101 **F. Hemans**, Angus Fletcher, 1829. Plaster cast of bust, height 705mm (27¾") © National Portrait Gallery. London (NPG 1046)

p.102 **J.M.W. Turner**, George Dance, 1800. Pencil and faint pink chalk on cream woven paper, 250 x 188mm (9⅞ x 7½") © Royal Academy of Arts, London; p.103 **J.M.W. Turner**, John Linnell, 1838. Oil on canvas, 460 x 384mm, (18⅛ x 15⅛") © National Portrait Gallery, London (NPG 6344)

p.104 **Mary Tighe**, attributed to John Comerford after George Romney, c.1794-5. Miniature on ivory, 89 x 72mm (3⅞ x 3") © National Portrait Gallery, London (NPG 1629); p.104 **Mary Tighe Memorial**, John Flaxman, 1815. Photo Conway Library, Courtauld Institute of Art; p.105 **Laetitia Landon**, Daniel Maclise, c.1830–35. Black chalk and stump, 273 x 216mm (10¾ x 8½") © National Portrait Gallery, London (NPG 1953); p.105 **Elizabeth Inchbald**, George Dance, 1794. Pencil 254 x 191mm (10 x 7½") © National Portrait Gallery, London (NPG 1144); p.105 **Ann Yearsley**, Henry R. Cook, published by I.W.A. Payne after Sarah Shiells, 28 February 1814. Stipple engraving, 174 x 123mm (6⅞ x 4⅞") © National Portrait Gallery, London (NPG D14829)

Index